T0246405

Modern Operating Systems

Modern Operating Systems

Nora Wilson

 Larsen & Keller
www.larsen-keller.com

Modern Operating Systems
Nora Wilson
ISBN: 978-1-64172-640-5 (Hardback)

© 2022 Larsen & Keller

 Larsen & Keller

Published by Larsen and Keller Education,
5 Penn Plaza,
19th Floor,
New York, NY 10001, USA

Cataloging-in-Publication Data

Modern operating systems / Nora Wilson.
    p. cm.
Includes bibliographical references and index.
ISBN 978-1-64172-640-5
1. Operating systems (Computers). 2. Systems software. I. Wilson, Nora.
QA76.77 .M63 2022
005.43--dc23

Table of Contents

Preface

The purpose of this book is to help students understand the fundamental concepts of this discipline. It is designed to motivate students to learn and prosper. I am grateful for the support of my colleagues. I would also like to acknowledge the encouragement of my family.

Operating systems are software that are used to manage the computer hardware and software resources. They also provide common services for computer programs. The operating system acts as an intermediary between programs and the computer hardware for hardware functions such as input and output, and memory allocation. They are found in many devices that contain a computer including cellular phones and video game consoles as well as web servers and supercomputers. There are numerous types of operating systems such as single-tasking system, multi-tasking operating system and distributed operating system. This book unfolds the innovative aspects of operating systems which will be crucial for the holistic understanding of the subject matter. Some of the diverse topics covered herein address the varied branches that fall under this category. This book is an essential guide for both academicians and those who wish to pursue this discipline further.

A foreword for all the chapters is provided below:

Chapter – What is Operating Systems?

The system software which is used to manage software resources and computer hardware is termed as an operating system. A few types of operating systems are mobile operating systems, batch processing operating systems and time sharing operating systems. This chapter briefly introduces operating systems and its various types.

Chapter – Mobile Operating Systems

The operating system which has been specifically designed to be used in phones, tablets and other mobile devices is known as a mobile operating system. Some of its common types are android and iOS. This chapter has been carefully written to provide an easy understanding of the varied facets of these types of mobile operating systems.

Chapter – Computer Operating Systems

A computer operating system is used to manage the software and hardware resources in a personal computer. A few of the popular operating systems are Microsoft Windows, Mac OS, Unix and Linux. The diverse applications of these types of computer operating systems have been thoroughly discussed in this chapter.

Chapter – Process and Threads

The smallest sequence of programmed instructions which can be independently managed by a scheduler is known as a thread. The instance of a computer program which is being executed by a single or multiple threads is termed as a process. The topics elaborated in this chapter will help in gaining a better perspective about processes and threads, as well as the difference between them.

Chapter – Deadlock in Operating Systems

The state in computing where each member within a group is waiting for another member including its own self to send a message is known as a deadlock. There are numerous methods of handling deadlocks, which are broadly categorized as prevention, avoidance, detection and recovery. This chapter discusses in detail the characterization of deadlocks as well as these methods of handling them.

Nora Wilson

1

What is Operating System?

The system software which is used to manage software resources and computer hardware is termed as an operating system. A few types of operating systems are mobile operating systems, batch processing operating systems and time sharing operating systems. This chapter briefly introduces operating systems and its various types.

An operating system (OS) is the program that, after being initially loaded into the computer by a boot program, manages all of the other application programs in a computer. The application programs make use of the operating system by making requests for services through a defined application program interface (API). In addition, users can interact directly with the operating system through a user interface such as a command line or a graphical user interface (GUI).

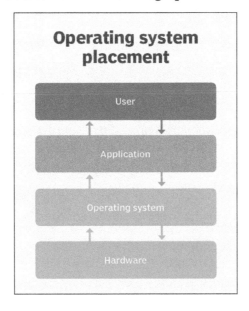

An operating system can perform the following services for applications:

- In a multitasking operating system, where multiple programs can be running at the same time, the OS determines which applications should run in what order and how much time should be allowed for each application before giving another application a turn.

- It manages the sharing of internal memory among multiple applications.

- It handles input and output to and from attached hardware devices, such as hard disks, printers and dial-up ports.

- It sends messages to each application or interactive user (or to a system operator) about the status of operation and any errors that may have occurred.

- It can offload the management of batch jobs (for example, printing) so that the initiating application is freed from this work.

- On computers that can provide parallel processing, an operating system can manage how to divide the program so that it runs on more than one processor at a time.

All major computer platforms (hardware and software) require and sometimes include an operating system, and operating systems must be developed with different features to meet the specific needs of various form factors.

Types of Operating Systems

- A mobile OS allows smartphones, tablet PCs and other mobile devices to run applications and programs. Mobile operating systems include Apple iOS, Google Android, BlackBerry OS and Windows 10 Mobile.

- An embedded operating system is specialized for use in the computers built into larger systems, such as cars, traffic lights, digital televisions, ATMs, airplane controls, point of sale (POS) terminals, digital cameras, GPS navigation systems, elevators, digital media receivers and smart meters.

- A network operating system (NOS) is a computer operating system system that is designed primarily to support workstation, personal computer, and, in some instances, older terminals that are connected on a local area network (LAN).

- A real-time operating system (RTOS) is an operating system that guarantees a certain capability within a specified time constraint. For example, an operating system might be designed to ensure that a certain object was available for a robot on an assembly line.

Examples of Operating Systems

Common desktop operating systems include:

- Windows is Microsoft's flagship operating system, the de facto standard for home and business computers. Introduced in 1985, the GUI-based OS has been released in many versions since then. The user-friendly Windows 95 was largely responsible for the rapid development of personal computing.

- Mac OS is the operating system for Apple's Macintosh line of personal computers and workstations.

- Unix is a multi-user operating system designed for flexibility and adaptability. Originally developed in the 1970s, Unix was one of the first operating systems to be written in C language.

- Linux is a Unix-like operating system that was designed to provide personal computer users a free or very low-cost alternative. Linux has a reputation as a very efficient and fast-performing system.

KERNEL

The kernel is a computer program that is the core of a computer's operating system, with complete control over everything in the system. On most systems, it is one of the first programs loaded on start-up (after the bootloader). It handles the rest of start-up as well as input/output requests from software, translating them into data-processing instructions for the central processing unit. It handles memory and peripherals like keyboards, monitors, printers, and speakers.

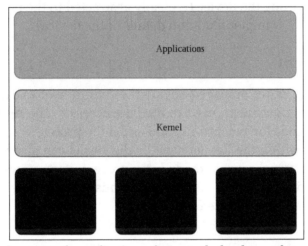

A kernel connects the application software to the hardware of a computer.

The critical code of the kernel is usually loaded into a separate area of memory, which is protected from access by application programs or other, less critical parts of the operating system. The kernel performs its tasks, such as running processes, managing hardware devices such as the hard disk, and handling interrupts, in this protected kernel space. In contrast, application programs like browsers, word processors, or audio or video players use a separate area of memory, user space. This separation prevents user data and kernel data from interfering with each other and causing instability and slowness, as well as preventing malfunctioning application programs from crashing the entire operating system.

The kernel's interface is a low-level abstraction layer. When a process makes requests of the kernel, it is called a system call. Kernel designs differ in how they manage these system calls and resources. A monolithic kernel runs all the operating system instructions in the same address space for speed. A microkernel runs most processes in user space, for modularity.

Functions

The kernel's primary function is to mediate access to the computer's resources, including:

- The central processing unit (CPU): This central component of a computer system is responsible for running or executing programs. The kernel takes responsibility for deciding at any time which of the many running programs should be allocated to the processor or processors.

- Random-access memory (RAM): Random-access memory is used to store both program instructions and data. Typically, both need to be present in memory in order for a program to execute. Often multiple programs will want access to memory, frequently demanding more memory than the computer has available. The kernel is responsible for deciding which memory each process can use, and determining what to do when not enough memory is available.

- Input/output (I/O) devices: I/O devices include such peripherals as keyboards, mice, disk drives, printers, USB devices, network adapters, and display devices. The kernel allocates requests from applications to perform I/O to an appropriate device and provides convenient methods for using the device (typically abstracted to the point where the application does not need to know implementation details of the device).

Resource Management

Key aspects necessary in resource management are the definition of an execution domain (address space) and the protection mechanism used to mediate access to the resources within a domain. Kernels also provide methods for synchronization and inter-process communication (IPC). These implementations may be within the Kernel itself or the kernel can also rely on other processes it is running. Although the kernel must provide inter-process communication in order to provide access to the facilities provided by each other, kernels must also provide running programs with a method to make requests to access these facilities.

Memory Management

The kernel has full access to the system's memory and must allow processes to safely access this memory as they require it. Often the first step in doing this is virtual addressing, usually achieved by paging and/or segmentation. Virtual addressing allows the kernel to make a given physical address appear to be another address, the virtual address. Virtual address spaces may be different for different processes; the memory that one process accesses at a particular (virtual) address may be different memory from what another process accesses at the same address. This allows every program to behave as if it is the only one (apart from the kernel) running and thus prevents applications from crashing each other.

On many systems, a program's virtual address may refer to data which is not currently in memory. The layer of indirection provided by virtual addressing allows the operating system to use other data stores, like a hard drive, to store what would otherwise have to remain in main memory (RAM). As a result, operating systems can allow programs to use more memory than the system has physically available. When a program needs data which is not currently in RAM, the CPU signals to the kernel that this has happened, and the kernel responds by writing the contents of an inactive memory block to disk (if necessary) and replacing it with the data requested by the program. The program can then be resumed from the point where it was stopped. This scheme is generally known as demand paging.

Virtual addressing also allows creation of virtual partitions of memory in two disjointed areas, one being reserved for the kernel (kernel space) and the other for the applications (user space). The applications are not permitted by the processor to address kernel memory, thus preventing an application from damaging the running kernel. This fundamental partition of memory space has contributed much to the current designs of actual general-purpose kernels and is almost universal in such systems, although some research kernels (e.g. Singularity) take other approaches.

Device Management

To perform useful functions, processes need access to the peripherals connected to the computer, which are controlled by the kernel through device drivers. A device driver is a computer program that enables the operating system to interact with a hardware device. It provides the operating system with information of how to control and communicate with a certain piece of hardware. The driver is an important and vital piece to a program application. The design goal of a driver is abstraction; the function of the driver is to translate the OS-mandated abstract function calls (programming calls) into device-specific calls. In theory, the device should work correctly with the suitable driver. Device drivers are used for such things as video cards, sound cards, printers, scanners, modems, and LAN cards. The common levels of abstraction of device drivers are:

On the hardware side:

- Interfacing directly.

- Using a high level interface (Video BIOS).

- Using a lower-level device driver (file drivers using disk drivers).

- Simulating work with hardware, while doing something entirely different.

On the software side:

- Allowing the operating system direct access to hardware resources.

- Implementing only primitives.

- Implementing an interface for non-driver software (Example: TWAIN).

- Implementing a language, sometimes high-level (Example PostScript).

For example, to show the user something on the screen, an application would make a request to the kernel, which would forward the request to its display driver, which is then responsible for actually plotting the character/pixel.

A kernel must maintain a list of available devices. This list may be known in advance (e.g. on an embedded system where the kernel will be rewritten if the available hardware changes), configured by the user (typical on older PCs and on systems that are not designed for personal use) or detected by the operating system at run time (normally called plug and play). In a plug and play system, a device manager first performs a scan on different hardware buses, such as Peripheral Component Interconnect (PCI) or Universal Serial Bus (USB), to detect installed devices, then searches for the appropriate drivers.

As device management is a very OS-specific topic, these drivers are handled differently by each kind of kernel design, but in every case, the kernel has to provide the I/O to allow drivers to physically access their devices through some port or memory location. Very important decisions have to be made when designing the device management system, as in some designs accesses may involve context switches, making the operation very CPU-intensive and easily causing a significant performance overhead.

System Calls

In computing, a system call is how a process requests a service from an operating system's kernel that it does not normally have permission to run. System calls provide the interface between a process and the operating system. Most operations interacting with the system require permissions not available to a user level process, e.g. I/O performed with a device present on the system, or any form of communication with other processes requires the use of system calls.

A system call is a mechanism that is used by the application program to request a service from the operating system. They use a machine-code instruction that causes the processor to change mode. An example would be from supervisor mode to protected mode. This is where the operating system performs actions like accessing hardware devices or the memory management unit. Generally the operating system provides a library that sits between the operating system and normal programs. Usually it is a C library such as Glibc or Windows API. The library handles the low-level details of passing information to the kernel and switching to supervisor mode. System calls include close, open, read, wait and write.

To actually perform useful work, a process must be able to access the services provided by the kernel. This is implemented differently by each kernel, but most provide a C library or an API, which in turn invokes the related kernel functions.

The method of invoking the kernel function varies from kernel to kernel. If memory isolation is in use, it is impossible for a user process to call the kernel directly, because that would be a violation of the processor's access control rules. A few possibilities are:

- Using a software-simulated interrupt: This method is available on most hardware, and is therefore very common.

- Using a call gate: A call gate is a special address stored by the kernel in a list in kernel memory at a location known to the processor. When the processor detects a call to that address, it instead redirects to the target location without causing an access violation. This requires hardware support, but the hardware for it is quite common.

- Using a special system call instruction: This technique requires special hardware support, which common architectures (notably, x86) may lack. System call instructions have been added to recent models of x86 processors, however, and some operating systems for PCs make use of them when available.

- Using a memory-based queue: An application that makes large numbers of requests but does not need to wait for the result of each may add details of requests to an area of memory that the kernel periodically scans to find requests.

Kernel Design Decisions

Issues of Kernel Support for Protection

An important consideration in the design of a kernel is the support it provides for protection from faults (fault tolerance) and from malicious behaviours (security). These two aspects are usually not clearly distinguished, and the adoption of this distinction in the kernel design leads to the rejection of a hierarchical structure for protection.

The mechanisms or policies provided by the kernel can be classified according to several criteria, including: static (enforced at compile time) or dynamic (enforced at run time); pre-emptive or post-detection; according to the protection principles they satisfy (e.g. Denning); whether they are hardware supported or language based; whether they are more an open mechanism or a binding policy; and many more. Support for hierarchical protection domains is typically implemented using CPU modes.

Many kernels provide implementation of "capabilities", i.e. objects that are provided to user code which allow limited access to an underlying object managed by the kernel. A common example occurs in file handling: a file is a representation of information stored on a permanent storage device. The kernel may be able to perform many different operations (e.g. read, write, delete or execute the file contents) but a user level application may only be permitted to perform some of these operations (e.g. it may only be allowed to read the file). A common implementation of this is for the kernel to provide an object to the application (typically called a "file handle") which the application may then invoke operations on, the validity of which the kernel checks at the time the operation is requested. Such a system may be extended to cover all objects that the kernel manages, and indeed to objects provided by other user applications.

An efficient and simple way to provide hardware support of capabilities is to delegate to the MMU the responsibility of checking access-rights for every memory access, a mechanism called capability-based addressing. Most commercial computer architectures lack such MMU support for capabilities.

An alternative approach is to simulate capabilities using commonly supported hierarchical domains; in this approach, each protected object must reside in an address space that the application does not have access to; the kernel also maintains a list of capabilities in such memory. When an application needs to access an object protected by a capability, it performs a system call and the kernel then checks whether the application's capability grants it permission to perform the requested action, and if it is permitted performs the access for it (either directly, or by delegating the request to another user-level process). The performance cost of address space switching limits the practicality of this approach in systems with complex interactions between objects, but it is used in current operating systems for objects that are not accessed frequently or which are not expected to perform quickly. Approaches where protection mechanism are not firmware supported but are instead simulated at higher levels (e.g. simulating capabilities by manipulating page tables on hardware that does not have direct support), are possible, but there are performance implications. Lack of hardware support may not be an issue, however, for systems that choose to use language-based protection.

An important kernel design decision is the choice of the abstraction levels where the security mechanisms and policies should be implemented. Kernel security mechanisms play a critical role in supporting security at higher levels.

One approach is to use firmware and kernel support for fault tolerance, and build the security policy for malicious behavior on top of that (adding features such as cryptography mechanisms where necessary), delegating some responsibility to the compiler. Approaches that delegate enforcement of security policy to the compiler and/or the application level are often called language-based security.

The lack of many critical security mechanisms in current mainstream operating systems impedes the implementation of adequate security policies at the application abstraction level. In fact, a common misconception in computer security is that any security policy can be implemented in an application regardless of kernel support.

Hardware-based or Language-based Protection

Typical computer systems today use hardware-enforced rules about what programs are allowed to access what data. The processor monitors the execution and stops a program that violates a rule (e.g., a user process that is about to read or write to kernel memory, and so on). In systems that lack support for capabilities, processes are isolated from each other by using separate address spaces. Calls from user processes into the kernel are regulated by requiring them to use one of the described system call methods.

An alternative approach is to use language-based protection. In a language-based protection system, the kernel will only allow code to execute that has been produced by a trusted language compiler. The language may then be designed such that it is impossible for the programmer to instruct it to do something that will violate a security requirement.

Advantages of this approach include:

- No need for separate address spaces. Switching between address spaces is a slow operation that causes a great deal of overhead, and a lot of optimization work is currently performed in order to prevent unnecessary switches in current operating systems. Switching is completely unnecessary in a language-based protection system, as all code can safely operate in the same address space.

- Flexibility. Any protection scheme that can be designed to be expressed via a programming language can be implemented using this method. Changes to the protection scheme (e.g. from a hierarchical system to a capability-based one) do not require new hardware.

Disadvantages include:

- Longer application start up time. Applications must be verified when they are started to ensure they have been compiled by the correct compiler, or may need recompiling either from source code or from bytecode.

- Inflexible type systems. On traditional systems, applications frequently perform operations that are not type safe. Such operations cannot be permitted in a language-based protection system, which means that applications may need to be rewritten and may, in some cases, lose performance.

Examples of systems with language-based protection include JX and Microsoft's Singularity.

Process Cooperation

Edsger Dijkstra proved that from a logical point of view, atomic lock and unlock operations operating on binary semaphores are sufficient primitives to express any functionality of process cooperation. However this approach is generally held to be lacking in terms of safety and efficiency, whereas a message passing approach is more flexible. A number of other approaches (either lower- or higher-level) are available as well, with many modern kernels providing support for systems such as shared memory and remote procedure calls.

I/O Devices Management

The idea of a kernel where I/O devices are handled uniformly with other processes, as parallel co-operating processes, was first proposed and implemented by Brinch Hansen (although similar ideas were suggested in 1967). In Hansen's description of this, the "common" processes are called internal processes, while the I/O devices are called external processes.

Similar to physical memory, allowing applications direct access to controller ports and registers can cause the controller to malfunction, or system to crash. With this, depending on the complexity of the device, some devices can get surprisingly complex to program, and use several different controllers. Because of this, providing a more abstract interface to manage the device is important. This interface is normally done by a Device Driver or Hardware Abstraction Layer. Frequently, applications will require access to these devices. The Kernel must maintain the list of these devices by querying the system for them in some way. This can be done through the BIOS, or through one of the various system buses (such as PCI/PCIE, or USB). When an application requests an operation on a device (Such as displaying a character), the kernel needs to send this request to the current active video driver. The video driver, in turn, needs to carry out this request. This is an example of Inter Process Communication (IPC).

Operating System Design/Kernel Architecture

An operating system is a construct that allows the user application programs to interact with the system hardware. Operating system by itself does not provide any function but it provides an atmosphere in which different applications and programs can do useful work.

There are many problems that can occur while designing and implementing an operating system. These are covered in operating system design and implementation.

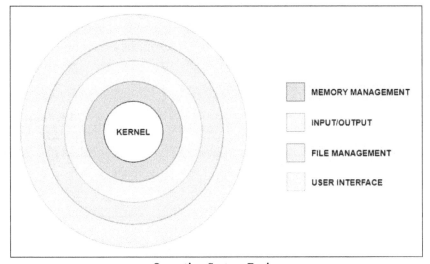

Operating System Design.

Operating System Design Goals

It is quite complicated to define all the goals and specifications of the operating system while designing it. The design changes depending on the type of the operating system i.e if it is batch system, time shared system, single user system, multi user system, distributed system etc.

There are basically two types of goals while designing an operating system. These are:

- User Goals: The operating system should be convenient, easy to use, reliable, safe and fast according to the users. However, these specifications are not very useful as there is no set method to achieve these goals.

- System Goals: The operating system should be easy to design, implement and maintain. These are specifications required by those who create, maintain and operate the operating system. But there is not specific method to achieve these goals as well.

Operating System Mechanisms and Policies

There is no specific way to design an operating system as it is a highly creative task. However, there are general software principles that are applicable to all operating systems.

A subtle difference between mechanism and policy is that mechanism shows how to do something and policy shows what to do. Policies may change over time and this would lead to changes in mechanism. So, it is better to have a general mechanism that would require few changes even when a policy change occurs.

For example - If the mechanism and policy are independent, then few changes are required in mechanism if policy changes. If a policy favours I/O intensive processes over CPU intensive processes, then a policy change to preference of CPU intensive processes will not change the mechanism.

Operating System Implementation

The operating system needs to be implemented after it is designed. Earlier they were written in assembly language but now higher level languages are used. The first system not written in assembly language was the Master Control Program (MCP) for Burroughs Computers.

Advantages of Higher Level Language

There are multiple advantages to implementing an operating system using a higher level language such as: the code is written more fast, it is compact and also easier to debug and understand. Also, the operating system can be easily moved from one hardware to another if it is written in a high level language.

Disadvantages of Higher Level Language

Using high level language for implementing an operating system leads to a loss in speed and increase in storage requirements. However in modern systems only a small amount of code is needed for high performance, such as the CPU scheduler and memory manager. Also, the bottleneck routines in the system can be replaced by assembly language equivalents if required.

Monolithic Kernel

A monolithic kernel is an operating system architecture where the entire operating system works in kernel space. It is a very basic operating system which performs tasks like file management, device management, memory management, and process management. All these processes are directly controlled within the kernel. This also manages resources between hardware and application along with User service and kernel services that are implemented under the same address space. It also increases the size of the kernel and thus increases the size of the operating system as well. This kernel was one of the most used and preferred OS architecture of the late 1980s and many operating systems have built upon this. Operating systems such as Linux, Solaris, AIX, OpenVMS, HP-UX, DOS, etc leverages Monolithic Kernel OS architecture.

The architecture diagram of a Monolithic Kernel, as you can see the IPC, file system, device drivers, etc. is working in the kernel space and thus have a larger kernel than Microkernel and hybrid kernel OS.

To understand any operating system it's very important to understand the architecture of the OS and the different components and how do they communicate with each other. As you can see from the architecture diagram shown, the monolithic kernel is a very old and basic operating system that perform tasks like batch processing, file transfer, etc. it works as a virtual machine and takes control over all the hardware components.

Key things to notice in Monolithic kernel architecture is:

- All the hardware components which are needed for processing is embedded inside the kernel.

- Since all the components are present inside the kernel, they can communicate with each other directly and also with the kernel.

- It can handle very limited resources and are ideal for performing smaller tasks.

- It can load modules dynamically, dynamically loadable modules incur a very small overhead as compared to build the module into the operating system image.

- It also helps to keep the amount of code running in kernel space to a minimum.

This kernel has a very simple architecture and that makes it so easy to work and understand. It also requires less code to write a monolithic kernel than other kernels like Microkernel. Monolithic kernel leverages one address space running in kernel mode for its functioning with all of the kernel and device drivers. The main advantage of this approach is effective especially with the x86 architecture was switching a task is an expensive operation.

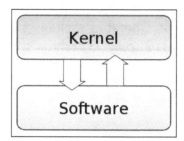

Graphical overview of Monolithic Kernel.

It offers high speed and is ideal for smaller tasks as it can handle limited resources. With a monolithic kernel, you can perform tasks like CPU scheduling, file management, memory management, and other functions via system calls.

Advantages

So far we have seen the architecture of the Monolithic kernel and what it can do, now let's see the advantages:

- The execution speed is faster in the monolithic kernel as compared to the microkernel.

- Less coding is required to write this kernel as compared to the microkernel.

- It is one single piece of software and thereby both source and compiled code is smaller.

- Monolithic Kernel consists of the core functions of the operating system and device drivers and capable of loading modules at runtime.

- Also loading the modules dynamically helps to keep the amount of code running in the kernel to a minimum.

Use this kernel when you need the execution to be fast and fewer resources need to be handled. Also if modules need to be load dynamically one can go with the Monolithic kernel OS, dynamic loading of modules is a more flexible way of handling the operating system image at runtime as compare to rebooting operating system image.

Scope

This OS has a very confined scope as it was only capable of performing smaller tasks. Also, there are certain limitations of Monolithic kernel OS that you should be well aware of while making a decision on the OS.

- This kernel is hard to extend.

- If any service crashes the whole system can get crashed in a monolithic kernel. This is the major drawback of Monolithic kernel.

- Coding in kernel space is hard as you can not make use of common libraries and debug is also hard.

- If a user wants to add a new service then the entire operating system has to be modified.

Microkernel

Microkernel is one of the classification of the kernel. Being a kernel it manages all system resources. But in a microkernel, the user services and kernel services are implemented in different address space. The user services are kept in user address space, and kernel services are kept under kernel address space, thus also reduces the size of kernel and size of operating system as well.

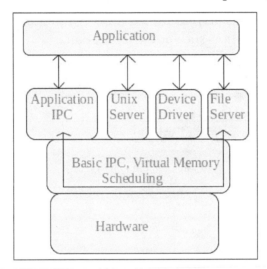

It provides minimal services of process and memory management. The communication between client program/application and services running in user address space is established through message passing, reducing the speed of execution microkernel. The Operating System remains unaffected as user services and kernel services are isolated so if any user service fails it does not affect kernel service. Thus it adds to one of the advantages in a microkernel. It is easily extendable i.e. if any new services are to be added they are added to user address space and hence requires no modification in kernel space. It is also portable, secure and reliable.

Microkernel Architecture

Since kernel is the core part of the operating system, so it is meant for handling the most important services only. Thus in this architecture only the most important services are inside kernel and rest of the OS services are present inside system application program. Thus users are able to interact with those not-so important services within the system application. And the microkernel is solely responsible for the most important services of operating system they are named as follows:

- Inter process-Communication,

- Memory Management,

- CPU-Scheduling.

Advantages of Microkernel

- The architecture of this kernel is small and isolated hence it can function better.

- Expansion of the system is easier, it is simply added in the system application without disturbing the kernel.

  Eclipse IDE is a good example of Microkernel Architecture.

Exokernel

Exokernel is an operating system developed at the MIT that provides application-level management of hardware resources. This architecture is designed to separate resource protection from management to facilitate application-specific customization.

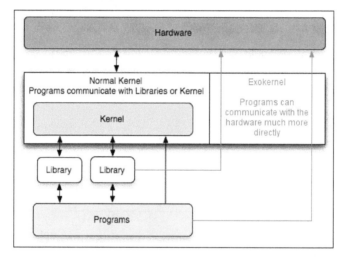

The ultimate idea behind the development of exokernel is to impose as few abstractions as possible on the developers of the applications by providing them with the freedom to use the abstractions as and when needed. This ensures that there is no forced abstraction, which is what makes exokernel different from micro-kernels and monolithic kernels.

This is done by moving all the hardware abstractions into untrusted user-space libraries called "library operating systems" (libOS), which are linked to applications call the operating system on their behalf. So basically, the kernel allocates the basic physical resources of the machine (disk blocks, memory, and processor time) to multiple application programs, and each program decides on what to do with these resources.

For an example, an application can manage its own disk-block cache, it can also share the pages with the other applications, but the exokernel allows cached pages to be shared securely across all applications. Thus, the exokernel protects pages and disk blocks, but applications manage them.

Of course, not all applications need customized resource management. At these instances, the applications can be linked with the support libraries that implement the abstractions that the applications need. However, library implementations are unprivileged and can therefore be modified or replaced at the user's needs as well. This helps the programmers to choose what level of abstraction they want, high, or low.

Principles of Exokernels

- Separate protection and management: Resource management is restricted to functions necessary for protection.

- Expose allocation: Applications allocate resources explicitly.

- Expose name: Exokernels use physical names wherever possible.

- Expose revocation: Exokernels let applications to choose which instance of a resource to give up.

- Expose information: Exokernels expose all system information and collect data that applications cannot easily derive locally.

Advantages of Exokernels

- Significant performance increase.

- Applications can make more efficient and intelligent use of hardware resources by being aware of resource availability, revocation and allocation.

- Ease development and testing of new operating system ideas. (New scheduling techniques, memory management methods, etc.)

Disadvantages of Exokernels

- Complexity in design of exokernel interfaces.

- Less consistency.

Hybrid Kernel

A hybrid kernel is an operating system kernel architecture that attempts to combine aspects and benefits of microkernel and monolithic kernel architectures used in computer operating systems.

The traditional kernel categories are monolithic kernels and microkernels (with nanokernels and exokernels seen as more extreme versions of microkernels). The "hybrid" category is controversial, due to the similarity of hybrid kernels and ordinary monolithic kernels; the term has been dismissed by Linus Torvalds as simple marketing.

The idea behind a hybrid kernel is to have a kernel structure similar to that of a microkernel, but to implement that structure in the manner of a monolithic kernel. In contrast to a microkernel, all (or nearly all) operating system services in a hybrid kernel are still in kernel space. There are none of the reliability benefits of having services in user space, as with a microkernel. However, just as with an ordinary monolithic kernel, there is none of the performance overhead for message passing and context switching between kernel and user mode that normally comes with a microkernel.

NT kernel

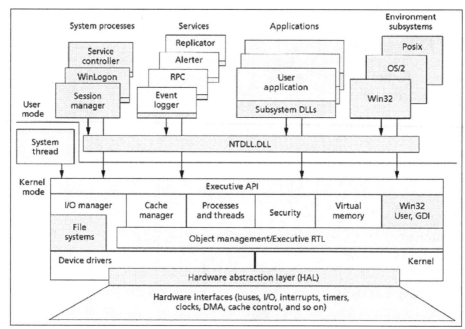

The Windows NT operating system family's architecture consists of two layers (user mode and kernel mode), with many different modules within both of these layers.

One prominent example of a hybrid kernel is the Microsoft Windows NT kernel that powers all operating systems in the Windows NT family, up to and including Windows 10 and Windows Server 2019, and powers Windows Phone 8, Windows Phone 8.1, and Xbox One. NT-based Windows is classified as a hybrid kernel (or a macrokernel) rather than a monolithic kernel because the emulation subsystems run in user-mode server processes, rather than in kernel mode as on a monolithic kernel, and further because of the large number of design goals which resemble design goals of Mach (in particular the separation of OS personalities from a general kernel design). Conversely, the reason NT is not a microkernel system is because most of the system components run in the same address space as the kernel, as would be the case with a monolithic design (in a traditional monolithic design, there would not be a microkernel per se, but the kernel would implement broadly similar functionality to NT's microkernel and kernel-mode subsystems).

The Windows NT design includes many of the same objectives as Mach, the archetypal microkernel system, one of the most important being its structure as a collection of modules that communicate via well-known interfaces, with a small microkernel limited to core functions such as first-level interrupt handling, thread scheduling and synchronization primitives. This allows for the possibility of using either direct procedure calls or interprocess communication (IPC) to communicate between modules, and hence for the potential location of modules in different address spaces (for example in either kernel space or server processes). Other design goals shared with Mach included support for diverse architectures, a kernel with abstractions general enough to allow multiple operating system personalities to be implemented on top of it and an object-oriented organisation.

The primary operating system personality on Windows is the Windows API, which is always present. The emulation subsystem which implements the Windows personality is called the Client/ Server Runtime Subsystem (csrss.exe). On versions of NT prior to 4.0, this subsystem process also contained the window manager, graphics device interface and graphics device drivers. For performance reasons, however, in version 4.0 and later, these modules (which are often implemented in user mode even on monolithic systems, especially those designed without internal graphics support) run as a kernel-mode subsystem.

Applications that run on NT are written to one of the OS personalities (usually the Windows API), and not to the native NT API for which documentation is not publicly available (with the exception of routines used in device driver development). An OS personality is implemented via a set of user-mode DLLs, which are mapped into application processes' address spaces as required, together with an emulation subsystem server process. Applications access system services by calling into the OS personality DLLs mapped into their address spaces, which in turn call into the NT run-time library (ntdll.dll), also mapped into the process address space. The NT run-time library services these requests by trapping into kernel mode to either call kernel-mode Executive routines or make Local Procedure Calls (LPCs) to the appropriate user-mode subsystem server processes, which in turn use the NT API to communicate with application processes, the kernel-mode subsystems and each other.

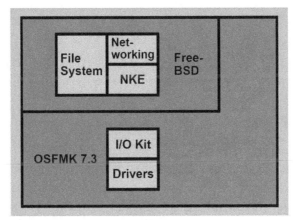

The XNU Kernel

XNU Kernel

XNU is the kernel that Apple Inc. acquired and developed for use in the macOS, iOS, watchOS, and tvOS operating systems and released as free and open source software as part of the Darwin operating system. *XNU* is an acronym for X is Not Unix.

Originally developed by NeXT for the NeXTSTEP operating system, XNU was a hybrid kernel combining version 2.5 of the Mach kernel developed at Carnegie Mellon University with components from 4.3BSD and an object-oriented API for writing drivers called Driver Kit.

After Apple acquired NeXT, the Mach component was upgraded to OSFMK 7.3, which is a microkernel. Apple uses a heavily modified OSFMK 7.3 functioning as a hybrid kernel with parts of FreeBSD included. (OSFMK 7.3 includes applicable code from the University of Utah Mach 4 kernel and applicable code from the many Mach 3.0 variants that sprouted off from the original Carnegie Mellon University Mach 3.0 kernel.) The BSD components were upgraded with code from the FreeBSD project and the Driver Kit was replaced with a C++ API for writing drivers called I/O Kit.

Like some other modern kernels, XNU is a hybrid, containing features of both monolithic and microkernels, attempting to make the best use of both technologies, such as the message passing capability of microkernels enabling greater modularity and larger portions of the OS to benefit from protected memory, as well as retaining the speed of monolithic kernels for certain critical tasks. XNU runs on ARM as part of iOS, IA-32, and x86-64 based processors.

TYPES OF OPERATING SYSTEMS

Mobile Operating System

A mobile operating system, also called a mobile OS, is an operating system that is specifically designed to run on mobile devices such as mobile phones, smartphones, PDAs, tablet computers and other handheld devices.

Much like the Linux or Windows operating system controls your desktop or laptop computer, a mobile operating system is the software platform on top of which other programs can run on mobile devices. The operating system is responsible for determining the functions and features available on your device, such as thumb wheel, keyboards, WAP, synchronization with applications, email, text messaging and more. The mobile OS will also determine which third-party applications (mobile apps) can be used on your device.

Types of Mobile Operating Systems

When you purchase a mobile device the manufacturer will have chosen the operating system for that specific device. Often, you will want to learn about the mobile operating system before you purchase a device to ensure compatibility and support for the mobile applications you want to use.

Android OS (Google Inc.)

The Android mobile operating system is Google's open and free software stack that includes an operating system, middleware and also key applications for use on mobile devices, including smartphones. Updates for the open source Android mobile operating system have been developed under "dessert-inspired" version names (Cupcake, Donut, Eclair, Gingerbread, Honeycomb, Ice Cream Sandwich) with each new version arriving in alphabetical order with new enhancements and improvements.

Bada (Samsung Electronics)

Bada is a proprietary Samsung mobile OS that was first launched in 2010. The Samsung Wave was the first smartphone to use this mobile OS. Bada provides mobile features such as multi-point-touch, 3D graphics and of course, application downloads and installation.

BlackBerry OS (Research in Motion)

The BlackBerry OS is a proprietary mobile operating system developed by Research In Motion for use on the company's popular BlackBerry handheld devices. The BlackBerry platform is popular with corporate users as it offers synchronization with Microsoft Exchange, Lotus Domino, Novell GroupWise email and other business software, when used with the BlackBerry Enterprise Server.

iPhone OS/iOS (Apple)

Apple's iPhone OS was originally developed for use on its iPhone devices. Now, the mobile operating system is referred to as iOS and is supported on a number of Apple devices including the iPhone, iPad, iPad 2 and iPod Touch. The iOS mobile operating system is available only on Apple's own manufactured devices as the company does not license the OS for third-party hardware. Apple iOS is derived from Apple's Mac OS X operating system.

MeeGo OS (Nokia and Intel)

A joint open source mobile operating system which is the result of merging two products based on open source technologies: Maemo (Nokia) and Moblin (Intel). MeeGo is a mobile OS designed to work on a number of devices including smartphones, netbooks, tablets, in-vehicle information systems and various devices using Intel Atom and ARMv7 architectures.

Palm OS (Garnet OS)

The Palm OS is a proprietary mobile operating system (PDA operating system) that was originally released in 1996 on the Pilot 1000 handheld. Newer versions of the Palm OS have added support for expansion ports, new processors, external memory cards, improved security and support for ARM processors and smartphones. Palm OS 5 was extended to provide support for a broad range of screen resolutions, wireless connections and enhanced multimedia capabilities and is called Garnet OS.

Symbian OS (Nokia)

Symbian is a mobile operating system (OS) targeted at mobile phones that offers a high-level of integration with communication and personal information management (PIM) functionality. Symbian OS combines middleware with wireless communications through an integrated mailbox and the integration of Java and PIM functionality (agenda and contacts). Nokia has made the Symbian platform available under an alternative, open and direct model, to work with some OEMs and the small community of platform development collaborators. Nokia does not maintain Symbian as an open source development project.

WebOS (Palm/HP)

WebOS is a mobile operating system that runs on the Linux kernel. WebOS was initially developed by Palm as the successor to its Palm OS mobile operating system. It is a proprietary Mobile OS which was eventually acquired by HP and now referred to as webOS (lower-case w) in HP literature. HP uses webOS in a number of devices including several smartphones and HP TouchPads. HP has pushed its webOS into the enterprise mobile market by focusing on improving security features and management with the release of webOS 3.x. HP has also announced plans for a version of webOS to run within the Microsoft Windows operating system and to be installed on all HP desktop and notebook computers in 2012.

Windows Mobile (Windows Phone)

Windows Mobile is Microsoft's mobile operating system used in smartphones and mobile devices – with or without touchscreens. The Mobile OS is based on the Windows CE 5.2 kernel. In 2010 Microsoft announced a new smartphone platform called Windows Phone 7.

Batch Processing Operating System

To avoid the problems of early systems the batch processing systems were introduced. The problem of early systems was more setup time. So the problem of more set up time was reduced by processing the jobs in batches, known as batch processing system. In this approach similar jobs were submitted to the CPU for processing and were run together.

The main function of a batch processing system is to automatically keep executing the jobs in a batch. This is the important task of a batch processing system i.e. performed by the 'Batch Monitor' resided in the low end of main memory.

This technique was possible due to the invention of hard-disk drives and card readers. Now the jobs could be stored on the disk to create the pool of jobs for its execution as a batch. First the pooled jobs are read and executed by the batch monitor, and then these jobs are grouped; placing the identical jobs (jobs with the similar needs) in the same batch, So, in the batch processing system, the batched jobs were executed automatically one after another saving its time by performing the activities (like loading of compiler) only for once. It resulted in improved system utilization due to reduced turn around time.

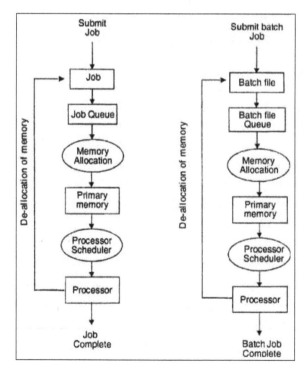

In the early job processing systems, the jobs were placed in a job queue and the memory allocateor managed the primary memory space, when space was available in the main memory, a job was selected from the job queue and was loaded into memory.

Once the job loaded into primary memory, it competes for the processor. When the processor became available, the processor scheduler selects job that was loaded in the memory and execute it.

In batch strategy is implemented to provide a batch file processing. So in this approach files of the similar batch are processed to speed up the task.

Traditional Job Processing

Batch File Processing

In batch processing the user were supposed to prepare a program as a deck of punched cards. The header cards in the deck were the "job control" cards which would indicate that which compiler was to be used (like FORTRAN, COBOL compilers etc). The deck of cards would be handed in to an operator who would collect such jobs from various users. Then the submitted jobs were 'grouped as FORTRAN jobs, COBOL jobs etc. In addition, these jobs were classified as 'long jobs' that required more processing time or short jobs which required a short processing time. Each set of jobs was considered as a batch and the processing would be done for a batch. For instance, there maybe a batch of short FORTRAN jobs. The output for each job would be separated and turned over to users in a collection area. So in this approach, files of the similar batch were processed to speed up the task.

In this environment there was no interactivity and the users had no direct control. In this system, only one job could engage the processor at a time and if there was any input/ output operation the processor had to sit idle till the completion of I/O job. So it resulted to the underutilization of CPU time.

In batch processing system, earlier; the jobs were scheduled in the order of their arrival i.e. First Come First Served (FCFS). Even though this scheduling method was easy and simple to implement but unfair for the situations where long jobs are queued ahead of the short jobs. To overcome this problem, another scheduling method named as 'Shortest Job First' was used. As memory management is concerned, the main memory was partitioned into two fixed partitions. The lower end of this partition was assigned to the resident portion of the OS i.e. named as Batch Monitor. Whereas, the other partition (higher end) was assigned to the user programs.

Though, it was an improved technique in reducing the system setup time but still there were some limitations with this technique like as under-utilization of CPU time, non-interactivity of user with the running jobs etc. In batch processing system, the jobs of a batch were executed one after another. But while these jobs were performing I/O operations; meantime the CPU was sitting idle resulting to low degree of resource utilization.

Time Sharing Operating System

Time-sharing means to share the time in among processes. When there are many processes and each process wants to loads on to the memory and each process wants to execute on the CPU then what operating system can do?

Simply, the time-sharing operating system tries to satisfy every process. When there are fewer resources and many processes are waiting for getting the resources comma that time sharing is the best solution for this problem. Time-sharing operating systems equally distribute the time among each of the processes.

Time-sharing systems are the interactive systems and support the multiprocessing and multi-programming. The time-sharing system allows multiple users to access and to share the computer concurrently. The time-sharing system can execute multiple processes together at the same time.

The time-sharing systems play a very important role when multiple computers are connected with a communication network. The time-sharing operating system can facilitate different processes to execute together. Time-sharing operating systems share the time between all the processes.

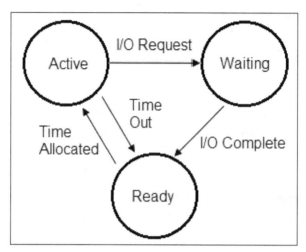

Each process is assigned a small amount of time, and this time is known as Time slice. Round Robin scheduling is a very famous scheduling algorithm of a time-sharing system. Any of the processes can execute in the CPU if a process has a time slice. When time slice of a process expires, then that process needs to leave the CPU. All this mechanism continues in a regular cycle.

Example of Time-sharing Operating Systems

For example, there are three users working on the same operating system, and suppose there are three processes. The process one is for user one and process 3 is for user 3. Keep in mind that the time-sharing operating system will manage all this process in such a way that every user feels that all the operating system is dedicated to him but actually it is not dedicated. We can load multiple processes together on the main memory.

When there are many processes to be load on the memory and the memory is not free, then the Operating System needs to move that process to the hard disk. Operating System maintains a job pool.

There are many examples of time-sharing operating systems. Some common examples are mentioned below; Windows 2000 server:

- Windows NT server,

- Unix ,

- Linux.

Advantages of Time-sharing Operating System

There are many advantages of time-sharing operating systems. Some of the most common advantages are mentioned:

- The time-sharing system helps to reduce the CPU idle time.

- Time-sharing systems improve response time.

- Time-sharing system avoids duplication of software.

Disadvantages of Time-sharing Operating Systems

Some common disadvantages of time-sharing operating systems are mentioned:

- When we share the time among different process, the problem of reliability can occur.

- When we share the time among different process then the problem of data communication can occur.

- Some questions of security and integrity of data in time-sharing systems are still under question.

Challenges of Time-sharing Systems

There are some challenges for the time sharing systems. If there are multiple processes in the system, then each process can interfere with each other, and sometimes this is not a good situation. First time sharing system was developed by IBM.

Distributed Operating Systems

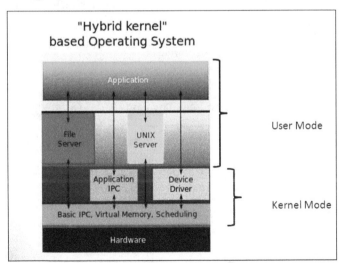

Structure of monolithic kernel, microkernel and hybrid kernel-based operating systems

A distributed operating system is a software over a collection of independent, networked, communicating, and physically separate computational nodes. They handle jobs which are serviced by multiple CPUs. Each individual node holds a specific software subset of the global aggregate operating system. Each subset is a composite of two distinct service provisioners. The first is a ubiquitous minimal kernel, or microkernel, that directly controls that node's hardware. Second is a higher-level collection of system management components that coordinate the node's individual and collaborative activities. These components abstract microkernel functions and support user applications.

The microkernel and the management components collection work together. They support the system's goal of integrating multiple resources and processing functionality into an efficient and stable system. This seamless integration of individual nodes into a global system is referred to as transparency, or single system image; describing the illusion provided to users of the global system's appearance as a single computational entity.

A distributed OS provides the essential services and functionality required of an OS but adds attributes and particular configurations to allow it to support additional requirements such as increased scale and availability. To a user, a distributed OS works in a manner similar to a single-node, monolithic operating system. That is, although it consists of multiple nodes, it appears to users and applications as a single-node.

Separating minimal system-level functionality from additional user-level modular services provides a "separation of mechanism and policy". Mechanism and policy can be simply interpreted as "what something is done" versus "how something is done," respectively. This separation increases flexibility and scalability.

Kernel

At each locale (typically a node), the kernel provides a minimally complete set of node-level utilities necessary for operating a node's underlying hardware and resources. These mechanisms include allocation, management, and disposition of a node's resources, processes, communication, and input/output management support functions. Within the kernel, the communications sub-system is of foremost importance for a distributed OS.

System management components overview.

In a distributed OS, the kernel often supports a minimal set of functions, including low-level address space management, thread management, and inter-process communication (IPC). A kernel of this design is referred to as a microkernel. Its modular nature enhances reliability and security, essential features for a distributed OS. It is common for a kernel to be identically replicated over all nodes in a system and therefore that the nodes in a system use similar hardware. The combination of minimal design and ubiquitous node coverage enhances the global system's extensibility, and the ability to dynamically introduce new nodes or services.

System Management

System management components are software processes that define the node's policies. These components are the part of the OS outside the kernel. These components provide higher-level communication, process and resource management, reliability, performance and security. The components match the functions of a single-entity system, adding the transparency required in a distributed environment.

The distributed nature of the OS requires additional services to support a node's responsibilities to the global system. In addition, the system management components accept the "defensive" responsibilities of reliability, availability, and persistence. These responsibilities can conflict with each other. A consistent approach, balanced perspective, and a deep understanding of the overall system can assist in identifying diminishing returns. Separation of policy and mechanism mitigates such conflicts.

Working together as an Operating System

The architecture and design of a distributed operating system must realize both individual node and global system goals. Architecture and design must be approached in a manner consistent with separating policy and mechanism. In doing so, a distributed operating system attempts to provide an efficient and reliable distributed computing framework allowing for an absolute minimal user awareness of the underlying command and control efforts.

The multi-level collaboration between a kernel and the system management components, and in turn between the distinct nodes in a distributed operating system is the functional challenge of the distributed operating system. This is the point in the system that must maintain a perfect harmony of purpose, and simultaneously maintain a complete disconnect of intent from implementation. This challenge is the distributed operating system's opportunity to produce the foundation and framework for a reliable, efficient, available, robust, extensible, and scalable system. However, this opportunity comes at a very high cost in complexity.

Price of Complexity

In a distributed operating system, the exceptional degree of inherent complexity could easily render the entire system an anathema to any user. As such, the logical price of realizing a distributed operation system must be calculated in terms of overcoming vast amounts of complexity in many areas, and on many levels. This calculation includes the depth, breadth, and range of design investment and architectural planning required in achieving even the most modest implementation.

These design and development considerations are critical and unforgiving. For instance, a deep understanding of a distributed operating system's overall architectural and design detail is required at an exceptionally early point. An exhausting array of design considerations are inherent in the development of a distributed operating system. Each of these design considerations can potentially affect many of the others to a significant degree. This leads to a massive effort in balanced approach, in terms of the individual design considerations, and many of their permutations. As an aid in this effort, most rely on documented experience and research in distributed computing power.

Distributed Computing Models

Three basic Distributions

To better illustrate this point, examine three system architectures; centralized, decentralized, and distributed. In this examination, consider three structural aspects: organization, connection, and control. Organization describes a system's physical arrangement characteristics. Connection covers the communication pathways among nodes. Control manages the operation of the earlier two considerations.

Organization

A centralized system has one level of structure, where all constituent elements directly depend upon a single control element. A decentralized system is hierarchical. The bottom level unites subsets of a system's entities. These entity subsets in turn combine at higher levels, ultimately culminating at a central master element. A distributed system is a collection of autonomous elements with no concept of levels.

Connection

Centralized systems connect constituents directly to a central master entity in a hub and spoke fashion. A decentralized system (aka network system) incorporates direct and indirect paths between constituent elements and the central entity. Typically this is configured as a hierarchy with only one shortest path between any two elements. Finally, the distributed operating system requires no pattern; direct and indirect connections are possible between any two elements. Consider the 1970s phenomena of "string art" or a spirograph drawing as a fully connected system, and the spider's web or the Interstate Highway System between U.S. cities as examples of a partially connected system.

Control

Centralized and decentralized systems have directed flows of connection to and from the central entity, while distributed systems communicate along arbitrary paths. This is the pivotal notion of the third consideration. Control involves allocating tasks and data to system elements balancing efficiency, responsiveness and complexity.

Centralized and decentralized systems offer more control, potentially easing administration by limiting options. Distributed systems are more difficult to explicitly control, but scale better horizontally and offer fewer points of system-wide failure. The associations conform to the needs imposed by its design but not by organizational chaos.

Design Considerations

Transparency

Transparency or single-system image refers to the ability of an application to treat the system on which it operates without regard to whether it is distributed and without regard to hardware or other implementation details. Many areas of a system can benefit from transparency, including access, location, performance, naming, and migration. The consideration of transparency directly affects decision making in every aspect of design of a distributed operating system. Transparency can impose certain requirements and/or restrictions on other design considerations.

Systems can optionally violate transparency to varying degrees to meet specific application requirements. For example, a distributed operating system may present a hard drive on one computer as "C:" and a drive on another computer as "G:". The user does not require any knowledge of device drivers or the drive's location; both devices work the same way, from the application's perspective. A less transparent interface might require the application to know which computer hosts the drive. Transparency domains:

- Location transparency: Location transparency comprises two distinct aspects of transparency, naming transparency and user mobility. Naming transparency requires that nothing in the physical or logical references to any system entity should expose any indication of the entity's location, or its local or remote relationship to the user or application. User mobility requires the consistent referencing of system entities, regardless of the system location from which the reference originates.

- Access transparency: Local and remote system entities must remain indistinguishable when viewed through the user interface. The distributed operating system maintains this perception through the exposure of a single access mechanism for a system entity, regardless of that entity being local or remote to the user. Transparency dictates that any differences in methods of accessing any particular system entity—either local or remote—must be both invisible to, and undetectable by the user.

- Migration transparency: Resources and activities migrate from one element to another controlled solely by the system and without user/application knowledge or action.

- Replication transparency: The process or fact that a resource has been duplicated on another element occurs under system control and without user/application knowledge or intervention.

- Concurrency transparency: Users/applications are unaware of and unaffected by the presence/activities of other users.

- Failure transparency: The system is responsible for detection and remediation of system failures. No user knowledge/action is involved other than waiting for the system to resolve the problem.

- Performance Transparency: The system is responsible for the detection and remediation of local or global performance shortfalls. Note that system policies may prefer some users/ user classes/tasks over others. No user knowledge or interaction is involved.

- Size/Scale transparency: The system is responsible for managing its geographic reach, number of nodes, level of node capability without any required user knowledge or interaction.

- Revision transparency: The system is responsible for upgrades and revisions and changes to system infrastructure without user knowledge or action.

- Control transparency: The system is responsible for providing all system information, constants, properties, configuration settings, etc. in a consistent appearance, connotation, and denotation to all users and applications.

- Data transparency: The system is responsible for providing data to applications without user knowledge or action relating to where the system stores it.

- Parallelism transparency: The system is responsible for exploiting any ability to parallelize task execution without user knowledge or interaction.

Inter-process Communication

Inter-Process Communication (IPC) is the implementation of general communication, process interaction, and dataflow between threads and/or processes both within a node, and between nodes in a distributed OS. The intra-node and inter-node communication requirements drive low-level IPC design, which is the typical approach to implementing communication functions that support transparency. In this sense, Interprocess communication is the greatest underlying concept in the low-level design considerations of a distributed operating system.

Process Management

Process management provides policies and mechanisms for effective and efficient sharing of resources between distributed processes. These policies and mechanisms support operations involving the allocation and de-allocation of processes and ports to processors, as well as mechanisms to run, suspend, migrate, halt, or resume process execution. While these resources and operations can be either local or remote with respect to each other, the distributed OS maintains state and synchronization over all processes in the system.

As an example, load balancing is a common process management function. Load balancing monitors node performance and is responsible for shifting activity across nodes when the system is out of balance. One load balancing function is picking a process to move. The kernel may employ several selection mechanisms, including priority-based choice. This mechanism chooses a process based on a policy such as 'newest request'. The system implements the policy.

Resource Management

Systems resources such as memory, files, devices, etc. are distributed throughout a system, and at any given moment, any of these nodes may have light to idle workloads. Load sharing and load balancing require many policy-oriented decisions, ranging from finding idle CPUs, when to move, and which to move. Many algorithms exist to aid in these decisions; however, this calls for a second level of decision making policy in choosing the algorithm best suited for the scenario, and the conditions surrounding the scenario.

Reliability

Distributed OS can provide the necessary resources and services to achieve high levels of reliability, or the ability to prevent and/or recover from errors. Faults are physical or logical defects that can cause errors in the system. For a system to be reliable, it must somehow overcome the adverse effects of faults.

The primary methods for dealing with faults include fault avoidance, fault tolerance, and fault detection and recovery. Fault avoidance covers proactive measures taken to minimize the occurrence of faults. These proactive measures can be in the form of transactions, replication and backups. Fault tolerance is the ability of a system to continue operation in the presence of a fault. In the event, the system should detect and recover full functionality. In any event, any actions taken should make every effort to preserve the single system. Availability is the fraction of time during which the system can respond to requests.

Performance

Many benchmark metrics quantify performance; throughput, response time, job completions per unit time, system utilization, etc. With respect to a distributed OS, performance most often distills to a balance between process parallelism and IPC. Managing the task granularity of parallelism in a sensible relation to the messages required for support is extremely effective. Also, identifying when it is more beneficial to migrate a process to its data, rather than copy the data, is effective as well.

Synchronization

Cooperating concurrent processes have an inherent need for synchronization, which ensures that changes happen in a correct and predictable fashion. Three basic situations that define the scope of this need:

- One or more processes must synchronize at a given point for one or more other processes to continue,

- One Or more processes must wait for an asynchronous condition in order to continue,

- Or A Process must establish exclusive access to a shared resource.

Improper synchronization can lead to multiple failure modes including loss of atomicity, consistency, isolation and durability, deadlock, livelock and loss of serializability.

Flexibility

Flexibility in a distributed operating system is enhanced through the modular and characteristics of the distributed OS, and by providing a richer set of higher-level services. The completeness and quality of the kernel/microkernel simplifies implementation of such services, and potentially enables service providers greater choice of providers for such services.

Network Operating System

Network Operating System is an operating system that includes special functions for connecting computers and devices into a local-area network (LAN) or Inter-network. Short form of Network Operating system is NOS. Some popular network operating systems are Novell Netware, Windows NT/2000, Linux, Sun Solaris, UNIX, and IBM OS/2. The network operating system which was first developed is Novell Netware. It was developed in 1983.

An operating system that provides the connectivity among a number of autonomous computers is called a network operating system. A typical configuration for a network operating system is a collection of personal computers along with a common printer, server and file server for archival storage, all tied together by a local network.

Some of the features of Network Operating System are to:

- It allows multiple computers to connect so that they can share data, files and hardware devices.

- Provide basic operating system features such as support for processors, protocols, automatic hardware detection and support multi-processing of applications.

- Provide security features such as authentication, logon restrictions and access control.

- Provide name and directory services.

- Provide file, print, web services and back-up services.

- Support Internetworking such as routing and WAN ports.

- User management and support for logon and logoff, remote access; system management, administration and auditing tools with graphical interfaces.

- It has clustering capabilities.

- It has internetworking features. Example: Routing.

- In this, the users can remotely access each other.

- It also includes security features. Example: authentication of data, restrictions on required data, authorisations of users etc.

- It can also manage directory and name services.

- It also provides basic network administration utilities like access to the user.

- It also provides priority to the printing jobs which are in the queue in the network.

- It detects the new hardware whenever it is added to the system.

Types of Network Operating Systems

Peer-to-peer network operating systems allow users to share resources and files located on their computers and to access shared resources found on other computers. In a peer-to-peer network, all computers are considered equal; they all have the same privileges to use the resources available on the network. Peer-to-peer networks are designed primarily for small to medium local area networks. Windows for Workgroups is an example of the program that can function as peer-to-peer network operating systems.

Advantages of Peer-to-Peer(P2P) Operating System are as follows:

- Less requirement of hardware is there.

- No server needs to be established.

- Its setup process is natural.

Disadvantages of Peer-to-Peer(P2P) Operating System are as follows:

- It has no central location for storage, i.e. different systems have different storage capacity.

- It has less security as compared to the client-server model.

Client/server network operating systems allow the network to centralise functions and applications in one or more dedicated file servers. The file servers become the heart of the system, providing access to resources and providing security. The workstations (clients) have access to the resources available on the file servers. The network operating system allows multiple users to share the same resources irrespective of physical location simultaneously. Novell Netware and Windows 2000 Server are examples of client/ server network operating systems.

Each computer in the workgroup run an autonomous operating system; yet cooperate to allow a variety of facilities including sharing of files, sharing of hardware resources and execution of remote machines etc.

Network operating systems are implementations of loosely coupled operating systems on top of loosely coupled hardware. Network operating systems is the software that supports the use of a network of machines and provides users that are aware of using a set of computers, with facilities designed to ease the use of remote resources located over the network. These resources are made available as services and might be printers, processors, file systems or other devices. Some resources, of which dedicated hardware devices such as printers, tape drives are connected to and managed by a particular machine and are made available to other machines in the network via a service. A typical example of such a system is a set of workstations connected through a local area network (LAN). Every workstation has its operating system every user has its workstation in exclusive use and cooperates to allow a variety of facilities including sharing of files, sharing of hardware resources and execution of remote machines etc. A user can execute a login command to connect to another station and also can access a set of shared files maintained by a workstation named/file server.

Advantages of Client Server Operating System are as follows:

- In this, security to the machines is provided through the server.

- Here, hardware can be easily connected to the system.

- Also, new technology is easily integrated into the system.

- The central server is more stable in a client-server model.

- Hardware and the operating system can be specialised.

- In this model, different machines can remotely access the server from different locations.

Disadvantages Client Server Operating System is as follows:

- It seems to be costly as buying and running a server is cost effective.
- Also, here we always have to depend on the central location for any type of operation like for storage, for accessing of data etc.
- It requires regular maintenance.
- Daily updation is required as per requirement.

Embedded Operating Systems

Embedded Systems are a specially designed computer system that essentially contains software and hardware for performing specific tasks. Mobile Phones, Laptops, Cameras, Washing Machines, ATMS, and Hair Straightener etc., are examples of Embedded System.

As the name suggests Embedded Operating System is an Embedded System's Operating System. It has limited features. It is usually designed for some particular operations to control an electronic device. For instance, all mobile phones essentially consist of an operating system that always boots up when the mobile phone is in running condition. It controls all the features and basic interface of the mobile phone. There are some other programs that can be loaded onto the mobile phones. Mostly, JAVA Apps run on the top. Embedded operating systems runs on embedded processors.

Characteristics of Embedded Operating Systems

The main characteristics of Embedded Operating Systems are as follows:

- Direct use of interrupts,
- Reactive operation,
- Real-time operation,
- Streamlined protection mechanisms,
- I/O device flexibility,
- Configurability.

There are two different kinds of operating system, either general purpose operating system that is modified in such a way that it runs on top of a device or the operating system can be custom written. The approaches for the design of operating system include that either we take embedded Operating System that is existing and adapt it to our embedded application or we can design and use a new operating system that is particularly for our Embedded System.

We can adapt the existing Operating System to our embedded application by streamline operation, real-time capability and be adding other necessary functions. The advantage of this approach that it has a familiar interface and its disadvantage is that it is not optimized for real-time.

The most common examples of embedded operating system around us include Windows Mobile/CE (handheld Personal Data Assistants), Symbian (cell phones) and Linux. Flash Memory Chip is added on a motherboard in case of the embedded operating system of your personal computer to boot from the Personal Computer.

Types of Embedded Operating Systems

Single System Control Loop

Single system control loop is the simplest type of embedded operating system. It is so like operating system but it is designed to run the only single task. It still under debate that this system should be classified as a type of operating system or not.

Multi-tasking Operating System

As the name suggests that this operating system can perform multiple tasks. In multi-tasking operating system there are several tasks and processes that execute simultaneously. More than one function can be performed if the system has more than one core or processor.

The operating system is switched between tasks. Some tasks wait for events while other receive events and become ready to run. If one is using a multitasking operating system, then software development is simplified because different components of software can be made independent to each other.

Rate Monotonic Operating System

It is a type of operating system that ensures that task runs in a system can run for a specific interval of time and for a specific period of time. When it is not ensured, there comes a notification of failure to system software to take suitable action. This time limit cannot be ensured if the system is oversubscribed, at this point another event may occur during run time and the failure notification comes.

Preemptive Operating System

A preemptive operating system is a type of multitasking operating system that interprets the preemptive predominance for tasks. A higher priority is task is always defined and run before a lower priority task. Such multi-tasking operating systems are efficient in increasing system response to events and also simplify the development of software making the system more reliable. The designer of the system may be able to calculate the time required for the service interprets in a system and also the time is taken by the scheduler for switching tasks. Such systems may fail to meet the deadline of a system and the software is unaware of the missed deadline. CPU loading in a preemptive operating system can be measured naturally by defining a lower priority task that only increments counter and do nothing else.

Real Time Operating System

A real-time operating system is the one which serves real time applications. It processes data as it comes in. The time requirements for processing of operating system are usually measured in shorter increments or in 10th of seconds. They may be time sharing or driven by events. Real time Operating systems are used in small embedded systems.

The main features of real-time operating system include:

- Process threads that can be defined,

- Multitasking,

- Interrupt levels.

The RTOS is an operating system, it is a brain of the real-time system and its response to inputs immediately. In the RTOS, the task will be completed by the specified time and its responses in a predictable way to unpredictable events. The structure of the RTOS is shown.

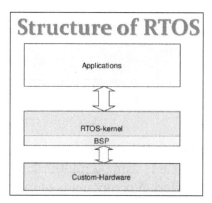

Types of RTOS

There are three different types of RTOS which are following:

- Soft real-time operating system,

- Hard real-time operating system,

- Firm real-time operating system.

Soft Real-time Operating System

The soft real-time operating system has certain deadlines, may be missed and they will take the action at a time t=0+. The soft real-time operating system is a type of OS and it does not contain constrained to extreme rules. The critical time of this operating system is delayed to some extent. The examples of this operating system are the digital camera, mobile phones and online data etc.

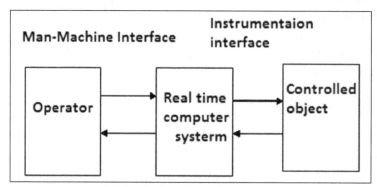

Soft Real-Time Operating System.

Hard Real-time Operating System

This is also a type of OS and it is predicted by a deadline. The predicted deadlines will react at a time t = 0. Some examples of this operating system are air bag control in cars, anti-lock brake, and engine control system etc.

Firm Real-time Operating System

In the firm real-time, an operating system has certain time constraints, they are not strict and it may cause undesired effects. Examples of this operating system are a visual inspection in industrial automation.

Working with Real-time Operating System

There are different types of basic functionalities of an RTOS are following:

- Priority based scheduler,

- System clock interrupt routine,

- Deterministic behavior,

- Synchronization and Messaging,

- RTOS service.

Priority based Scheduler

In the priority-based scheduler, most of the RTOS is between 32 and 256 possible priorities for the individual tasks or processes. This scheduler will run the process with the highest priority. If the task is running on the CPU, then the next highest priority task runs and continuous the processes.

In the system, the highest priority process will have the CPU:

- It runs to close,

- If the original task is pre-empted by the new then a high priority process is made ready.

There are three states of the tasks or processes which are like ready to run and the other one is blocked and description of each state is given.

Ready to Run

The ready to run is said to be when the process has all the resources to run, but it should not be in the running state. Then it is called as a ready to run.

Running

If the task is executing then it is said to have a running state.

Blocked

In this state, if it doesn't have the enough resources to run, then it is sent to blocked state. Three techniques are modified to schedule the task, there are following with their description.

Cooperating Scheduling

In this type of scheduling, the task will run until the execution is completed.

Round Robin Scheduling

In this scheduling, each process is assigned a fixed time slot and the process needs to complete its execution or else the task loses its flow and data generation.

Preemptive Scheduling

The preemptive scheduling involves in the priority time-dependent time allocation. In generally 256 priority levels are used and each task has a unique priority level. There are some systems which support the more priority level and multiple tasks have some priorities.

System Clock Interrupt Routine

To perform the time sensitive operation the RTOS will provide some sort of system clocks. If there is a 1ms system clock, then you have to complete the task in 50ms. Usually, there is an API that follows you to say "In 50ms wake me up". Hence the task would be in sleeping position until the RTOS will wake up. We have two notices that the woken up will not ensure to run exactly at that time, it depends on the priority and if the higher priority is running currently it would be delayed.

Deterministic Behavior

The RTOS moves to great length to protect that whether you have taken 100 tasks or 10 tasks, it does not make any difference in the distance to switch context and it determines the next highest priority task. In the prime area deterministic the RTOS is the interrupt handling, when the interrupt line is signaled them the RTOS immediately takes the action of the correct interrupt service routine and interrupt is handled without any delay.

We have to noise that the developers of the project will write the hardware specific ISR's. Before now the RTOS gives the ISR's for the serial ports, system clocks and it may be a networking hardware, but if there is anything specialized like pacemaker signals, actuators, etc., are not be a part of the RTOS.

This is all about the gross generalizations and there is a large variety implementation in the RTOS. Some of the RTOS are operated differently and the above description is capable for the large portion of existing RTOS.

Synchronization and Messaging

The synchronization and messaging provides the communication between the task of one system to another system and the messaging services are following. To synchronize the internal activities the event flag is used and to send the text messages we can use in the mailbox, pipes and message queues. In the common data areas, the semaphores are used.

- Semaphores;
- Event flags;
- Mailboxes;
- Pipes;
- Message queues.

RTOS Service

The most important part of the operating system is the Kernel. To monitor the hardware the task should be relieved and the responsibilities kernel manages & allocate the resources. If the task can't obtain the CPU attention for every time, then there are some other services provide by the kernel. The following are:

- Time services;
- Interrupt handling services;
- Device management services;
- Memory management services;
- Input-output services.

Advantages of RTOS

- When all the resources and devices are inactive, then the RTOS gives maximum consumption of the system and more output.
- When a task is performing there is a no chance to get the error because the RTOS is an error free.
- Memory allocation is the best type to manage in this type of system.
- In this type of system, the shifting time is very less.
- Because of the small size of the program, the RTOS is used in the embedded system like transport and others.

References

- Operating-system-design-and-implementation: tutorialspoint.com, Retrieved 5 January, 2019
- Hansen, Per Brinch (2001). "The evolution of operating systems" (PDF). Retrieved 2006-10-24. Included in book: Per Brinch Hansen, ed. (2001). "1" (PDF). Classic operating systems: from batch processing to distributed systems. New York: Springer-Verlag. Pp. 1–36. ISBN 978-0-387-95113-3

- Operating-system-microkernel: geeksforgeeks.org, Retrieved 6 February, 2019

- Ball, Stuart R. (2002) [2002]. Embedded Microprocessor Systems: Real World Designs (first ed.). Elsevier Science. ISBN 978-0-7506-7534-5

- Mobile-operating-systems-mobile-os-explained, Hardware-Software: webopedia.com, Retrieved 7 March, 2019

- L.B. Ryzhyk, A.Y. Burtsev. Architectural design of de1 distributed operating system. System Research and Information Technologies international scientific and technical journal, October 2004, Kiev, Ukraine

- Batch-processing-operating-system, disk-operating-system, fundamental: ecomputernotes.com, Retrieved 8 April, 2019

- Hansen, Per Brinch, ed. (2001). Classic Operating Systems: From Batch Processing to Distributed Systems. Springer. ISBN 978-0-387-95113-3

- Time-sharing-operating-systems: t4tutorials.com, Retrieved 9 May, 2019

2

Mobile Operating Systems

The operating system which has been specifically designed to be used in phones, tablets and other mobile devices is known as a mobile operating system. Some of its common types are android and iOS. This chapter has been carefully written to provide an easy understanding of the varied facets of these types of mobile operating systems.

ANDROID

Android is a software package and linux based operating system for mobile devices such as tablet computers and smartphones.

It is developed by Google and later the OHA (Open Handset Alliance). Java language is mainly used to write the android code even though other languages can be used.

The goal of android project is to create a successful real-world product that improves the mobile experience for end users.

There are many code names of android such as Lollipop, Kitkat, Jelly Bean, Ice cream Sandwich, Froyo, Ecliar, Donut etc.

Open Handset Alliance (OHA)

It's a consortium of 84 companies such as google, samsung, AKM, synaptics, KDDI, Garmin, Teleca, Ebay, Intel etc.

It was established on 5th November, 2007, led by Google. It is committed to advance open standards, provide services and deploy handsets using the Android Plateform.

Features of Android

The important features of android are given below:

- It is open-source.

- Anyone can customize the Android Platform.

- There are a lot of mobile applications that can be chosen by the consumer.

- It provides many interesting features like weather details, opening screen, live RSS (Really Simple Syndication) feeds etc.

It provides support for messaging services(SMS and MMS), web browser, storage (SQLite), connectivity (GSM, CDMA, Blue Tooth, Wi-Fi etc.), media, handset layout etc.

Categories of Android applications

There are many android applications in the market. The top categories are:

- Entertainment
- Tools
- Communication
- Productivity
- Personalization
- Music and Audio
- Social
- Media and Video
- Travel and Local etc.

Android Pie

Android Pie (codenamed Android P during development) is the ninth major release and the 16th version of the Android mobile operating system. It was first released as a developer preview on March 7, 2018, and released publicly on August 6, 2018.

As of May 2019, 10.4% of Android devices checking in with Google Play run Pie.

Features

User Experience

Android Pie utilizes a refresh of Google's "material design" language, unofficially referred to as "Material Design 2.0". The revamp provides for more variance in aesthetics, encouraging the creation of custom "themes" for the base guidelines and components rather than a standardized appearance. Bottom-aligned navigation bars are also more prominent. As applied to Android Pie's interface, rounded corners (influenced by the proprietary Google theme used by in-house software implementing Material Design 2.0) are more prominent. In addition, Pie contains official support for screen cutouts ("notches"), including APIs and system behaviors depending on their size and position. Android certification requirements restrict devices to two cutouts, which may only be along the top or bottom of the screen.

The most significant user interface change on Pie is a redesigned on-screen navigation bar. Unlike previous versions of Android, it only consists of a slim home button, and a back button rendered only when available. The bar utilizes gesture navigation: swiping up opens the "Overview" screen, a redesign of the existing recent apps menu. Swiping the handle to the right activates application switching. The gesture bar is used primarily on new devices such as the Pixel 3; existing devices may either use the previous navigation key setup or offer the ability to opt into gesture navigation. As opposed to the previous recent apps menu, Overview utilizes a horizontal layout rather than vertical, and text may also be selected and copied from apps appearing there. The Pixel Launcher exclusively supports the ability to access the app drawer and most recently used apps from the overview as well. However, this integration is proprietary, as there are no current plans to offer the necessary integration to third-party software due to security concerns. In addition, when rotation lock is enabled, rotating the device causes a screen rotation button to appear on the navigation bar.

The notification area was redesigned, with the clock moved to the left, and the number of icons that may be displayed at once limited to four, in order to accommodate displays that may have "notch" cutouts in the center. The drop-down panels attached to quick settings items have been removed; long-pressing a toggle directs users to the relevant settings screen. Notifications for chats can now be threaded, displaying previous messages within (complementing the existing inline reply functionality). If a particular type of notification is frequently dismissed, the user will now be offered to disable it. The do not disturb mode has been overhauled with a larger array of settings.

The power menu now contains a screenshot button (which itself now supports cropping an image after taking one), and an optional "lockdown" mode that disables biometric unlock methods. The volume pop-up now only controls media volume, as well as the choice of sound, vibrate, or silent modes for notifications. Users are directed to the settings menu to change the volume of notifications. A magnifier display has been added to text selection, and "smart linkify" offers access to relevant apps if particular types of text (such as phone numbers or addresses) are highlighted.

Platform

Android Pie introduces a major change to power management, using algorithms to prioritize background activity by apps based on long-term usage patterns and predictions, dividing apps into "Active", "Working Set" (run often), "Frequent", "Rare", and "Never". Similar "adaptive brightness" settings are adjusted automatically based on detected lighting conditions. Both of these features were developed in collaboration with DeepMind.

The "PrecomputedText" API (also available as a compatibility library compatible with Android 4.0 and newer) can be used to perform text display processing in a background thread as opposed to a UI thread to improve performance. The fingerprint authentication API has also been revamped to account for different types of biometric authentication experiences (including face scanning and in-screen fingerprint readers).

Android Runtime can now create compressed bytecode files, and profiler data can be uploaded to Google Play servers to be bundled with apps when downloaded by users with a similar device.

Apps targeting older Android API levels (beginning with Android 4.2) display a warning when launched. Google Play Store is now requiring all apps to target an API level released within the past year, and will also mandate 64-bit support in 2019.

Android Pie supports IEEE 802.11mc, including Wi-Fi Round Trip Time for location positioning.

The camera API now supports accessing multiple cameras at once. Apps may no longer perform background audio or video recording unless they run a foreground service. There is support for the High Efficiency Image Format (subject to patent licensing and hardware support) and VP9 Profile 2.

DNS over TLS is supported under the name "Private DNS".

Android Go for Android Pie uses less storage than the previous release, and has enhancements to security and storage tracking.

Android Oreo

Android "Oreo" (codenamed Android O during development) is the eighth major release and the 15th version of the Android mobile operating system. It was first released as an alpha quality developer preview in March 2017 and released to the public on August 21, 2017.

It contains a number of major features, including notification grouping, picture-in-picture support for video, performance improvements and battery usage optimization, and support for autofillers, Bluetooth 5, system-level integration with VoIP apps, wide color gamuts, and Wi-Fi Aware. Android Oreo also introduces two major platform features: Android Go – a software distribution of the operating system for low-end devices – and support for implementing a hardware abstraction layer.

As of May 2019, 28.3% of Android devices run Oreo, with 12.9% on 8.0 and 15.4% on 8.1, making the Oreo major release the most commonly used version of Android.

Features

User Experience

Notifications can be snoozed, and batched into topic-based groups known as "channels". The 'Major Ongoing' feature orders the alerts by priority, pinning the most important application to the top slot. Android Oreo contains integrated support for picture-in-picture modes (supported in the YouTube app for YouTube Premium subscribers). The "Settings" app features a new design, with a white theme and deeper categorization of different settings, while its ringtone, alarm and notification sound settings now contain an option for adding custom sounds to the list.

The Android 8.1 update supports the display of battery percentages for connected Bluetooth devices, makes the notification shade slightly translucent, and dims the on-screen navigation keys in order to reduce the possibility of burn-in.

Platform

Android Oreo adds support for Neighborhood Aware Networking (NAN) for Wi-Fi based on Wi-Fi Aware, Bluetooth 5, wide color gamuts in apps, an API for autofillers, multiprocess and Google Browsing support for WebViews, an API to allow system-level integration for VoIP apps, and launching activities on remote displays. Android Runtime (ART) features performance improvements. Android Oreo contains additional limits on apps' background activities in order to improve battery life. Apps can specify "adaptive icons" for differently-shaped containers specified by themes, such as circles, squares, and squircles.

Android Oreo supports new emoji that were included in the Unicode 10 standard. A new emoji font was also introduced, which notably redesigns its face figures to use a traditional circular shape, as opposed to the "blob" design that was introduced on KitKat.

The underlying architecture of Android was revised so that low-level, vendor-specific code for supporting a device's hardware can be separated from the Android OS framework using a hardware abstraction layer known as the "vendor interface". Vendor interfaces must be made forward compatible with future versions of Android. This new architecture, called Project Treble, allows the quicker development and deployment of Android updates for devices, as vendors would only need to make the necessary modifications to their bundled software. All devices shipping with Oreo must support a vendor interface, but this feature is optional for devices being updated to Oreo from an earlier version. The "seamless updates" system introduced in Android 7.0 was also modified to download update files directly to the system partition, rather than requiring them to be downloaded to the user partition first. This reduces storage space requirements for system updates.

Android Oreo introduces a new automatic repair system known as "Rescue Party"; if the operating system detects that core system components are persistently crashing during startup, it will automatically perform a series of escalating repair steps. If all automatic repair steps are exhausted, the device will reboot into recovery mode and offer to perform a factory reset.

The Android 8.1 update also introduces a neural network API, which is designed to "[provide] apps with hardware acceleration for on-device machine learning operations." This API is designed for use with machine learning platforms such as TensorFlow Lite, and specialized co-processors such as the Pixel Visual Core (featured in Google's Pixel 2 smartphones, but dormant until 8.1 is installed), but it also provides a CPU fallback mode.

Android Go

A tailored distribution for low-end devices known as Android Go was unveiled for Oreo; it is intended for devices with 1 GB of RAM or less. This mode has platform optimizations designed to reduce mobile data usage (including enabling Data Saver mode by default), and a special suite of Google Mobile Services designed to be less resource- and bandwidth-intensive. The Google Play Store will also highlight lightweight apps suited for these devices. The operating system's interface is also modified, with the quick settings panel providing greater prominence to information regarding the battery, mobile data limit, and available storage, the recent apps menu using a modified layout and being limited to four apps (in order to reduce RAM consumption), and an API for allowing mobile carriers to implement data tracking and top-ups within the Android settings menu. Google Play Services was also modularized to reduce its memory footprint.

Android Go was made available to OEMs for Android 8.1.

Security

Android Oreo re-brands automatic scanning of Google Play Store and sideloaded apps as "Google Play Protect", and gives the feature, as well as Find My Device (formerly Android Device Manager) higher prominence in the Security menu of the Settings app. As opposed to a single, system-wide setting for enabling the installation of apps from sources outside of the Google Play Store, this function is now implemented as a permission that can be granted to individual apps (i.e. clients for third-party app repositories such as Amazon Appstore and F-Droid). Verified boot now includes a "Rollback Protection" feature, which enforces a restriction on rolling back the device to a previous version of Android, aimed at preventing a potential thief from bypassing security measures by installing a previous version of the operating system that doesn't have them in place.

Android Nougat

Android "Nougat" (codenamed Android N during development) is the seventh major version and 14th original version of the Android operating system. First released as an alpha test version on March 9, 2016, it was officially released on August 22, 2016, with Nexus devices being the first to receive the update. The LG V20 was the first smartphone released with Nougat.

Nougat introduces notable changes to the operating system and its development platform, including the ability to display multiple apps on-screen at once in a split-screen view, support for inline replies to notifications, and an expanded "Doze" power-saving mode that restricts device functionality once the screen has been off for a period of time. Additionally, the platform switched to an OpenJDK-based Java environment and received support for the Vulkan graphics rendering API, and "seamless" system updates on supported devices.

Nougat received positive reviews. The new app notification format received particular praise, while the multitasking interface was seen as a positive change, but reviewers experienced incompatible apps. Critics had mixed experiences with the Doze power-saving mode, but faster app installs and "tweaks" to the user interface were also reviewed positively.

As of May 2019, 19.2% of devices that access Google Play run Nougat, with 11.4% on Android 7.0 (API 24) and 7.8% on Android 7.1 (API 25).

Features

User Experience

Nougat redesigns the notification shade, which now features a smaller row of icons for settings, replacing notification cards with a new "sheet" design, and allowing inline replies for notifications. Multiple notifications from a single app can also be "bundled", and there is greater per-app control over notifications.

A split-screen display mode was introduced for phones, in which two apps can be snapped to occupy halves of the screen. An experimental multi-window mode is also available as a hidden feature, where multiple apps can appear simultaneously on the screen in overlapping windows.

The "Doze" power saving mechanism introduced in Android Marshmallow was expanded to include a state activated when the device is running on battery and the screen has been off for a period of time but is not stationary. In this state, network activity is restricted, and apps are granted "maintenance windows" in which they can access the network and perform background tasks. As in Marshmallow, the full Doze state is activated if the device is stationary with its screen off for a period of time. A new "Data Saver" mode restricts background mobile data usage, and can trigger internal functions in apps that are designed to reduce bandwidth usage, such as capping the quality of streaming media.

The updated notification shade on Nougat.

Platform

In December 2015, Google announced that Android Nougat would switch its Java Runtime Environment from the defunct Apache Harmony to OpenJDK—the official open source implementation of the Java platform maintained by Oracle Corporation and the Java community. The Android Runtime (ART) now incorporates a profile-guided compilation system, utilizing a JIT compiler and profiling alongside its current ahead-of-time compiler to further optimize apps for a device's hardware and other conditions in the background.

Nougat introduces a system for enabling "seamless", automatic system updates, based upon and sharing some code with the implementation of similar functionality on Chrome OS. The system uses a pair of SquashFS partitions; the Android system executes from an "online" partition, while updates are applied in the background to a redundant "offline" partition. On the next boot following the installation of an update, the redundant partition is designated as active, and the device henceforth boots into the updated system. The previous system partition is kept as a backup in case of update failure, and to serve as the "offline" partition for the next update. This system removes the requirement for the device to reboot into the system recovery environment to apply the update (which prevents the device from being used until the update is complete) and also provides the ability for an update to be automatically rolled back in case of a failure. Google chose to enable seamless updates only for devices shipped with Nougat (or later), rather than enabling earlier devices to support the feature after repartitioning. Additionally, due to the ART changes on Nougat, apps no longer need to be re-compiled upon the first boot after a system update.

Developer Preview 2 added platform support for Vulkan, a new low-level 3D-rendering API alternative to OpenGL ES with higher graphics performance.

Nougat is the first version featuring Unicode 9.0 support, and comes with updated emoji, plus support for emoji skin tones.

Android 7.1 adds native API support for implementing image keyboards; multi-endpoint telephony; shortcut menus and rounded icon assets for apps on launchers; and support for the Google Daydream virtual reality platform. The Daydream environment includes a "sustained performance mode" to assist developers in optimizing apps to a device's thermal profile, a new head tracking algorithm which combines the input from various device sensors, and integration of system notifications into the VR user interface.

Security

In response to the Stagefright family of bugs disclosed and fixed in 2015, several changes were made to harden the media stack against future vulnerabilities. Runtime integer overflow detection was implemented, preventing the majority of Stagefright-like programming bugs from becoming vulnerabilities, in addition to helping fix and prevent such bugs. Android's monolithic MediaServer process was redesigned to better adhere to the principle of least privilege. MediaServer is now split into several separate processes, each running in its own unprivileged sandbox, and granted only the permissions required for its task. For example, only the AudioServer can access Bluetooth, and libstagefright now runs within the MediaCodecService sandbox, which is only granted GPU access. Further constraints were placed on the media stack through seccomp.

Various mechanisms were enabled to reduce the possibility of malicious code being injected and/ or executed inside the Linux kernel, including dividing kernel memory into logical segments for code and data, with page access permissions of read-only and no-execute as appropriate. The kernel was also restricted from directly accessing user space memory, and stronger stack protection was enabled in the GCC compiler to reduce stack smashing. To limit exposure of the kernel to potentially malicious code, perf was disabled by default, ioctl commands were restricted by SELinux, and seccomp-bpf was enabled to grant processes the ability to restrict system calls.

On devices shipping with Android Nougat, the "Verified Boot" policy (introduced partially on Kit-Kat, and displaying notifications on startup on Marshmallow) must be strictly enforced. If system files are corrupted or otherwise modified, the operating system will only allow operation in a limited-use mode or will refuse to boot at all.

Android Marshmallow

Android "Marshmallow" (codenamed Android M during development) is the sixth major version of the Android operating system and the 13th version of Android. First released as a beta build on May 28, 2015, it was officially released on October 5, 2015, with Nexus devices being the first to receive the update.

Marshmallow primarily focuses on improving the overall user experience of its predecessor, Lollipop. It introduced a new permissions architecture, new APIs for contextual assistants (first used by a new feature "Now on Tap" to provide context-sensitive search results), a new power management system that reduces background activity when a device is not being physically handled, native support for fingerprint recognition and USB-C connectors, the ability to migrate data and applications to a microSD card, and other internal changes.

As of May 2019, 16.9% of devices accessing Google Play run Android 6.0. It is the single most popular point release of Android, while the Android Nougat and Oreo major releases, 7.x and 8.x, both have larger install bases.

Features

User Experience

A new "Assist" API allows information from a currently opened app, including text and a screenshot of the current screen, to be sent to a designated "assistant" application for analysis and processing. This system is used by the Google Search app feature "Google Now on Tap", which allows users to perform searches within the context of information currently being displayed on-screen. While the "Home" button was used in Android 5 to show available apps, the "Home" button is used now (together with a voice command) to generate on-screen cards which display information, suggestions, and actions related to the content. "Direct Share" allows Share menus to display recently used combinations of contacts and an associated app as direct targets.

"Adoptable storage" allows a newly inserted SD card or other secondary storage media to be designated as either "portable" or "internal" storage. "Portable" maintains the default behavior of previous Android versions, treating the media as a secondary storage device for storage of user files, and the storage media can be removed or replaced without repercussions, but is subject to access restrictions by apps. When designated as "Internal" storage, the storage media is reformatted with an encrypted ext4 file system, and is "adopted" by the operating system as the primary storage partition. Existing data (including applications and "private" data folders) are migrated to the external storage, and normal operation of the device becomes dependent on the presence of the media. Apps and operating system functions will not function properly if the adopted storage device is removed. If the user loses access to the storage media, the adopted storage can be "forgotten", which makes the data permanently inaccessible. Samsung and LG have, however, removed the ability to use an SD card as "internal" storage on their Galaxy S7 and G5 devices, with Samsung arguing that the feature could result in unexpected losses of data, and prevents users from being able to transfer data using the card.

Platform

Android Marshmallow introduces a redesigned application permissions model; apps are no longer automatically granted all of their specified permissions at installation time. An opt-in system is now used, in which users are prompted to grant or deny individual permissions (such as the ability to access the camera or microphone) to an application when they are needed for the first time. Applications remember the grants, which can be revoked by the user at any time. The new permissions model is used only by applications developed for Marshmallow using its software development kit (SDK), and older apps will continue to use the previous all-or-nothing approach. Permissions can still be revoked for those apps, though this might prevent them from working properly, and a warning is displayed to that effect.

Marshmallow introduces new power management schemes known as "Doze" and "App Standby"; when running on battery power, a device will enter a low-power state if it is inactive and not being physically handled. In this state, network connectivity and background processing is restricted, and only "high-priority" notifications are processed. Additionally, network access by apps is deferred if the user has not recently interacted with the app. Apps may request a permission to exempt themselves from these policies, but will be rejected from Google Play Store as a violation of its "Dangerous Products" policy if their core functionality is not "adversely affected" by them.

Android Marshmallow provides native support for fingerprint recognition on supported devices via a standard API, allowing third-party applications to implement fingerprint-based authentication. Fingerprints can be used for unlocking devices and authenticating Play Store and Google Pay purchases. Android Marshmallow supports USB-C, including the ability to instruct devices to charge another device over USB. Marshmallow also introduces "verified links" that can be configured to open directly in their specified application without further user prompts. User data for apps targeting Marshmallow can be automatically backed up to Google Drive over Wi-Fi. Each application receives up to 25 MB of storage, which is separate from a user's Google Drive storage allotment.

As of Marshmallow, the Android Compatibility Definition Document contains new security mandates for devices, dictating that those that are capable of accessing encrypted data without affecting performance must enable secure boot and device encryption by default. These conditions comprise part of a specification that must be met in order to be certified for the operating system, and be able to license Google Mobile Services software. The requirement for mandatory device encryption was originally intended to take effect on Lollipop, but was delayed due to performance issues.

IOS

IOS is a mobile operating system for Apple-manufactured devices. iOS runs on the iPhone, iPad, iPod Touch and Apple TV.

iOS is best known for serving as the underlying software that allows iPhone users to interact with their phones using gestures such as swiping, tapping and pinching. These finger actions are typically performed on multitouch capacitive touch screen displays, which provide fast response and accept inputs from multiple fingers. Although it is not the No. 1 mobile OS globally, iOS dominates the North American market by a large margin, with a 60 percent market share as of May 2010.

iOS is derived from Mac OS X and is a Unix-like OS. There are four abstraction layers within iOS:

- Core OS Layer: Provides low-level features as well as frameworks for security and interaction with external hardware.
- Core Services Layer: Provides services required by upper layers.
- Media Layer: Provides the necessary technologies for graphics, audio and video.
- Coca Touch Layer: Where frameworks are located, which are often used when creating an application.

iOS comes with a lot of default apps, including an email client, a Safari Web browser, a portable media player (iPod) and the phone app.

Developers can use the iOS software development kit (SDK) to create applications for Apple mobile devices. The SDK includes tools and interfaces for developing, installing, running and testing apps.

Native apps can be written using the iOS system frameworks and the Objective-C programming language. Included in the iOS SDK are Xcode Tools, which include an integrated development environment (IDE) for managing application projects, a graphical tool for creating the user interface and a debugging tool for analyzing runtime performance. It also includes an iOS simulator, which allows developers to test apps on a Mac, and an iOS developer library, which provides all the necessary documentation and reference material.

iOS 13

iOS 13 is the thirteenth major release of the iOS mobile operating system developed by Apple Inc., being the successor to iOS 12. It was announced at the company's Worldwide Developers Conference on June 3, 2019, and is scheduled to be released in September 2019.

System Features

Privacy

iOS 13 contains changes to the handling of location data. When an app requests access to location, the user can choose whether to grant access whenever they are using the app, or only once. The user will also receive similar prompts for background location access, and if an app requests access to Bluetooth or Wi-Fi.

In August 2019, it was reported that beginning April 2020, the PushKit API for VoIP will be restricted to internet telephony usage only, closing a "loophole" that had been used by other apps for background data collection.

User Interface

A system-wide dark mode was implemented, allowing users to enable a light-on-dark color scheme for the entire iOS and iPadOS user interface and all native applications, as well as all supported third-party apps. It can be manually turned on or set to automatically switch between light and dark modes based on the time of day.

iOS 13 introduces an updated volume indicator which appears on the left side of the screen as opposed to previous versions where the indicator was located in the center of the screen. The user can slide their finger up and down the volume indicator to change the system volume.

Siri

Siri uses a software-generated voice called "Neural TTS" instead of using clips of human voices which will allow Siri to sound more natural. Siri will also become more functional and new sound control will be available. The Siri Shortcuts app is now installed by default. Siri will also use HomePods to learn and recognize voices of different people. It will also be possible for Siri to read messages aloud.

Keyboard

The QuickType virtual keyboard now features QuickPath, allowing the user to swipe their finger across the keyboard to complete words and phrases. This functionality was previously exclusively available via certain third-party keyboard applications such as SwiftKey or Gboard. Emoji stickers have been included on the emoji keyboard and so are available for use anywhere regular emoji can be input.

Text Manipulation

A new systemwide gesture interface was added for cut, copy, paste, undo, and redo for iOS 13 and iPadOS 13. A three-finger swipe left or up will undo and three fingers right or down will redo. A single three-finger pinch will copy, a second three-finger pinch will cut, and a three-finger spread pastes. A three-finger single tap will bring up a shortcut menu with all five options.

The blue text cursor can now be moved around text fields by pressing and holding to pick it up and move it. Many new options for text selection have also been added – double tapping a word will select it, triple tapping selects a sentence, and quadruple tapping a paragraph selects it.

Sign in with Apple

A new single sign-on implementation known as "Sign in with Apple" was implemented, allowing users to create accounts with third-party services with a minimal amount of information. Users have the option to generate a disposable email address for each site, improving privacy, anonymity, and further reduces the amount of information that can be associated with a single email address. All iOS applications that support third-party login methods, such as Facebook and Google, must support the "Sign in with Apple" system, and the iOS human interface guidelines recommend that developers place the "Sign in with Apple" option above other login methods.

Performance

Several improvements to performance in iOS 13 were implemented. Face ID on the iPhone X, XS / XS Max, and iPhone XR now unlocks the devices up to 30 percent faster than it does on iOS 12. App downloads will be up to 50 percent smaller due to a new format, and app updates will be up to 60 percent smaller.

Other changes

The version of iOS available for iPad devices was renamed iPadOS, noting the platform and functionality differences compared to iOS for iPhone and iPod touch.

iOS 13 adds official support for the Sony DualShock 4 and the Microsoft Xbox One controller. iOS 13 also adds support for wireless audio sharing for AirPods and certain Beats headphones.

A new multi-select gesture is available in supported applications such as Files and Mail. Multiple items, such as files or emails, can be quickly selected by dragging two fingers over the desired items.

App Features

Messages and Memoji

User profiles can now be created and Memoji can be used as an iMessage profile picture. All iOS devices with an A9 processor or newer can now create custom Memoji. Memoji and Animoji can now be used as a sticker in iMessage and other apps; they are also available as regular emoji for use anywhere the emoji keyboard is available. There are a variety of new customization options for Memoji.

Maps

The Maps app features a redesigned maps UI, featuring more detailed maps and Look Around, a street level imagery implementation similar to Google Street View.

Reminders

Redesigned and rebuilt from the ground up with new features such as the ability to suggest when a reminder should be delivered to the user, and the ability to tag contacts so that references to reminders can be surfaced elsewhere, such as in Messages.

Photos

The Photos app includes a redesigned UI and uses machine learning to auto-hide "clutter" images such as screenshots and documents.

Photos now has a redesigned interface showing users photos they took in the past year, month, week and day. Bringing all photos to one page and showing you photos based on what your device suggests you.

Supported Devices

iOS 13 drops support for several devices, including all devices with an Apple A8 chip or earlier, and devices with only 1 GB of RAM. This also marks the first time any 64-bit devices were dropped. Devices no longer supported by iOS 13 include the iPhone 5S, iPhone 6 / 6 Plus, and the sixth-generation iPod touch.

To further differentiate features between iPhones and iPads, iOS 13 is now specific to the iPhone and iPod touch, and Apple has rebranded the tablet oriented platform with its own operating system, iPadOS.

iPhone

- iPhone 6S
- iPhone 6S Plus
- iPhone SE
- iPhone 7
- iPhone 7 Plus
- iPhone 8
- iPhone 8 Plus
- iPhone X
- iPhone XS
- iPhone XS Max
- iPhone XR

iPod Touch

- iPod Touch (7th generation).

iOS 12

iOS 12 is the twelfth and current major release of the iOS mobile operating system developed by Apple Inc., being the successor to iOS 11. It was announced at the company's Worldwide Developers Conference on June 4, 2018. It is aesthetically similar to iOS 11 but contains numerous performance and battery life improvements, security updates, and additional functions within native applications. It was released to the public on September 17, 2018.

iOS 12 focuses on performance and quality improvements.

System Features

Performance

Performance optimizations were made in order to speed up common tasks across all supported iOS devices. Tests done by Apple on an iPhone 6 Plus showed apps launching 40 percent faster, the system keyboard activating 50 percent faster, and the camera opening 70 percent faster.

Screen Time

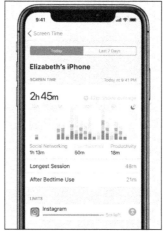

The Screen Time usage information screen in iOS 12 on iPhone X.

Screen Time is a new feature in iOS 12 that records the amount of time a user spent on the device. The feature also displays the amount of time the user used particular apps, the amount of time the user used particular categories of apps (such as games), and the number of notifications the user received.

Screen Time also provides blocking features to limit usage of apps (with time limits) or set other restrictions such as on purchases or explicit content. It replaces Parental Controls in the iOS Settings app, but can also be used by adults to limit their own usage. These features can be used with or without a passcode. Without setting a passcode, the limits can easily be bypassed but may serve as a useful reminder of usage goals.

Shortcuts

A dedicated application in iOS 12 allows users to set up Shortcuts, automated actions that the user can ask Siri to perform. Using the Shortcuts app, you can create phrases and type in the action you want

Siri to do for you. Once you say the phrase to Siri, Siri will automatically do the task you set for it in the Shortcuts app. The Shortcuts app replaces the Workflow app that Apple acquired in March 2017.

ARKit 2

ARKit now allows users to share their view with other iOS 12-supported devices. ARKit 2 additionally allows full 2D image tracking and incorporates the ability to detect 3D objects.

CarPlay

CarPlay can now run third-party navigation applications. (Waze, Google Maps, etc).

iPad

The Voice Memos and Stocks apps are now available for iPads.

Control Center is separated from the app switcher on iPad and can be opened with a swipe down on the top right corner. In addition, iPhone X-style gestures are introduced across all iPads running iOS 12.

Keyboard

In iOS 12, the trackpad mode (which allows the user to freely move the cursor) is enabled by long-pressing the space bar on devices without 3D Touch.

App Switcher

For devices with gesture navigation and no home button (iPhone X and later), users can now force quit applications by swiping up from the bottom of the screen (without having to press and hold on them when in the app switcher).

App Features

Messages

Messages in iOS 12 introduces a new type of customizable Animoji called "Memoji" which allows a user to create a 3D character of themselves. Apple also introduced Koala, Tiger, Ghost and T-Rex Animojis. In addition, Apple added new text and GIF effects similar to those found on other social media applications.

Face Time

FaceTime gains support for Animoji and Memoji, as well as new text and GIF effects similar to those found on other social media applications and in the Messages application.

iOS 12.1, released on October 30, 2018, adds the ability to include up to 32 people in a FaceTime conversation. This feature is only supported with video by devices with the Apple A8X or Apple A9 chip or later; it is only supported for audio on iPhone 5S, iPhone 6, and iPhone 6 Plus, and is not available at all on iPad Mini 2, iPad Mini 3, and iPad Air. Group FaceTime was disabled on January 28, 2019 due to a software bug that allowed calls to be answered by the caller rather than the recipient, allowing video and audio to be transmitted unless the call was declined. The functionality was restored on February 7, 2019 with the release of iOS 12.1.4. Group FaceTime remains disabled on devices running iOS 12 that are affected by the bug.

Measure

Measure is a native AR application that allows the user to take measurements of real objects. It also works as a level, a feature that was originally packaged as part of the Compass app.

Photos

Apple Photos has been completely redesigned with four new tabs, including "Photos", "For You", "Albums", and "Search". The new "For You" tab replaces the "Memories" tab previously found in iOS 11 and makes sharing recommendations, creates short length video collages, photo editing suggestions, as well as featured photos from a specific day.

While the "Photos" and "Albums" tabs received only a few cosmetic changes, the "Search" tab includes new Artificial Intelligence and Machine Learning features which show the user photos by place and categories (e.g. animals, cars, objects).

Notifications

Notifications are now grouped by application and have a "manage" button to turn off notifications for that app or to deliver them quietly right from the notification center without having to go into the Settings application.

Do not Disturb

Do Not Disturb gives users more options for automation. Users can hide notifications indefinitely or scheduled like previously, but can also hide notifications for 1 hour, until a time of day, until leaving a location, or until the end of a scheduled event in Calendar.

Voice Memos and Stocks

Voice Memos and Stocks are supported on iPad, and have a newer design. Stocks was integrated with Apple News to show financial and other related news.

Apple Books

iBooks was renamed Apple Books, and the app was redesigned, with five new tabs, including "Reading Now", "Library", "Book Store", "Audio Books", and "Search". The new app design is similar to that of Apple Music, and has been praised for its simplicity in allowing users to easily navigate their book library.

Safari

Safari receives an update to Intelligent Tracking Prevention. This includes a feature which allows the user to disable social media "like" and "share" buttons.

Maps

Apple Maps has started to be rebuilt from the ground up by relying on first-party map data instead of using map data provided by third parties. This allows for more accurate directions and predictions on the fastest routes. The new maps will be rolled out in sections and Apple expects to have the entire US completed by the end of 2019. As of April 2019, Arizona, California, Hawaii and New Mexico are the only states to have completely first party map data.

Problems

Rainbow Flag Emoji

After a rainbow flag emoji with an interdictory sign over it appeared on Twitter, several users accused Apple of encouraging anti-LGBT attitudes. However, Emojipedia has clarified that this occurs when a user tweets the two emojis together and is not an intended feature. This can be used with other emojis as well.

Facetime Eavesdropping Issue

Earlier this year Apple acknowledged a widespread eavesdropping FaceTime issue impacting several versions of iOS 12 (versions 12.1–12.1.3) that allowed users to call someone via FaceTime and hear the audio coming from their phone before answering the call.

Supported Devices

Any device that supports iOS 11 can be upgraded to iOS 12. This includes:

iPhone	iPod Touch	iPad
• iPhone 5S	• iPod Touch (6th generation)	• iPad Air
• iPhone 6	• iPod Touch (7th generation)	• iPad Air 2
• iPhone 6 Plus		• iPad Air (2019)
• iPhone 6S		• iPad (2017)
• iPhone 6S Plus		• iPad (2018)
• iPhone SE		• iPad Mini 2
• iPhone 7		• iPad Mini 3
• iPhone 7 Plus		• iPad Mini 4
• iPhone 8		• iPad Mini (2019)
• iPhone 8 Plus		• iPad Pro (9.7-inch)
• iPhone X		• iPad Pro (10.5-inch)
• iPhone XS		• iPad Pro (11-inch)
• iPhone XS Max		• iPad Pro (12.9-inch 1st generation)
• iPhone XR		• iPad Pro (12.9-inch 2nd generation)
		• iPad Pro (12.9-inch 3rd generation)

iOS 11

iOS 11 is the eleventh major release of the iOS mobile operating system developed by Apple Inc., being the successor to iOS 10. It was announced at the company's Worldwide Developers Conference on June 5, 2017, and released on September 19, 2017. It was succeeded by iOS 12 on September 17, 2018.

Among iOS 11's changes: the lock screen and Notification Center were combined, allowing all notifications to be displayed directly on the lock screen. The various pages of the Control Center were unified, gaining custom settings and the ability to 3D Touch icons for more options. The App Store received a visual overhaul to focus on editorial content and daily highlights. A "Files" file manager app allowed direct access to files stored locally and in cloud services. Siri was updated to translate between languages and use a privacy-minded "on-device learning" technique to better understand a user's interests and offer suggestions. The camera had new settings for improved portrait-mode photos and utilised new encoding technologies to reduce file sizes on newer devices. In a later release, Messages was integrated with iCloud to better synchronize messages across iOS and macOS devices. A previous point release also added support for person-to-person Apple Pay payments. The operating system also introduced the ability to record the screen, limited forms of drag-and-drop functionality, and support for augmented reality. Certain new features appeared only on iPad, including an always-accessible application dock, cross-app drag-and-drop, and a new user interface to show multiple apps at once.

Shortly after release, it was discovered that disabling Wi-Fi and Bluetooth connections through the Control Center does not disable the respective chips in the device in order to remain functional for background connectivity, a design decision sparking criticism for "misleading" users and reducing security due to potential vulnerabilities in inactive open connections. The iOS 11.2 update added warning messages and a new toggle color to explain the new functions. iOS 11 has also received continuous criticism from critics and end-users for its perceived stability and performance issues, particularly on older devices; Apple has issued numerous software updates to address such issues and has dedicated iOS 12 mainly toward stability and performance improvements in response.

Two months after release, 52% of iOS devices were running iOS 11, a slower adoption rate than previous iOS versions. The number increased to 85% of devices by September 2018.

On June 4, 2018, at the Worldwide Developers Conference, Apple announced its successor, iOS 12.

System Features

Lock Screen

The lock screen and Notification Center are combined, allowing users to see all notifications directly on the lock screen. Scrolling up and down will either show or hide notifications.

Control Center

The Control Center redesign unifies its pages and allows users to 3D Touch (or long press on devices without 3D Touch) buttons for more options. Sliders adjust volume and brightness. The Control

Center is customizable via the Settings app, and allows more settings to be shown, including cellular service, Low Power Mode, and a shortcut to the Notes app.

The default Control Center on an iPhone 7 Plus.

Siri

The Siri intelligent personal assistant has a more human voice and supports language translation, with English, Chinese, French, German, Italian and Spanish available at launch. It will also support follow-up questions by users. Users will also be able to type to Siri.

Siri will be able to use "on-device learning", a privacy-minded local learning technique to understand a user's behavior and interests inside different apps, to offer better suggestions and recommendations.

Settings

A new "Do Not Disturb While Driving" mode lets users block unnecessary notifications as long as their iPhone is connected to a vehicle through Bluetooth. An auto-reply feature sends a specific reply to senders of messages to let them know the user is currently unavailable through text. Passengers can be granted full notification access to the phone.

A new "Smart Invert" feature, dubbed a "dark mode" by some publications, inverts the colors on the display, except for images, some apps, and some user interface elements. Using the iPhone X, which utilizes OLED technology, some news outlets have reported that this feature can conserve battery life by turning off pixels when black, saving energy by preventing itself from displaying a white pixel.

Users get expanded control over apps' location usage, with every app featuring a "While Using the App" location toggle in Settings. This differs from previous iOS versions, in which apps were only required to have "Never" or "Always" location options.

Users can remove rarely-used apps without losing the app's data using the "Offload App" button. This allows for a later reinstallation of the app (if available on the App Store), in which data returns and usage can continue. Users can also have those apps removed automatically with the "Offload Unused Apps" setting. When an app is offloaded, the app appears on the home screen as a grayed-out icon.

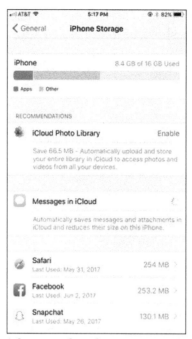

Storage settings on an iPhone 6S Plus, showing personalized recommendations.

Personalized suggestions will help the user free up storage space on their device, including emptying Photos trash, backing up messages, and enabling iCloud Photo Library for backing up photos and videos.

iPad

Multitasking interface on a 9.7-inch iPad Pro.

Certain new iOS 11 features will appear only on iPad. The application dock gets an overhaul, bringing it closer to the design seen on macOS, and is accessible from any screen, letting users more easily open apps in split-screen view. Users can also drag-and-drop files across different apps. A new multitasking interface shows multiple apps on the screen at the same time in floating "windows". Additionally, through a combination of "slide over", "split view", and "picture-in-picture" modes, users can have up to four active apps on-screen at the same time.

Each letter on the iPad keyboard features an alternative background number or symbol, accessible by pulling down on the respective key and releasing.

The Control Center is visible in the multitasking window on iPads. Running iOS 11, the 9.7-inch, 10.5-inch and the 2nd-generation 12.9-inch iPad Pros now have flashlight support.

Camera

iOS 11 introduces optical image stabilization, flash photography and high dynamic range for portrait photos.

Live Photos receives new "Loop", "Bounce" and "Long Exposure" effects, and uses High Efficiency Image File Format to decrease photo sizes.

On devices with an Apple A10 chip or newer, photos can be compressed in the new High Efficiency Image File Format and videos can be encoded in the new High Efficiency Video Coding video compression format, enabling improved quality while also decreasing size by half.

Wallpapers

Apple significantly changed the wallpapers available for use with iOS 11. In the initial beta version, released after Apple's developer conference, Apple included one new wallpaper, and removed all the six "Live" animated fish wallpapers, introduced with the iPhone 6S in 2015. The iOS 11.2 release later brought iPhone X/8/8 Plus-exclusive wallpapers to older iPhones.

iPhone X exclusively features six "Live" wallpapers and seven new "Dynamic" wallpapers.

Other Changes

The default system keyboard, in one-handed mode, on an iPhone 7 Plus.

iOS 11 introduces native support for QR code scanning, through the Camera app. Once a QR code is positioned in front of the camera, a notification is created offering suggestions for actions based on the scanned content. Twitter users have so far discovered that joining Wi-Fi networks and adding someone to the contacts list are supported through QR codes.

Third-party keyboards can add a one-handed mode. Users are able to record the screen natively. In order to record the screen, users must first add the feature to the Control Center through the

Settings app. Once added, users can start and stop recordings from a dedicated Control Center icon, with a distinctly colored bar appearing at the top of the screen indicating active recording. Pressing the bar gives the option to end recording, and videos are saved to the Photos app.

When an iOS 11 device is attempting to connect to a Wi-Fi network, nearby iOS 11 or macOS High Sierra devices already connected can wirelessly send the password, streamlining the connection process.

The volume change overlay no longer covers the screen while playing video, and a smaller scrubber appears on the top right of the screen.

After a user takes a screenshot, a thumbnail of the screenshot will appear at the bottom left of the screen. The user can then tap the thumbnail to bring up an interface that allows them to crop, annotate, or delete the screenshot.

Third-party apps are also able to take advantage of iCloud Keychain to allow autofilling passwords. The user's airline flight information can be viewed in Spotlight through a dedicated widget.

iOS 11 switches the top-left cellular network strength icons from five dots to four signal bars, similar to that before iOS 7.

A new "Automatic Setup" feature aims to simplify the first-time setup of new devices, with wireless transfer between the old and new device, transferring preferences, Apple ID and Wi-Fi info, preferred Settings, and iCloud Keychain passwords.

Similar to iPad, drag-and-drop file support is available on iPhone, though with more limitations, specifically only supported within apps, not between.

Many of Apple's pre-installed applications, including Notes, Contacts, Reminders, Maps, and App Store, have redesigned home screen icons.

An "Emergency SOS" feature was added that disables Touch ID after pressing the Sleep/Wake button five times in quick succession. It prevents Touch ID from working until the iPhone's passcode has been entered.

iOS 11 adds support for 8-bit and 10-bit HEVC. Devices with an Apple A9 chip or newer support hardware decoding, while older devices support software-based decoding.

App Features

Mail

Where there is empty space in the Mail app, users can draw inline.

Messages

The Messages application synchronizes messages across iOS and macOS through iCloud, reflecting message deletion across devices. This feature was temporarily removed in the fifth beta release and returned on May 29, 2018 when iOS 11.4 was released.

At the time of the iOS 11 announcement in June 2017, Apple presented functionality letting users send person-to-person payments with Apple Pay through Messages. By the time of the iOS 11 release in September 2017, the feature was not present, having been removed in an earlier beta version, with Apple announcing the feature as "coming this fall with an update to iOS 11". It was launched a few days after the iOS 11.2 update went live, although initially only available in the United States.

A new app drawer for iMessage apps aims to simplify the experience of using apps and stickers, and an optimized storage system reduces the backup size of messages.

The Messages app also incorporates a "Business Chat" feature for businesses to communicate directly with customers through the app. This can be accessed through a message icon next to search results of businesses. However, this feature was not included with the initial release of iOS 11 (instead launching with iOS 11.3).

The Messages app on the iPhone X introduces face-tracking emoji called "Animoji" (animated emoji), using Face ID.

App Store

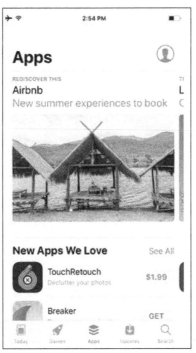

The "Apps" tab in the App Store on an iPhone 7 Plus.

The App Store receives a complete redesign, with a greater focus on editorial content such as daily highlights, and a design described as "cleaner and more consistent" to other apps developed by Apple. The app's design mimics the design seen in the Apple Music app in iOS 10.

Maps

At select locations, Apple Maps will offer indoor maps for shopping malls and airports. New lane guidance and speed limit features aim to guide drivers on unfamiliar roads.

Photos

The Photos app in iOS 11 gains support for viewing animated GIFs. Users can access GIF images inside an album titled "Animated". Memories can be viewed while the phone is in portrait orientation.

Podcasts

The Podcasts app receives a redesign similar to the App Store, with a focus on editorial content.

Notes

The Notes app has a built-in document scanner using the device's camera, and the feature removes artifacts such as glare and perspective.

An "Instant Notes" feature on the iPad Pro allows the user to start writing a note from the lock screen by putting the Apple Pencil onto the screen.

The app also allows users to input inline tables. Where there is open space in the Notes app, the user can draw inline.

Files

The layout of the "Files" app on an iPad.

A new "Files" app lets users browse the files stored on their device, as well as those stored across various cloud services, including iCloud Drive, Dropbox, OneDrive, and Google Drive. The app supports organization through structured sub-folders and various file-based options. The "Files" app also includes a built-in player for FLAC audio files. The Files app is available on both iPad and iPhone.

Safari

The user's flight information can be found in the Safari app.

Calculator

The Calculator app receives a redesign, with rounded buttons, replacing the grid ones seen on iOS 7.

Developer APIs

A new "ARKit" application programming interface (API) lets third-party developers build augmented reality apps, taking advantage of a device's camera, CPU, GPU, and motion sensors. The ARKit functionality is only available to users of devices with Apple A9 and later processors. According to Apple, this is because "these processors deliver breakthrough performance that enables fast scene understanding and lets you build detailed and compelling virtual content on top of real-world scenes."

A new "Core ML" software framework will speed up app tasks involving artificial intelligence, such as image recognition.

A new "Depth" API allows third-party camera app developers to take advantage of the iPhone 7 Plus, iPhone 8 Plus, and iPhone X's dual-camera "Portrait mode". This will let apps implement the same depth-sensing technology available in the default iOS Camera app, to simulate a shallow depth-of-field.

A new "Core NFC" framework gives developers limited access to the near field communication (NFC) chip inside supported iPhones, opening potential use cases in which apps can scan nearby environments and give users more information.

Removed Functionality

Apps must be compiled for 64-bit architecture in order to be supported on iOS 11. 32-bit apps are not supported or shown in the App Store in iOS 11, and users who attempt to open such apps receive an alert about the app's incompatibility.

iOS 11 drops the native system integration with Twitter, Facebook, Flickr, and Vimeo.

The iCloud Drive app is removed and replaced by the Files app.

The ability to trigger multitasking using 3D Touch was removed from the original iOS 11 release. In response to a bug report, an Apple engineer wrote that "Please know that this feature was intentionally removed". Apple's software engineering chief Craig Federighi wrote in reply to an email that the company had to "temporarily drop support" due to a "technical constraint", pledging to bring it back in a future update to iOS 11. It was brought back in iOS 11.1.

In iOS 11.2 the toggle switch for Wi-Fi and Bluetooth were unexpectedly changed to not completely turning off those two things but temporarily until the next day. The real turn off is in the Settings app.

Problems

Wi-Fi and Bluetooth Control Center toggles

Shortly after iOS 11 was released, Vice's Motherboard discovered new behaviors by the Wi-Fi and Bluetooth toggles in the Control Center. When users tap to turn off the features, iOS 11 only disconnects the chips from active connections, but does not disable the respective chips in the device.

The report further states that "it's a feature, not a bug", referencing documentation pages by Apple confirming the new toggle behaviors as a means to disconnect from connections but remain active for AirDrop transfers, AirPlay streaming, Apple Pencil input, handoff and other features. Security researcher Andrea Barisani told Motherboard that the new user interface was "not obvious at all", making the user experience "more uncomfortable". In October 2017, the Electronic Frontier Foundation published an article, calling the interface "misleading" and "bad for user security", due to a higher risk of security vulnerabilities with Wi-Fi and Bluetooth chips activated while not in active use. The Foundation recommended that Apple fix the "loophole in connectivity", writing that "It's simply a question of communicating better to users, and giving them control and clarity when they want their settings off - not "off-ish"".

iOS 11.2 changes this behavior slightly, by turning the toggles white and showing a warning message that explains the functions of the toggles in the Control Center, when the toggles are turned off.

Battery Drain Issues

Some users have experienced battery drain problems after updating to iOS 11. In a poll on its website, 70% of *9to5Mac* visitors reported decreased battery life after updating to the new operating system. However, in an article featuring Twitter complaints of battery life, *Daily Express* wrote that "honestly, this is to be expected. It happens every year, and it's completely normal. Major iOS releases will hammer the battery on your device much faster during the first few days of use", with *Forbes* stating in an article that "The days after you install a new version of iOS, your iDevice is busy doing all sorts of housekeeping. Practically all of your apps have updates, so iOS is busy downloading and installing them in the background. Additionally, after you install a new version of iOS, it has to do something called "re-indexing." During this process, iOS 11 will comb through all of the data on your device so that it can be cataloged for quick Spotlight searching." The article further states that "The good news is that both of these things are temporary".

Within a week of the launch of the 11.3.1 update, users began reporting continued issues with this update regarding battery drainage. Some of these reports indicated drains from 57% down to 3% in just 3 minutes. Even users with the health of the battery measuring 96% noticed iPhones draining at around 1% per minute. In addition to battery drains, some iPhone users noticed their devices having excessive heat buildup.

It has been recommended by technology experts that users not upgrade their software until the release of a version subsequent to 11.3.1 unless specifically plagued by the 'third party display issue'.

Calculator Bug

In October 2017, users reported on Reddit that quickly typing in an equation in the built-in iOS calculator app gives incorrect answers, most notably making the query "1+2+3" result in "24" rather than "6". Analysts have blamed an animation lag caused during the redesign of the app in iOS 11. The problem can be worked around by typing the numbers slowly, or by downloading alternative calculator apps from the App Store that do not have this problem. With a large amount of bug reports filed, Apple employee Chris Espinosa indicated on Twitter that the company was aware of the issue. iOS 11.2 fixed the issue.

Keyboard Autocorrect Bugs

In November 2017, users reported a bug in the default iOS keyboard, in which pressing "I" resulted in the system rendering the text as "!" or "A" along with an incomprehensible symbol featuring a question mark in a box. The symbol is known as Variation Selector 16 for its intended purpose of merging two characters into an emoji. Apple acknowledged the issue in a support document, advising users to set up a Text Replacement feature in their device's keyboard settings as a temporary workaround. The company confirmed to The Wall Street Journal that devices using older iOS 11 versions, as opposed to just the latest 11.1 version at the time of the publication, were affected by the issue, and an Apple spokesperson announced that "A fix will be released very soon". iOS 11.1.1 was released on November 9, 2017, fixing the issue.

At the end of the month, another keyboard autocorrection bug was reported, this time replacing the word "It" with "I.T". *MacRumors* suggested users set up the Text Replacement feature the same way they did for the earlier autocorrection issue, though its report notes that "some users insist this solution does not solve the problem". It was fixed with the release of iOS 11.2.

December 2 Crashes

In early December, users wrote on Twitter and Reddit that, at exactly 12:15 a.m. local time on December 2, any App Store app that sends local notifications would cause the device to repeatedly restart. Reddit users reported that disabling notifications or turning off background app refresh would stop the issue, while Apple staff on Twitter reported that it was a bug in date handling, recommending users to manually set the date prior to December 2. *MacRumors* wrote that the issue "looks like it's limited to devices running iOS 11.1.2", with users on the 11.2 beta release not affected. iOS 11.2, released on the same day, fixed the issue.

iOS 11.2 HomeKit Vulnerability

In December 2017, 9to5Mac uncovered a security vulnerability in iOS 11.2 within Apple's HomeKit smart home system, allowing unauthorized access to smart locks and garage door openers. It noted that Apple had already issued a server-side fix that, while preventing unauthorized access, also limited HomeKit functionality, with an upcoming software fix for the iOS operating system intended to restore the lost functionality. On December 13, Apple released iOS 11.2.1, which fixed the limitation on remote access.

Supported Devices

iOS 11 drops support for devices with a 32-bit processor: specifically the iPhone 5, iPhone 5C, and the fourth-generation iPad. It is the first version of iOS to run exclusively on iOS devices with 64-bit processors.

iPhone	iPod Touch	iPad
• iPhone 5S	• iPod Touch (6th generation)	• iPad Air
• iPhone 6		• iPad Air 2
• iPhone 6 Plus		• iPad

•	iPhone 6S	•	iPad
•	iPhone 6S Plus	•	iPad Mini 2
•	iPhone SE	•	iPad Mini 3
•	iPhone 7	•	iPad Mini 4
•	iPhone 7 Plus	•	iPad Pro (9.7-inch)
•	iPhone 8	•	iPad Pro (10.5-inch)
•	iPhone 8 Plus	•	iPad Pro (12.9-inch)
•	iPhone X		

iOS 10

iOS 10 is the tenth major release of the iOS mobile operating system developed by Apple Inc., being the successor to iOS 9. It was announced at the company's Worldwide Developers Conference on June 13, 2016, and was released on September 13, 2016. It was succeeded by iOS 11 on September 19, 2017.

iOS 10 incorporates changes to 3D Touch and the lock screen. There are new features to some apps: Messages has additional emojis and third-party apps can extend functionality in iMessage, Maps has a redesigned interface and additional third-party functions, the Home app manages "Home-Kit"-enabled accessories, Photos has algorithmic search and categorization of media known as "Memories", and Siri is compatible with third-party app-specific requests, such as starting workouts apps, sending IMs, using Lyft or Uber or to use payment functions.

A month after release, iOS 10 was installed on 54% of iOS devices, a "slightly slower migration" than for the release of iOS 9, speculated as being caused by an early release issue that may have "put some [users] off downloading the update". User adoption of iOS 10 steadily increased in the following months, eventually totaling 89% of active devices in September 2017.

System Features

Control Center

The Control Center has been redesigned and split into three pages: one for general settings, such as quick toggles for airplane mode and orientation lock, one for audio controls and one for controlling HomeKit (internet of things) appliances, if used. 3D Touch capabilities have been added to several toggles.

Home screen

Apps can show a widget when their home-screen icon is accessed with 3D Touch. Most default apps included with iOS devices can be hidden from the home screen and 're-downloaded' from the App Store. Upon doing this, the sandbox of the respective app is removed, which contains user data, settings and caches. The app is also hidden from other places, such as the "Today" view, the Settings app and "Share Sheets", through which the user can interact with the app from within another app. This feature was first hinted at during an interview in September 2015, in which

Apple CEO Tim Cook stated that Apple was "looking at" allowing customers to remove unused stock apps. iOS 10 allows users to prioritize certain app downloads by using 3D Touch.

Keyboard

QuickType virtual keyboards, which provide word-completion capabilities, can predict answers to questions and suggest relevant information based on location, calendar availability or contacts.

The "Define" feature in previous iOS versions has been replaced by "Look Up", and now expands its use from just providing definitions to retrieving information from locations, web browsing history, downloaded apps, suggested websites, and more.

The QuickType keyboard will allow the user to type in multiple languages if the user selects the desired languages in the "Dictionary" and "Keyboard" settings menus.

The user has the ability to change keyboard settings specifically for physical keyboards (such as autocorrect and auto-capitalization).

Lock Screen

The "slide to unlock" mechanism on the lock screen has been removed in favor of pressing the home button.

Similar to the feature on the Apple Watch, "Raise to Wake" wakes up the device when the user lifts it. This function requires a device with an M9 motion coprocessor or newer.

The "Today" view of Notification Center has been replaced by widgets, and is accessible by swiping from left to right. On the iPad, widgets can be displayed in a two-column layout.

Notification Center

The Notification Center no longer has a "Today" view. Notifications, now larger, can expand to display more information and all unread notifications can be cleared at once, using 3D Touch. Apps that need to be updated frequently can now have notifications that update live. The Notification Center contains a Spotlight search bar.

Settings

A new Magnifier setting was added which allows users to triple-click the home button and iOS will open the Camera app with magnification on.

There are also new "Color Filters" settings to compensate for a user's color blindness. Color Filters options include grayscale, red/green filter for protanopia, green/red filter for deuteranopia, and blue/yellow filter for tritanopia.

For the Messages application, users can now turn on Low Quality Image mode, which saves "your poor iPhone from stuffing itself full of images" based on new animated stickers and GIFs that can be sent in iMessage.

The Wi-Fi menu in Settings now shows warnings about the security of a network and if a network is not connected to the Internet. This is shown to the user as small subtext under the Wi-Fi's network's name. "Raise to Wake" can be enabled or disabled in Settings.

In iOS 10.2, a "Preserve Settings" feature allows users to set up the Camera app to launch with certain settings by default. Options include launching with the Video or Square mode rather than the Photo mode, preserving the last used filter, and preserving the capture settings for Live Photos.

Music added to Apple Music on one device can now be automatically downloaded to other devices using the Automatic downloads setting. The Settings allows the user the option to have routes in the Maps app avoid toll roads and highways.

In iOS 10.3, Settings was updated to feature information relating to a user's Apple ID account in the main menu, and features a section that allows users to see which old, unmaintained apps won't work in future versions of iOS.

Additionally, users can now see a breakdown of their iCloud storage. The user can enable a setting to have Siri announce who's calling, with options for "Always", "Headphones and Car", "Headphones Only", and "Never".

CarPlay

iOS 10 now allows users to rearrange and remove apps from their CarPlay display, through Settings. In iOS 10.3, Maps on CarPlay added electric vehicle charging stations.

Universal Clipboard

As part of the overall Continuity features introduced in iOS 8, a new Universal Clipboard feature allows users of Mac personal computers running macOS Sierra and iOS devices running iOS 10 to easily copy material to and from different devices through iCloud.

As part of Continuity, a new "Continuity Keyboard" feature allows users to type text on an iPhone and have the text appear on an Apple TV running tvOS 10, avoiding the Siri Remote for text input.

Other Changes

- iOS 10 features new sound effects for locking the device and for keyboard clicks.
- Whenever a device detects liquid in the Lightning port, a notice warns the user to disconnect the Lightning cable and allow the port to dry.
- iOS 10 also allows TTY calls to be made without any additional hardware.
- iOS 10 allows users to find their Apple Watch using Find My iPhone.
- Spotlight can now search the contents of users' iCloud Drive.

- Storage is reported to the user in the base 10 (1 kilobyte equals 1000 bytes) format instead of base 2, which was used in older iOS versions.

App Features

App Store

iOS 10 allows developers to buy advertisement spots in the App Store when users search for content. It also adds back the "Categories" section, which replaces the "Explore" section introduced in iOS 8.

In iOS 10.3, developers are able to respond to user reviews, and "Helpful" and "Not Helpful" review labels can help surface the most relevant customer reviews.

Calendar

In iOS 10, users can now change what day of the week the calendar starts on, as well as alert settings for birthdays and events, and calendar type (Gregorian, Chinese, Hebrew, Islamic).

Camera

Music will no longer stop playing when the Camera app is launched, unless users decide to record a video, or to take a Live Photo. Live Photos can be taken with filters.

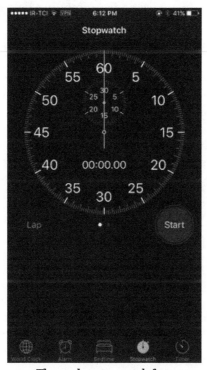

The analog stopwatch face.

In iOS 10.1, the iPhone 7 Plus received a new depth of field portrait camera mode, using both the wide-angle and telephoto lenses on the phone to "create shallow depth of field portrait photos with blurred backgrounds".

Clock

The Clock app now has a dark theme. A new "Bedtime" feature reminds the user when to go to bed to get the desired amount of sleep. There is also a new stopwatch face, accessed by swiping to the left.

Contacts

The Contacts app in iOS 10 allows users to set default phone numbers and email addresses for contacts who have multiple numbers or addresses. The app also allows the user to add and remove contacts from the Favorite Contacts list.

Home

Home is a new app that allows users to manage appliances compatible with HomeKit, Apple's API for home automation. In the app, users can add compatible HomeKit accessories, such as locks, lights, and thermostats, and then directly control the appliances through the app.

A "Scenes" panel allows many devices to be controlled at once to fit a mood or setting. Geo-fencing activates scheduled sequences following the user's location.

Mail

The Mail app now allows users to unsubscribe from mailing lists with an Unsubscribe button. Users can dismiss the message to unsubscribe for a particular mailing list by tapping the "X" at the top right corner, preventing the Mail app from displaying the unsubscribe button for that mailing list again later.

Apple has added back support for HTML5 video in Mail, which was previously stopped in iOS 8. Mail can filter messages, either by unread/read, or by categories.

iOS 10 also changes how email threading works, by placing the oldest email at the top by default. An option in Settings lets users revert to the previous threading system with the most recent message on top. Additionally, the new threaded conversations allow users to tap a message to see a scrollable stream of messages inside the thread.

Maps

Maps has been redesigned and updated with additional features, including scanning calendar events for locations, learning from a user's typical actions, and a redesigned driving view.

A marker can be automatically placed to indicate the user's parked car. The marker can also tell the user when they last parked their car, and a Notes field allows the user to enter information, such as parking garage number, in the app.

The app now helps users find the nearest gas station, fast-food restaurant or coffee shop, by swiping up from the bottom of the screen. Maps also estimates how long the detour will take.

Users can add third-party extensions to the Maps app, which enable additional functionality, such as a restaurant-booking extension can help the user reserve a table from inside the Maps app. Users can now pan and zoom while in navigation mode.

The app displays the current temperature and weather conditions in the bottom right corner. In iOS 10.3, the app also allows the user to see a weather forecast by using 3D Touch on the current temperature. This functionality allows users to see an hour-by-hour breakdown of the area that they are looking at.

Messages

The Messages app incorporates its own App Store, which lets users download third-party iMessage apps that can be accessed within iMessage conversations. Users can use them to send stickers, play games or send rich content, such as media previews, to recipients. The Messages App Store has three navigation fields: Featured, Categories, and Manage.

The app has been updated to include many visual effects. Chat bubbles, for example, can be sent with a "loud" or "gentle" animation that the recipient sees upon receiving. "Invisible ink" effect obscures the message until the recipient swipes across it. Full-screen effects like balloons, confetti or fireworks can be sent. There is also support for interactions similar to the Apple Watch, such as sending quick sketches and recording and sending the user's heartbeat. In order to use the screen and bubble effects, the Reduce Motion setting needs to be turned off.

Messages now allows users to send handwritten notes. This is done by turning the device to landscape mode for iPhones (landscape or portrait for iPad users) and then tapping the handwriting squiggle. The Messages app automatically saves recently used notes, to make it easier to send them again. A handwritten message can be deleted in the same way an app is deleted; by holding down on the message and pressing Delete. The message can also be saved as a picture file.

New emojis have been added, as well as additional features related to emoji. Emojis appear 3x bigger if messages are sent with up to three emojis and no text, the keyboard can now predict emojis to use, and an emoji replacement feature attempts to match words in messages and replace them with emojis of the same meaning.

Since the Game Center app has been removed, Messages now handles actions such as inviting friends to a game. Read receipts can now be turned on or off for individual contacts rather than for all contacts.

Music

The Music app has been redesigned, with an emphasis placed on usability. The "For You" section has been reorganized, with a playlist offering daily music recommendations. The "New" tab has been renamed "Browse". A new tab for music that has been downloaded called "Downloaded Music" has been added.

Lyrics are viewable for songs in-app in iOS 10. The "Search" tab includes recent and trending searches. An "Optimized Storage" option removes downloaded music that the user hasn't played in a while.

News

The News app, taking cues from the Music layout, has been redesigned to incorporate bold headings and a newspaper-esque layout in the redesigned "For You" tab. News also features support for subscriptions and provides notifications for breaking news.

Notes

Notes now has a collaboration feature. This allows users to share a note and collaborate with other users, who can add and remove text from a note. Users tap a "round yellow badge with a person and a plus sign" and can then send invitations through text, email, or by link.

Photos

Apple added deep learning capabilities for sorting and searching in the Photos app.

A new "Memories" feature can automatically recognize and compile related photos and create short, shareable music videos. local facial recognition functionality was added to bundle together pictures of certain people.

iOS 10 allows users to add doodles and text on a photo, using a new "Markup" feature. If the user edits a Live Photo using Markup, the image will be turned into a still image.

Live Photos can now be edited by the Photos app. This allows users to trim the clip, change the still frame, add a filter and add digital image stabilization to the Live Photo so it is "buttery smooth".

The app also has an upgraded auto-enhance feature and adds a "Brilliance" slider.

Phone

The Phone app can transcribe received visual voicemails.

Siri can announce the name and phone number of incoming calls. The system can mark suspected spam callers on the call screen upon incoming calls.

Contacts can be enabled for "Emergency Bypass", in which the phone will always make sounds and vibrations when receiving notifications from the chosen contacts, even during Do Not Disturb mode.

In the Favorites screen, users can customize what action each favorited contact will enable from a click, including call, FaceTime, SMS, or email.

Users can save voicemails through AirDrop, iMessage, iCloud Drive and other apps through a share menu.

Safari

Apple Pay is now available through the Safari app. There is no limit to how many tabs users can have open at the same time.

On supported iPads, Safari has a unique "Split View" for viewing two Safari browser tabs in 50/50 mode next to each other.

Users can also search for keywords in specific tabs, close all tabs with a single click, and reopen recently closed tabs by long-pressing on the plus icon. Users can also search for items in the Bookmarks and Reading List.

TV

Included in the iOS 10.2 update is a "TV" app. The app, which is only available in the United States, offers a simple, unified experience of content from different video apps, as long as each service supports the feature. The new app replaces the Videos app found in previous iOS versions.

Developer APIs

iOS 10 gives third-party developers access to APIs to three major iOS system apps and services: Siri, iMessage, and Maps. Developers can:

- Turn certain activities into Siri voice commands, allowing users to speak voice queries into the Siri personal assistant and Siri returning results from the respective apps. Apps that can integrate with Siri are limited to: sending messages, starting calls, sending and requesting payments, search for photos and videos, ordering taxicab or ride-sharing services, and managing workouts.

- Add dedicated apps to the iMessage App Store, that lets users add unique sticker packs, share rich content, or interact with certain app functions entirely within an iMessage conversation.

- Add extensions to Apple Maps, so apps with specific functionality useful in a map, such as a restaurant-booking app, can integrate with the mapping service to handle app functionality directly in the Maps app.

iOS 10 allows third-party camera apps to capture RAW image format pictures. Support for shooting photos in Adobe's DNG RAW format is limited to devices with at least a 12MP camera and a third-party app that supports it, as Apple did not enable the feature in the native Camera app.

iOS 10 allows VoIP apps to have the same functionality and interface as the Phone and FaceTime apps have, through the use of a CallKit API.

Removed Functionality

Native support for the VPN protocol PPTP was removed. Apple recommends alternatives which it considers to be more secure.

The options to group notifications by app in Notification Center and customize the order of notifications were removed. The Game Center app has been removed, as is the case on macOS Sierra.

Problems

Initial Release Bricking Issue

The initial public release of iOS 10 on September 13, 2016 saw many iPhones and iPads temporarily disabled, or "bricked", by the over-the-air update, requiring bricked devices to be connected to a Mac or PC with iTunes in order to retry the update or restore the device to factory settings. Apple quickly released iOS 10.0.1, and issued a statement: "We experienced a brief issue with the software update process, affecting a small number of users during the first hour of availability. The problem was quickly resolved and we apologize to those customers."

Local Backup Encryption Issue

In September 2016, it was discovered that the encryption of local iOS backups made with iTunes is weaker for iOS 10 devices than for devices running iOS 9. Russian software firm ElcomSoft discovered that the iOS 10 backup process skips several security checks, making it "approximately 2,500 times" faster to try passwords, enabling 6 million password tries per second compared to the 2,400 password tries per second for the same process ElcomSoft has used on iOS 9. The firm stated that the impact is "severe". Apple acknowledged the problem, said it planned to issue a security update, but also stated that iCloud backups were not affected. The iOS 10.1 update subsequently fixed the issue.

Battery Shutdowns

The Next Web's Juan Buis wrote in late November 2016 that "complaints are shared [on Apple's support forums] about various iPhone models turning off when the battery falls below a certain percentage", and blames the iOS 10.1.1 update. He further wrote that "the original post [on support forums] explains that the phone dies when there's 30 percent charge left, and many others have since replied that they're experiencing the same." iOS 10.2, released in December 2016, adds a telemetry diagnostic tool that Apple can use to report battery consumption, for diagnosing reported issues with 30% battery shutdowns. In February 2017, Apple released a statement to TechCrunch, saying that the iOS 10.2.1 update, released on January 23, had reduced the occurrence of battery shutdowns by "more than 80%" on iPhone 6S devices and "over 70%" on iPhone 6 devices. In full, the statement read:

> "With iOS 10.2.1, Apple made improvements to reduce occurrences of unexpected shutdowns that a small number of users were experiencing with their iPhone. iOS 10.2.1 already has over 50% of active iOS devices upgraded and the diagnostic data we've received from upgraders shows that for this small percentage of users experiencing the issue, we're seeing a more than 80% reduction in iPhone 6s and over 70% reduction on iPhone 6 of devices unexpectedly shutting down. We also added the ability for the phone to restart without needing to connect to power, if a user still encounters an unexpected shutdown. It is important to note that these unexpected shutdowns are not a safety issue, but we understand it can be an inconvenience and wanted to fix the issue as quickly as possible. If a customer has any issues with their device they can contact AppleCare."

Supported Devices

With this release, Apple dropped support for devices with either an A5 or an A5X chip: the iPhone 4S, iPad 2, iPad (3rd generation), iPad Mini (1st generation) and iPod Touch (5th generation).

iPhone	iPod Touch	iPad
• iPhone 5	• iPod Touch (6th generation)	• iPad (4th generation)
• iPhone 5C		• iPad Air
• iPhone 5S		• iPad Air 2
• iPhone 6		• iPad (2017)
• iPhone 6 Plus		• iPad Mini 2
• iPhone 6S		• iPad Mini 3
• iPhone 6S Plus		• iPad Mini 4
• iPhone SE		• iPad Pro (12.9-inch)
• iPhone 7		• iPad Pro (9.7-inch)
• iPhone 7 Plus		• iPad Pro (10.5-inch)

iOS 9

iOS 9 is the ninth major update for Apple's iOS mobile operating system that runs on portable Apple devices like the iPhone, iPad and iPod Touch. Apple iOS 9 was introduced at the company's 2015 Worldwide Developers Conference (WWDC) in early June 2015 along with OS X El Capitan, with official availability expected in the fall.

Codenamed Monarch, Apple iOS9 builds on iOS 8 with new features and enhancements that are highlighted by "Proactive," a contextual, predictive personal assistant that's tied in with Siri to deliver personalized information based on a user's preferences, habits and location.

Additional new features in iOS 9 include a new News app, multitasking improvements (including a split-screen mode for iPads), tether-less CarPlay functionality, an updated Notes app and transit directions in the Maps app.

iOS 8

iOS 8 is the eighth major release of the iOS mobile operating system developed by Apple Inc., being the successor to iOS 7. It was announced at the company's Worldwide Developers Conference on June 2, 2014, and was released on September 17, 2014. It was succeeded by iOS 9 on September 16, 2015.

iOS 8 incorporated significant changes to the operating system. It introduced Continuity, a cross-platform (Mac, iPhone, and iPad) system that enables communication between devices in different product categories, such as the ability to answer calls and reply to SMS on the Mac and iPad. Continuity includes a "Handoff" feature that lets users start a task on one device and continue on another. Other changes included a new Spotlight Suggestions search results feature that provides more detailed results; Family Sharing, where a family can link together their accounts to share content, with one parent as the administrator with permission controls; an updated keyboard with QuickType, providing contextual predictive word suggestions; and Extensibility, which allows for easier sharing of content between apps. Third-party developers got additional features to integrate their apps deeper into the operating system, including support for widgets in the Notification Center, and the ability to make keyboards that users can replace the default iOS keyboard with.

App updates in the release included the new Health app, which can aggregate data from different fitness apps, as well as enabling a Medical ID accessible on the lock screen for emergencies; support for iCloud Photo Library in the Photos app, which enables photos to be synchronized and stored in the cloud; and iCloud Drive, which lets users store files in the cloud and browse them across devices. In iOS 8.4, Apple updated its Music app with a streaming service called Apple Music, and a 24-hour radio station called Beats 1.

Reception of iOS 8 was positive. Critics praised Continuity and Extensibility as major features enabling easier control and interaction between different apps and devices. They also liked the QuickType keyboard word suggestions, and highlighted Spotlight Suggestions for making the iPhone "almost a portable search portal for everything". However, reviewers noted that the full potential for iOS 8 would only be realized once third-party developers integrated their apps to support new features, particularly widgets in the Notification Center.

Roughly a week after release, iOS 8 had reached 46% of iOS usage share. In October 2014, it was reported that the adoption rate had "stalled", only increasing by "a single percentage point" from the previous month. This situation was blamed on the requirement of a high amount of free storage space to install the upgrade, especially difficult for iPhones sold with 8 or 16 gigabytes of maximum storage space. The following December, iOS 8 had reached 63% usage share, a notable 16% increase from the October measurement.

System Features

Continuity

iOS 8 introduced Continuity, a cross-platform (Mac, iPhone, and iPad) system that enables communication between devices in different product categories. Continuity enables phone call functionality for the iPad and Mac, in which calls are routed through the iPhone over to a secondary device. The secondary device then serves as a speaker phone. This also brings SMS support to the iPad and Mac, an extension of the iMessage feature in previous versions.

Continuity adds a feature called "Handoff", that lets users start a task on one device and continue on another, such as composing an e-mail on the iPhone and then continuing it on the iPad before sending it on the Mac. In order to support Handoff and Continuity, Macs needed to have the OS X Yosemite operating system, which was released in October 2014, as well as support for Bluetooth low energy.

Spotlight

iOS 8 introduced Spotlight Suggestions, a new search feature that integrates with many websites and services to show more detailed search results, including snippets, local news, quick access to apps installed on the device, iTunes content, movie showtimes, nearby places, and info from various websites. Spotlight Suggestions are available on the iOS home screen as well as in the Safari web browser search bar.

Notifications

The drop-down Notification Center has now been redesigned to allow widget functionality.

Third-party developers can add widget support to their apps that let users see information in the Notification Center without having to open each respective app. Users can add, rearrange, or remove any widgets, at any time. Examples of widgets include a Weather app showing current weather, and a Calendar app showing upcoming events.

Notifications are now actionable, allowing users to reply to a message while it appears as a quick drop-down, or act on a notification through the Notification Center.

Keyboard

iOS 8 includes a new predictive typing feature called QuickType, which displays word predictions above the keyboard as the user types.

Apple now allows third-party developers to make keyboard apps that users can replace the default iOS keyboard with. For added privacy, Apple added a settings toggle called "Allow Full Access", that optionally enables the keyboard to act outside its app sandbox, such as synchronizing keyboard data to the cloud, third-party keyboards are not allowed to use Siri for voice dictation, and some secure text fields do not allow input.

Family Sharing

iOS 8 introduced Family Sharing, which allows up to 6 people to register unique iTunes accounts that are then linked together, with one parent becoming the administrator, controlling the overall experience. Purchases made on one account can be shared with the other family members, but purchases made by kids under 13 years of age require parental approval. Purchases made by adults will not be visible for the kids at all.

Family Sharing also extends into apps; a Shared album is automatically generated in the Photos app of each family member, allowing everyone to add photos, videos, and comments to a shared place. An Ask to Buy feature allows anyone to request the purchase of items in the App Store, iTunes Store, and iBooks Store, as well as in-app purchases and iCloud storage, with the administrator having the option to either approve or deny the purchase.

Multitasking

The multitasking screen shows a list of recently called and favorited contacts. The feature can be turned off in Settings.

Other

iOS 8 includes an additional data roaming option in Settings for European users, allowing greater control over data usage abroad.

The Siri personal voice assistant now has integrated Shazam support. Asking Siri "What song is this?" will identify what song is playing.

Wi-Fi calling has been added to allow mobile phone calls over Wi-Fi. Mobile operator carriers can then enable the Voice-over-Wi-Fi functionality in their services.

App Features

Photos and Camera

- Camera app: The Camera app gets two new features; time-lapse and self-timer. Time-lapse records frames at shorter intervals than normal film frequencies and builds them into movies, showing events in a faster speed. Self-timer gives the user the option of a three-second or ten-second countdown before automatically taking a photo. iPads can now take pictures in panoramic mode.

- iCloud Photo Library: iOS 8 added iCloud Photo Library support to the Photos app, enabling photo synchronization between different Apple devices. Photos and videos were backed up in full resolution and in their original formats. This feature almost meant that lower-quality versions of photos could be cached on the device rather than the full-size images, potentially saving significant storage space on models with limited storage availability.

- Search: The Photos app received better search, with different search categorization options, including Nearby, One Year Ago, Favorites, and Home, based on geolocation and date of photo capture.

- Editing: Additionally, the Photos app gained more precise editing controls, including improved rotation; one-touch auto-enhancement tools; and deeper color adjustments, such as brightness, contrast, exposure, and shadows. There is also an option to hide a photo without deleting it.

- Extensions: Apple added an Extensibility feature in iOS 8, that allows filters and effects from third-party apps to be accessed directly from within a menu in the standard Photos app, rather than having to import and export photos through each respective app to apply effects.

- Camera Roll: In the initial release of iOS 8, Apple removed a "Camera Roll" feature from the Photos app. Camera Roll was an overview of all photos on the device, but was replaced by a "Recently Added" photo view displaying photos by how recently the user captured them.

Despite being replaced by a "Recently Added" album, the removal of Camera Roll sparked user complaints, which Apple returned the feature in the iOS 8.1 update.

Messages

In iOS 8, Messages gets new features for group conversations, including a Do Not Disturb mode that disables conversation notifications, as well as the ability to remove participants from the chat. A new Tap to Talk chat button lets users send quick voice comments to a recipient, and a Record button allows users to record short videos.

For interaction between two Apple users, the Messages app allows users to send short picture, video or audio clips with a 2-minute expiration time.

In the Settings app, the user has the option to have messages be automatically deleted after a certain time period.

Safari

In the Safari web browser, developers can now add support for Safari Password Sharing, which allows them to share credentials between sites they own and apps they own, potentially cutting down on the number of times users need to type in credentials for their apps and services. The browser also adds support for the WebGL graphics API.

iCloud Drive

In a similar style as a file manager, the iCloud Drive is a file hosting service that, once enabled in Settings, lets users save any kind of file in the app, and the media is synchronized to other iOS devices, as well as the Mac.

App Store

In iOS 8, Apple updated App Store with an "Explore" tab providing improved app discovery, trending searches in the "Search" tab, and the ability for developers to bundle multiple apps into a single discounted package. New "preview" videos allow developers to visually show an app's function.

Health

HealthKit is a service that allows developers to make apps that integrate with the new Health app. The Health app primarily aggregates data from fitness apps installed on the user's device, except for steps and flights climbed, which are tracked through the motion processor on the user's iPhone. Users can enter their medical history in Medical ID, which is accessible on the lock screen, in case of an emergency.

HomeKit

HomeKit serves as a software framework that lets users set up their iPhone to configure, communicate with, and control smart-home appliances. By designing rooms, items and actions in the HomeKit service, users can enable automatic actions in the house through a simple voice dictation to Siri or through apps.

Manufacturers of HomeKit-enabled devices are required to purchase a license, and all HomeKit products are required to have an encryption co-processor. Equipment manufactured without HomeKit-support can be enabled for use through a "gateway" product, such as a hub that connects between those devices and the HomeKit service.

Passbook

The Passbook app on iOS 8 was updated to include Apple Pay, a digital payment service, available on iPhone 6 and 6 Plus with the release of iOS 8.1.

Music

A new music streaming service, Apple Music, was introduced in the iOS 8.4 update. It allows subscribers to listen to an unlimited number of songs on-demand through subscriptions. With the release of the music service, the standard Music app on iOS was revamped both visually and functionally to include Apple Music, as well as the 24-hour live radio station Beats 1.

Notes

Notes received rich text editing support, with the ability to bold, italicize or underline text; and image support, allowing users to post photos in the app.

Weather

The Weather app now uses weather data from The Weather Channel instead of Yahoo!. The app also received slight changes in the user interface.

Tips

iOS 8 added a new "Tips" app, that shows tips and brief information about the features in iOS on a weekly basis.

Touch ID

iOS 8 allows Touch ID to be used in third-party apps.

Problems

App Crash Rate

A study by Apteligent (formerly Crittercism) found that the rate at which apps crashed in their tests was 3.56% on iOS 8, higher than the 2% found on iOS 7.1.

8.0.1 Update Issues

In September 2014, the iOS 8.0.1 update caused significant issues with Touch ID on iPhone 6 and cellular network connectivity on some models. Apple stated that affected users should reinstall the initial iOS 8 release until version 8.0.2 was ready.

iOS 8.0.2 was released one day after 8.0.1, with a fix for issues caused by the 8.0.1 update.

"Effective Power" Text Message Crash

In May 2015, news outlets reported on a bug where receiving a text message with a specific combination of symbols and Arabic characters, caused the Messages application to crash and the iPhone to reboot.

The bug, named "effective power", could potentially continuously reboot a device if the message was visible on the lock screen.

The flaw was exploited for the purpose of trolling, by intentionally causing others' phones to crash. The bug was fixed in iOS 8.4, an update released in June 2015.

Supported Devices

With this release, Apple dropped support for the iPhone 4.

iPhone	iPod Touch	iPad
• iPhone 4S	• iPod Touch (5th generation)	• iPad 2
• iPhone 5	• iPod Touch (6th generation)	• iPad (3rd generation)
• iPhone 5C		• iPad (4th generation)
• iPhone 5S		• iPad Air
• iPhone 6		• iPad Air 2
• iPhone 6 Plus		• iPad Mini (1st generation)
		• iPad Mini 2
		• iPad Mini 3

iOS 7

iOS 7 is the seventh major release of the iOS mobile operating system developed by Apple Inc., being the successor to iOS 6. It was announced at the company's Worldwide Developers Conference on June 10, 2013, and was released on September 18, 2013. It was succeeded by iOS 8 on September 17, 2014.

iOS 7 introduced a completely redesigned user interface, a design credited to a team led by Apple's senior vice president of design, Jony Ive. The new look, featuring flatter icons, a new slide-to-unlock function, and new animations, was described by Ive as "profound and enduring beauty in simplicity". The new design was implemented throughout the operating system, including the Notification Center, which was updated with three tabs offering different views of information; notifications visible on the lock screen; a redesigned Siri voice assistant offering visual indicators; and a Control Center offering easy access to the most commonly used features. iOS 7 also introduced AirDrop, a wireless sharing technology; CarPlay, phone and car integration; and automatic app updates in the App Store.

Reception of iOS 7 was mixed. The new design language was criticized, with critics noting the implementation of design changes rather than actual productivity improvements, and citing examples such as animations delaying access, lack of icon consistency, and buttons being hidden as negative aspects of the user experience. The addition of the Control Center was praised, as were updates to Siri and multitasking. Shortly after release, there were reports of the new design causing sickness, a trend explained as being caused by animations with similar effects as car sickness.

User adoption of iOS 7 was fast. Its iOS market share was reported to be as high as 35% after one day, and installed on 200 million devices within 5 days, which Apple claimed was "the fastest software upgrade in history."

System Features

Design

iOS 7 introduced a complete visual overhaul of the user interface. With "sharper, flatter icons, slimmer fonts, a new slide-to-unlock function, and a new control panel that slides up from the bottom of the screen for frequently accessed settings", the operating system also significantly redesigned the standard pre-installed apps from Apple. Jony Ive, Apple's head of design, commented that "There is a profound and enduring beauty in simplicity, in clarity, in efficiency. True simplicity is derived from so much more than just the absence of clutter and ornamentation - it's about bringing order to complexity. iOS 7 is a clear representation of these goals. It has a whole new structure that is coherent and applied across the entire system."

AirDrop

iOS 7 introduced AirDrop, a wireless sharing technology accessible from the share icon, which lets users send files from their local device to other, nearby iOS devices. It can be enabled in the Control Center, with options for controlling its discovery by other devices, including Off, Contacts Only, and Everyone.

At launch, AirDrop was only available on the iPhone 5 and later, fourth-generation iPad and later, all iPad Minis, and the fifth-generation iPod Touch.

Control Center

iOS 7 introduced the Control Center, a menu that users can access by swiping up from the bottom of the screen, providing access to frequently used settings such as Airplane Mode, Wi-Fi, Bluetooth, Do Not Disturb Mode, and Rotation Lock. There is a slider for adjusting screen brightness, controls for music playback, along with a volume slider. A Flashlight toggle is also available, as is an icon for quickly accessing the camera.

Notification Center

iOS 7 overhauled the Notification Center, with both visual and functional changes. It has three tabs; "Today" (information on what's coming during the day), "All", and "Missed". Notifications are now visible on the phone's lock screen, and notifications are synchronized across devices, so users don't need to dismiss the same notification multiple times on different devices.

App Switcher

iOS 7 expanded the screen for app switching. Users double-tapped the home button and were taken out of the current app for a view of full-screen thumbnails of recently accessed apps.

CarPlay

CarPlay (formerly iOS in the Car), released as part of iOS 7.1, integrates with selected car models to offer phone interaction, including music controls and Maps navigation, through the car's display. Users can also talk to Siri to send messages hands-free. It supports all Lightning-equipped iPhones with iOS 7.1 or later.

Siri

Siri features a new design where the assistant fades in with the background app being blurred.

While speaking, visual vocal waves appear, that form into a spinning circle as the device communicates with Apple's servers. Siri can now control a limited set of device settings, including Bluetooth. The assistant can alternatively send the user directly to the settings menu if their query cannot be controlled by voice, or otherwise, displays an error if the request can't be processed. For searching the Internet, Bing became the default search engine, and Siri's web resources were expanded to include Wikipedia. Siri was also more deeply connected into Twitter, offering full tweet search. iOS 7 also allowed the user to change Siri's gender, with new options for male and female voices.

Other

Spotlight search is accessed by holding and dragging down the home screen. iOS 7 came with new wallpapers that included a "Parallax" effect; the icons appear to be moving as the user moves the phone around, producing an "illusion that the icons are floating above the background wallpaper".

In Settings, users have the option to make custom vibrations for certain types of notifications, turn off the parallax wallpaper animation effect using a Reduce Motion setting, and block callers, with the block applying across multiple devices and apps, including Phone, Messages, and FaceTime.

On the home screen, newly installed apps and recently updated apps have a blue dot next to them until the user opens the app for the first time.

Folders are updated to incorporate different pages, similar to the home screen layout, allowing for a significant expansion of folder functionality. Each page of a folder can contain up to nine apps, and there can be 15 pages in total, allowing for a total of 135 apps in a single folder.

App Features

App Store

The App Store received several significant changes in iOS 7. Users can enable automatic app updates. Users can now view a history of updates to each installed app. With location services enabled, the App Store has a Near Me tab that recommends popular apps based on the user's geographic location. It also became possible to download older versions of apps, in case new iOS versions left older devices incompatible for system updates, allowing users to maintain a working copy of the last supported update of each app.

Photos and Camera

iOS 7 introduced a square photo mode for the Camera app, enabling "Instagram-style photos". Also new are live filters; nine different filter options that each change the photo's appearance. Further improvements to the camera included the ability to pinch-to-zoom during video recording, and a Burst mode for easily taking successive photos by holding the shutter button, causing the phone to take 10 frames per second. On the iPhone 5S, a slow-motion video option was added, with the ability to shoot a video at a high frame rate of 120 frames per second. It can be edited in the Photos app, where users can decide where to start and end the slow-motion part.

The Photos app was updated with new categorization options. Three tabs on the bottom, "Photos", "Shared", and "Albums", each open to different app sections featuring galleries. On the main Photos interface, the app displays a timeline of all photos, sorted into "Years", "Collections", and "Moments". Filters were added, allowing users to choose from several types of filters to add to their photos. Alongside existing options for sharing pictures, the app was updated with support for the new AirDrop functionality.

Music

The Music app integrated Apple's iTunes Radio service; a station-based music service that let users choose an artist, with the service generating a "station" based on that and similar artists' songs. Users were able to skip songs and search through the history of previous songs, in addition to being able to purchase the songs directly from the iTunes Store while playing. iTunes Radio also had a feature that showed songs currently trending on Twitter. iTunes Radio was free and ad-supported, but users could subscribe to iTunes Match, that enabled ad-free playback.

After more than two years of release, iTunes Radio was eventually discontinued in January 2016, with the features moving to the new Apple Music music subscription service and Beats 1 radio station.

Safari

In iOS 7, the Safari web browser received multiple significant updates. The two search bars found in previous iterations of the browser have been combined into a single "Smart Search" field. Tab management was improved to allow more than eight open tabs at once, as well as stacking tabs on top of each other vertically as opposed to a horizontal card view. The option to enter a Private tab was built into the app itself rather than in Settings menus, and a new "Do Not Track" button allows the user to further manage their privacy levels.

Maps

Apple Maps now features turn-by-turn walking directions. The design of Maps was updated to feature a full-screen view, where interface elements such as the search bar disappear from view, alongside new translucent search and lower toolbars, and a Night Mode that automatically activates when users drive at night. A separate Siri volume control is available in Maps, enabling users to "change the relative volume of Siri's voice feedback independently of the system volume, so it doesn't shout too loud over your background music".

Weather

The Weather app on iOS 7 received significant changes, including a new icon, the absence of a static weather indicator on the app thumbnail on the home screen, and new dynamic, visual representations of the current weather.

FaceTime

iOS 7 has its own FaceTime app on iPhone, with FaceTime Audio, a feature that allows users to call while on Wi-Fi. FaceTime Audio is accessible from the Phone app, the Contacts app, or the FaceTime app itself. It is available on devices running iOS 7 or later.

Messages

The Messages app allows users to see timestamps for every message they have sent or received.

Problems

Design Causing Sickness

In September 2013, Pranav Dixit of Fast Company reported about user complaints shared on Apple's support forums that the new design of iOS 7, including "many zoom animations while multitasking and opening and closing apps, in addition to a slight parallax effect" were causing users to feel sick. Dixit noted that while the parallax effect could be turned off, most animations did not have such an option.

Dr. George Kikano, "division chief of family medicine at UH Case Medical Center in Ohio", told Fox News that "There's some validity to this, for people who are susceptible." Fox News wrote that Dr. Kikano said "It's a new "parallax" function that causes the background of the phone to subtly move back and forth, a feature that leads to an effect not unlike car sickness. The inner ear is responsible for balance, the eyes for vision. When things are out of sync you feel dizzy, nauseous. Some people get it, some people don't, and some people get used to it."

Battery Drain

Adrian Kingsley-Hughes of *ZDNet* wrote in March 2014 that iPhone and iPad users reported battery drain with the iOS 7.1 update. In lab testing, Andrew Cunningham of *Ars Technica* found some hardware models experienced minor battery depletion, while others experienced no statistically significant changes.

Lock Screen Bypass

Dom Esposito of *9to5Mac* reported in June 2014 that a new lock screen bypass method had been discovered in iOS 7, allowing access to the phone in "5 seconds under certain circumstances". The issue was later fixed.

Supported Devices

With this release, Apple dropped support for older devices, specifically the iPhone 3GS and the fourth-generation iPod Touch.

iPhone	iPod Touch	iPad
• iPhone 4	• iPod Touch (5th generation)	• iPad 2
• iPhone 4S		• iPad (3rd generation)
• iPhone 5		• iPad (4th generation)
• iPhone 5C		• iPad Air
• iPhone 5S		• iPad Mini (1st generation)
		• iPad Mini 2

iOS 6

iOS 6 is the sixth major release of the iOS mobile operating system developed by Apple Inc, being the successor to iOS 5. It was announced at the company's Worldwide Developers Conference on June 11, 2012, and was released on September 19, 2012. It was succeeded by iOS 7 on September 18, 2013.

iOS 6 added a new Apple Maps app, replacing Google Maps as the default mapping service for the operating system; a dedicated Podcasts app, as a central location for podcasts; and a Passbook app, for managing different types of tickets, boarding passes, coupons, and loyalty cards. The App Store received a visual overhaul, bringing a card-based app layout as well as tweaks to search algorithms. Facebook was integrated into the operating system, incorporating status messages, like buttons, and contact and event synchronization to several of Apple's apps. New privacy controls allow users more fine-grained app permissions, as well as an option to prevent targeted advertising. Siri was added to more devices, and updated with more functionality, including the ability to make restaurant reservations, launch apps, retrieve movie reviews and sports statistics, and read items from the Notification Center.

Reception of iOS 6 was positive. Critics noted that the operating system did not offer any significant speed improvements or major redesigned elements, but instead focused on refinements, with a general consensus that Apple "isn't overhauling things for the sake of it". iOS 6 didn't "completely change the way you use your device", but "each of the tweaks will make many daily smartphone actions easier across the board", and critics noted that refinement of "something that already works extremely well" is "something other companies would do well to emulate".

The release of Apple Maps, however, attracted significant criticism, due to inaccurate or incomplete data. The issues prompted an open letter of apology from Apple CEO Tim Cook, and played a contributing role in the dismissal of Scott Forstall from the company, who had supervised iOS development since its inception.

While iOS 6 has seen no further updates since March 2014, two subversions of iOS 6 are still 'signed' by Apple Software Update: 6.1.3 for certain models of the iPad 2 and the iPhone 4S, and 6.1.6 for the iPhone 3GS and the iPod Touch (4th generation), meaning that it can be verified and installed on the mentioned devices provided the user has the necessary IPSW file.

System Features

Siri

Apple's Siri intelligent personal assistant, introduced in iOS 5 with the release of the iPhone 4S, was updated to include the ability to make restaurant reservations, launch apps, read items from Notification Center, dictate Facebook and Twitter updates, retrieve movie reviews, detailed sports statistics, and more.

Siri received language support for Italian, Korean, and Cantonese, and device support for iPhone 5, fifth-generation iPod Touch, and third-generation iPad.

In iOS 6.1, Siri was integrated with Fandango, allowing users to buy film tickets by voice. The feature was only available in the United States at launch.

Facebook Integration

Facebook came integrated in several of Apple's native apps with iOS 6. Facebook features could be directly accessed from within native apps such as Calendar, which could synchronize Facebook events; Contacts, which could show Facebook friend information; and the App Store and Game Center, which featured Facebook's like button; as well as through a widget in the Notification Center, which allowed users to post status updates to the social network.

Settings

The Settings app received multiple changes in iOS 6. The icon was revised to match the System Preferences icon used in the then-named OS X computer operating system developed by Apple; and a "Do Not Disturb" mode was added, which allows users to disable phone sounds. Additional options for Do Not Disturb mode include being able to allow phone calls from a specific group of contacts, and allowing sound on the second call if someone calls repeatedly. A crescent moon icon will appear in the status bar when Do Not Disturb mode is enabled.

New privacy settings became available to users. In addition to "Location Services", the following menus were added in iOS 6: "Contacts", "Calendars", "Reminders", and "Photos". The updated privacy menus allow users more fine-grained privacy permission controls for each app, with new notifications when apps want access to information in each of the categories.

iOS 6 also came with a "Limit ad tracking" user control setting to allow users the option to prevent targeted advertising. Apple's "Advertising Identifier" was described by Apple as "a non-permanent, nonpersonal, device identifier, that advertising networks will use to give you more control over advertisers' ability to use tracking methods. If you choose to limit ad tracking, advertising networks using the Advertising Identifier may no longer gather information to serve you targeted ads."

In iOS 6.1, a "Reset Advertising Identifier" setting was added to allow users to reset the identifier used by advertising companies.

Other

iOS 6 added a Twitter widget in the Notification Center, where users could tweet without going into the app. This saved resources.

The Share Sheet interface was updated to display a grid of icons, as opposed to a list, of different apps to which users could share content.

App Features

Maps

A new Apple Maps app replaced Google Maps as the default mapping app on the operating system. Apple Maps used Apple's vector-based engine, making for smoother zooming. New to Maps was turn-by-turn navigation with spoken directions and 3D views in certain countries, "Flyover" views in some major cities, and real-time traffic.

At launch, turn-by-turn navigation was only available for iPhone 4S and later, and iPad 2 (cellular capability required) and later, while "Flyover" view was only available for iPhone 4S and later, fifth-generation iPod Touch, and iPad 2 and later.

Passbook

A new Passbook app was added, to retrieve documents such as boarding passes, admission tickets, coupons and loyalty cards.

An iOS device with Passbook can replace a physical card when scanned to process a mobile payment at participating locations. The app has context-aware features such as notifications for relevant coupons when in the immediate vicinity of a given store, and automatic visibility of boarding passes when the user is at an airport, with notifications for gate changes.

Photos and Camera

The Camera app was updated to include a new Panorama mode that allowed users to take 240-degree panoramic photos.

The Photos app received updates to the Photo Stream functionality, letting users remove images, as well as share custom Photo Streams with other people or the public.

App Store

The App Store on iOS 6 had a brand new user interface that removed the "Categories" tab and replaced it with "Genius", Apple's search and recommendation engine. It also made use of cards rather than lists to present apps. There were also tweaks to the App Store's search algorithm, resulting in a "trend to favor newer companies", which sparked both developer concerns and praise.

The App Store also updated apps without requiring the iTunes password, and when installing or updating an app, users were no longer automatically returned to the home screen.

Phone

Upon receiving calls, iOS 6 enabled users to swipe up the lock screen to reveal "Reply with message" or "Remind me later". The "Reply with message" feature shows several pre-determined messages with an option for a custom message, while the "Remind me later" feature offers several options (such as an hour later, when the user gets home, or when the user leaves the current location) to enable a reminder.

Podcasts

Podcast functionality was separated from the iTunes app and received its own Podcasts app in iOS 6, in order to "centralize and promote podcast listening and downloading for users".

Safari

The Safari web browser was updated with a full-screen landscape view for iPhone and iPod Touch users.

Reading List, a feature introduced in iOS 5, received offline support, in which text, images, and layout from saved articles get stored on the user's device.

FaceTime

FaceTime video calling was updated to work over a cellular connection, in addition to Wi-Fi.

Clock

The Clock app, which had been on iPhone and iPod Touch since their original release, became available on iPad. The clock design looked similar to a Swiss railway clock, and Apple formed an agreement with the Swiss Federal Railways to license the design for its own use.

Removed Functionality

The YouTube app, which had been a default app on iOS developed by Apple, was removed. Apple told *The Verge* that the reason for the removal was due to an expired license, but that YouTube users could still view videos through the Safari web browser. The company also confirmed that Google, which owns YouTube, was developing its own app, with a then-upcoming release through App Store. The Apple-developed YouTube app remained on iOS 5 and previous iOS versions. In June 2017, former YouTube employee Hunter Walk tweeted that Apple contacted YouTube to make it a default app on the original iPhone to ensure mass market mobile launch for the video-sharing service, but required handling development efforts itself. In 2012, YouTube made the "gutsy move" to discontinue the license in an effort to "take back control of our app" by developing it themselves.

Problems

Maps App Launch

In iOS 6, Apple replaced Google Maps with its own Apple Maps as the default mapping service for the operating system, and immediately faced criticism for inaccurate or incomplete data, including a museum in a river, missing towns, satellite images obscured by clouds, missing local places, and more.

Apple CEO Tim Cook issued a letter on Apple's website apologizing for the "frustration caused by the Maps application", and recommended downloading alternative map apps from the App Store. Scott Forstall, the then-VP of iOS software engineering, was involuntarily dismissed from his role at Apple in October 2012 after he "refused to sign his name to a letter apologizing for shortcomings in Apple's new mapping service".

Advertising Identifier Privacy Skepticism

In September 2012, Sarah Downey, a "privacy expert" with the software company Abine expressed her concern that in spite of the new "Advertising Identifier", Apple didn't disclose details on what the identifier was actually based on. She stated: "I need them to tell me why it's not identifying because as we've seen from a lot other "non-identifying" pieces of data, they can identify you quite easily", and that "If you're using the opt-out, [Apple] may no longer gather information to serve you targeted ads. To me, that says they may still collect your information to do things other than serve you targeted ads, like build databases about you to send you marketing or to sell to third parties".

Abnormal Data Usage

Many users reported a higher-than-normal data usage after upgrading to iOS 6, causing some to be heavily billed for data largely exceeding their data plan. Steve Rosenbaum of *The Huffington Post* wrote that "The bug is the result of an iOS 6 problem that connects the phone to the cellular data network whenever the phone is connected to a WiFi signal", and also stated that Apple had released a patch.

FaceTime Certificate Expiration

In April 2014, users who were still running iOS 6 could not connect to FaceTime due to the expiration of a certificate. Apple released a support document explaining the problem, adding that devices capable of upgrading to iOS 7 must do so to fix the issue, while devices stuck on iOS 6 would receive an iOS 6.1.6 update.

Supported Devices

With this release, Apple dropped support for older devices, specifically the third-generation iPod Touch and the first-generation iPad.

iPhone	iPod Touch	iPad
• iPhone 3GS	• iPod Touch (4th generation)	• iPad 2
• iPhone 4	• iPod Touch (5th generation)	• iPad (3rd generation)
• iPhone 4S		• iPad (4th generation)
• iPhone 5		• iPad Mini (1st generation)

iOS 5

iOS 5 is the fifth major release of the iOS mobile operating system developed by Apple Inc., being the successor to iOS 4. It was announced at the company's Worldwide Developers Conference on June 6, 2011, and was released on October 12, 2011. It was succeeded by iOS 6 on September 19, 2012.

iOS 5 revamped notifications, adding temporary banners that appear at the top of screen and introducing the Notification Center, a central location for all recent notifications. The operating system also added iCloud, Apple's cloud storage service for synchronization of content and data across iCloud-enabled devices, and iMessage, Apple's instant messaging service. For the first time, system software updates can be installed wirelessly, without requiring a computer and iTunes. iOS 5 also featured deep integration with Twitter, introduced multitasking gestures on iPads, and added an easily accessible camera shortcut from the lock screen.

iOS 5 was the subject of criticism for iPhone 4S users, as the initial release had poor battery life, failures of SIM cards, and echoes during phone calls. These problems were fixed in subsequent releases.

System Features

Notifications

In previous iOS versions, notifications popped up on the screen as dialog boxes, interrupting the current activity. In iOS 5, notifications are revamped, and show up as a temporary banner at the top of the screen. Recent notifications can also be accessed by pulling a "Notification Center" down from the top of the screen. Users who prefer the old notification system can keep it by choosing the appropriate option in the Settings menu.

iCloud

iOS 5 introduces iCloud, Apple's cloud storage service. The new service allows users to synchronize their music, pictures, videos, and application data across all of their iCloud-enabled devices.

Wireless Updates

iOS 5 enables wireless system updates on supported devices, meaning a computer and iTunes aren't necessary to update devices. Both activation of new devices and updates can be done wirelessly.

Twitter Integration

iOS 5 features deep Twitter integration. Users are able to sign in to Twitter directly from the Settings menu. Photos can be "tweeted" directly from the Photos or Camera apps, and users are also able to tweet from the Safari, YouTube, and Google Maps apps.

Multitasking

Multitasking gestures debut on iPad with the release of iOS 5. Multitasking allows users to jump between apps without double-tapping the home button or first going to the home screen. Multitasking gestures were only available on the iPad 2.

Keyboard

The iPad keyboard could be undocked from the bottom of the screen, and could be split into two half-keyboards.

App Features

Photos and Camera

The first iOS 5 release allowed the Camera app to be easily accessed from the lock screen for the first time. Users double-clicked the home button, a camera icon would appear next to the "Slide to unlock" message, and users would click on it to directly access the camera. The iOS 5.1 update streamlined the process, dropping the home button double-click procedure, but requiring users to swipe up the camera icon. For security purposes when the device is locked with a passcode, this method of accessing the camera only allows access to the Camera app, and no other features of the device. Pressing the volume-up button allows the user to take a picture.

Messages

iMessage, a new instant messaging service built into the Messages app, allowed anyone with an iOS 5 device to send both basic and multimedia messages to anyone else with a compatible iOS 5 device. In contrast to SMS, messages sent through iMessage use the Internet rather than regular cellular texting, but also in contrast to regular SMS, Android and BlackBerry devices are not compatible with the service. iMessages are synchronized across the user's devices, and are color-coded blue, with regular SMS in green.

Mail

The iOS Mail app included rich text formatting, better indent control, flagging of messages, and the ability to drag addresses between To, CC, and BCC lines.

Reminders

Reminders allows users to create lists of tasks with alerts that can either be date-based or location-based.

Newsstand

Newsstand does not act as a native app, but rather a special folder. When selected, it shows icons for all of the periodicals that the user has subscribed to, such as newspapers and magazines. New issues are downloaded automatically.

Music and Videos

The iPod app was replaced by separate Music and Videos apps.

Problems

Initial Upgrade Issues

The initial October 2011 release of iOS 5 saw significant upgrade issues, with errors during installation and Apple server overload.

iPhone 4S Battery Life

Following user complaints, Apple officially confirmed that iOS 5 had poor battery life for some iPhone 4S users, and stated that an upcoming software update would fix the issues. The iOS 5.0.1 update fixed bugs related to battery issues.

Wi-Fi Connectivity Drops

In November 2011, Engadget reported that the iOS 5 update caused Wi-Fi connection drops for some users. The report also wrote that "The recent iOS 5.0.1 update certainly hasn't fixed the matter, either", and questioned whether the events were unrelated or part of a larger issue.

SIM Card Failure

Some users of the iPhone 4S reported issues with the SIM card in iOS 5, being given error messages about "Invalid SIM" and "SIM Failure". Apple released a second software build of the 5.0.1 update designed to fix SIM card issues.

Phone Call Echo

Some users of the iPhone 4S reported the random appearance of echoes during phone calls made with earphones in the initial release of iOS 5. The other party in the call was sometimes unable to hear the conversation due to this problem.

Supported Devices

With this release, Apple dropped support for older devices, specifically the iPhone 3G and the second-generation iPod Touch.

iPhone	iPod Touch	iPad	Apple TV
• iPhone 3GS	• iPod Touch (3rd generation)	• iPad (1st generation)	• Apple TV (2nd generation)
• iPhone 4	• iPod Touch (4th generation)	• iPad 2	• Apple TV (3rd generation)
• iPhone 4S		• iPad (3rd generation)	

iOS 4

iOS 4 is the fourth major release of the iOS mobile operating system developed by Apple Inc., being the successor to iPhone OS 3. It was announced at the company's Worldwide Developers Conference on June 7, 2010, and was released on June 21, 2010. iOS 4 is the first iOS version issued under the "iOS" rebranding, dropping the "iPhone OS" naming convention of previous versions. It was succeeded by iOS 5 on October 12, 2011.

iOS 4 introduced folders on the home screen, significantly increasing the number of apps that can be displayed. Support for custom wallpapers was also added, although limited to newer devices due to animation performance requirements. The operating system also added a multitasking feature, letting apps dealing with Internet calling, location and audio playback function in the background, whereas a similar but more restricted "Fast App Switching" technology enabled any app to be left inactive in the background while users switch to other apps. iOS 4 also added a system-wide spell checking feature, enabled iBooks on iPhone, unified the Mail inbox to combine content from different email providers, and introduced both Game Center for social gaming and FaceTime for video calling.

The iOS 4 update introduced performance and battery problems on iPhone 3G devices, with Apple investigating the matter and promising then-upcoming updates. However, the company became the subject of a lawsuit from an unsatisfied customer over the issues. Around the same time, the release of iPhone 4 and its subsequent antenna problems made Apple focus on unsuccessfully attempting to patch the issues with software updates.

System Features

Home Screen

iOS 4 raised the maximum number of home screen apps from 180 to 2,160 due to the addition of folders. These folders would automatically be named based on the containing apps' respective App

Store category. The ability to add custom wallpapers to the home screen was also added, though the feature was notably absent from iPhone 3G and the second-generation iPod Touch due to poor performance of icon animations.

Multitasking

iOS 4 introduced multitasking. The feature allowed users to switch between apps instantly by double-clicking the home button. It was implemented in such a way that did not cause excessive battery drain. Multitasking was limited to apps dealing with Internet calling, location, and audio playback, while a similar "Fast App Switching" technology meant users could leave an app and enter another, with the original app remaining in the background until the user returns. This feature was notably absent from iPhone 3G and the second-generation iPod Touch due to performance issues.

Spell Check

iOS 4 introduced a spell checking feature that underlined misspelled words in red. Tapping on the word would provide a pop-up with a recommended replacement.

Camera

The Camera app could take pictures with 5 times digital zoom.

App Features

iBooks

iOS 4 introduced iPhone and iPod Touch support in iBooks, which was already included on iPad. Though not a default app, it was available through App Store.

Mail

The Mail app featured a unified inbox on iOS 4, allowing users to see messages from all of their email accounts displayed together in a single inbox. It also gained support for MobileMe e-mail aliases and multiple Exchange accounts for business users.

Game Center

iOS 4.1 added a new app called Game Center, an online multiplayer social gaming network, which allows users to invite friends to play games and to compare their scores on a leaderboard. It was not available on the iPhone 3G.

FaceTime

iOS 4 introduced FaceTime, a videotelephony app that uses the device's camera to allow the user to make video calls with other FaceTime users. This feature was absent from the iPhone 3GS, and third-generation iPod Touch and lower due to the lack of required features, such as a front-facing camera.

Safari

The Safari mobile web browser on iOS 4 added Bing as a search option in addition to Google and Yahoo. On iOS 4.2, specific words or phrases on a page can searched.

Problems

iPhone 3G users reported performance and battery issues after upgrading to iOS 4. Apple started an investigation of the matter in July 2010. In November, Apple was sued for the issues, with an unsatisfied customer alleging "violating the Consumer Legal Remedies Act, unfair business practices, and false and deceptive advertising", with further allegations that Apple knew its software would cause problems on older models. Apple hasn't responded to the allegations, but wrote in a reply to another unsatisfied customer in August that updates were "coming soon".

In all versions of iOS 4, the alarm clock in the clock app had a problem in DST when it would go off an hour too early or too late.

Upon its release, some iPhone 4 users reported having technical problems with the phone's antennas. Apple attempted to fix the issue with iOS 4.0.1, but failed to do so.

Supported Devices

The first-generation iPhone and the first-generation iPod Touch cannot run iOS 4 and above due to hardware limitations. This marked the first time Apple dropped support for older devices.

iPhone	iPod Touch	iPad	Apple TV
• iPhone 3G	• iPod Touch (2nd generation)	• iPad (1st generation)	• Apple TV (2nd generation)
• iPhone 3GS	• iPod Touch (3rd generation)	• iPad 2	
• iPhone 4	• iPod Touch (4th generation)		

iPhone OS 3

iPhone OS 3 is the third major release of the iOS mobile operating system developed by Apple Inc., being the successor to iPhone OS 2. It was announced on March 17, 2009, and was released on June 17, 2009. It was succeeded by iOS 4 on June 21, 2010; the new version dropped the "iPhone OS" naming convention. iPhone OS 3 was the last version to use the "iPhone OS" naming convention.

iPhone OS 3 added a system-wide "cut, copy, or paste" dialog bubble, allowing users to more easily move content. It also introduced Spotlight, a search indexing feature designed to help users locate specific information on their device, such as contacts, email messages or apps. The home screen was expanded to let users add up to 11 pages, showcasing a total of 180 apps. The Messages app received support for MMS, while the Camera app received support for video recording on iPhone 3GS, and a new "Voice Memos" app let users record their voice.

System Features

Cut, Copy or Paste

iPhone OS 3 introduced a "cut, copy, or paste" bubble dialog when users double-tap text. The "paste" button would incorporate anything stored in the device's clipboard into the marked area.

Spotlight

Spotlight is a system-wide indexing and search feature, aiming to help users search their device for specific contacts, email messages, calendar appointments, multimedia files, apps and more. It is accessed by swiping to the right from the home screen.

Home Screen

iPhone OS 3 expands the maximum number of pages on the home screen to 11, for a total number of 180 apps.

App Features

Messages

The Messages app received native support for the Multimedia Messaging Service (MMS), allowing users to send and receive messages that also contain pictures, contacts, locations, voice recordings, and video messages.

Camera and Photos

The Camera app introduced video recording for iPhone 3GS.

The Photos app featured a new copy button and the ability to delete multiple photos at once.

Voice Memos

iPhone OS 3 added a "Voice Memos" app, allowing users to record their voice.

Cost

Upgrading to iPhone OS 3 was free for iPhone. Upgrading to iPhone OS 3 cost iPod Touch users $5 to $10, depending on device purchase date.

iPhone OS 3 was the last iOS to charge iPod Touch users to upgrade. Starting with iOS 4, iOS upgrades became free for all users, including users of iPod Touch.

Supported Devices

iPhone	iPod Touch	iPad
• iPhone (1st generation) • iPhone 3G • iPhone 3GS	• iPod Touch (1st generation) • iPod Touch (2nd generation) • iPod Touch (3rd generation)	• iPad (1st generation)

iPhone OS 2

iPhone OS 2 is the second major release of the iOS mobile operating system developed by Apple Inc., being the successor to iPhone OS 1. It was the first release of iOS to support third-party applications via the App Store. iPhone OS 2.2.1 was the final version of iPhone OS 2. It was succeeded by iPhone OS 3 on June 17, 2009.

iPhone OS 2.0 became available on July 11, 2008 with the release of the iPhone 3G. Devices running 1.x are upgradable to this version. This version of iOS introduces the App Store, making third-party applications available to the iPhone and iPod Touch. Prior to the public release of iPhone OS 2.0, Apple held a keynote event to announce the iPhone OS Software Development Kit ("SDK") to developers.

Features

App Store

The most notable feature of iPhone OS 2 was the App Store. Before this feature was introduced, the only way to install custom applications on the device was via jailbreaking, which is strongly discouraged and unsupported by Apple. There were 500 applications available for download at the launch of the App Store, though this amount has grown dramatically since then. Now, the App Store has more than 2 million apps as of 2016.

Mail

The Mail app had a makeover, having push-emails that provide an always-on capability. It also supports Microsoft Office attachments, as well as iWork attachments. Other new features including support for BCC, multiple email delete, and the ability to select an outgoing email.

Contacts

The Contacts app now has a new home screen icon that is only available on iPod Touch. Along with the release is the ability to search contacts without being searched one-by-one, as well as SIM contacts import ability.

Maps

New features were added to the Maps app in the iPhone OS 2.2 software update. Among the features added are the inclusion of Google Street View, directions to public transit and while walking, and the ability to display the address of a dropped pin.

Calculator

When the device is in landscape mode, the calculator app displays a scientific calculator. Also, the app icon is updated.

Settings

Settings now had an ability to turn Wifi back on while in Airplane mode, as well as the ability to turn on/off the Location Services within the app.

iPod Touch Price

iPhone OS 2 cost $9.95 for iPod Touch users; it was free for iPhone users.

Supported Devices

iPhone	iPod Touch
• iPhone (1st generation)	• iPod Touch (1st generation)
• iPhone 3G	• iPod Touch (2nd generation)

iPhone OS 1

iPhone OS 1 is the first major release of iOS, and shipped pre-installed on the original iPhone. This version of the operating system wasn't called the iOS at the time it launched.

Support for features like the multitouch screen, Visual Voicemail, and iTunes integration were significant advances.

While this initial release was a major breakthrough at the time, it lacked many of the features that would come to be closely associated with the iPhone in the future, including support for native, third-party apps. Pre-installed apps included Calendar, Photos, Camera, Notes, Safari, Mail, Phone, and iPod (which was later split into the Music and Videos apps).

Version 1.1, which was released in Sept. 2007 was the first version of the software compatible with the iPod touch.

References

- El Khoury, Rita. "Google announces Android P: Notch support, multi-camera API, indoor positioning, and more". Android Police. Illogical Robot LLC. Retrieved March 7, 2018

- Android-what-where-and-why: javatpoint.com, Retrieved 24 April, 2019

- Stern, Joanna (November 6, 2017). "Apple Working on Fix for iphone Autocorrect Bug". The Wall Street Journal. Dow Jones & Company. Archived from the original on November 7, 2017. Retrieved November 9, 2017. (subscription required)

- Ios, TERM: webopedia.com, Retrieved 25 May, 2019

- Cohen, Peter (March 17, 2009). "Cut and paste, MMS highlight iphone 3.0 improvements". Macworld. International Data Group. Retrieved July 20, 2017

- Ios-versions: lifewire.com, Retrieved 26 June, 2019

- Knutson, Ryan (March 31, 2017). "Apple Fixes 911 Flaw in Latest ios Update". The Wall Street Journal. Dow Jones & Company. Retrieved March 31, 2017. (subscription required)

3

Computer Operating Systems

A computer operating system is used to manage the software and hardware resources in a personal computer. A few of the popular operating systems are Microsoft Windows, Mac OS, Unix and Linux. The diverse applications of these types of computer operating systems have been thoroughly discussed in this chapter.

MICROSOFT WINDOWS

Windows is Microsoft's flagship operating system (OS), the de facto standard for home and business computers. The graphical user interface (GUI)-based OS was introduced in 1985 and has been released in many versions since then. Microsoft got its start with the partnership of Bill Gates and Paul Allen in 1975. Gates and Allen co-developed Xenix (a version of Unix) and also collaborated on a BASIC interpreter for the Altair 8800. The company was incorporated in 1981.

Microsoft gained prominence in the tech field with the release of MS-DOS, a text-based command-line-driven operating system. DOS was mostly based on a purchased intellectual property, QDOS. GUI-based operating systems of that time included Xerox's Alto, released in 1979, and Apple's LISA and Macintosh systems, which came later. Die-hard fans of MS-DOS referred to such systems as WIMPs, which stood for "windows, icons, mouse and pull-down menus (or pointers)."

However, Gates saw the potential in GUI-based systems and started a project he called Interface Manager. Gates thought he could bring the GUI to a wider audience at a lower cost than the $9,000 LISA. The rest of Microsoft supported this idea, and, in a somewhat ironic move, the project team selected "Windows" as the name of the new operating system.

Microsoft announced the impending release of Windows 1.0 in 1983. The company used some features it licensed from Apple for portions of its interface. Microsoft released Windows 1.0 in 1985. Apple sued Microsoft and Hewlett-Packard for $5.5 billion in 1988 claiming it did not give the companies authorization to use certain GUI elements. In 1992, a federal court concluded Microsoft and Hewlett-Packard did not go beyond the 1985 agreement. Apple appealed that decision, which was upheld in 1994.

Competitors to Windows include Apple's macOS and the open source Linux operating system from Linus Torvalds. The free price gives Linux an edge in availability, while macOS is known for its stability and user experience. However, Microsoft Windows continues to maintain its dominance

- a June 2018 report from the NetMarketShare site shows Windows installed on nearly 88% of desktops and laptops - with a steady rollout of new versions to support advances in hardware.

Windows Versions through the Years

1985: Windows 1.0

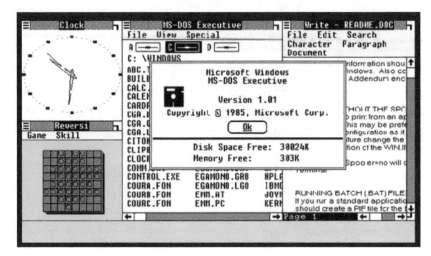

Like many early versions of Microsoft's GUI operating systems, Windows 1.0 was essentially a program that ran on top of DOS. Microsoft did not release the system until two years after its first announcement, leading to suggestions that Windows was vaporware. The release was a shaky start for the tech giant. Users found the software unstable. However, the point-and-click interface made it easier for new users to operate a computer. The user-friendly nature of Windows also drew interest from customers who might have been intimidated by a command-line interface. Windows 1.0 offered many of the common components found in today's graphical user interface, such as scroll bars and "OK" buttons.

1987: Windows 2.0 and 2.11

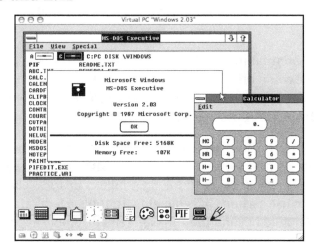

Windows 2.0 was faster, more stable and had more GUI features in common with the Apple LISA. The system introduced the control panel and ran the first versions of Excel and Word. Windows 2.0 supported extended memory, and Microsoft updated it for compatibility with Intel's 80386

processor. It was during this time that Microsoft became the largest software vendor in the world, just as computers were becoming more commonplace. The fact that Windows systems were user-friendly and relatively affordable was a contributing factor to the growing PC market.

1990: Windows 3.0

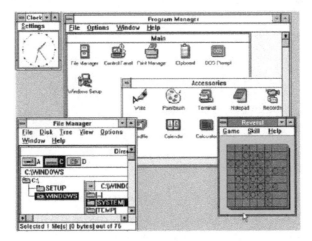

Microsoft optimized the Windows 3.0 operating system, which still ran on top of DOS, for the 386 processor for a more responsive system. Windows 3.0 supported 16 colors and included the casual games familiar to most Windows users: Solitaire, Minesweeper and Hearts. Games that required more processing power still ran directly on MS-DOS. Exiting to DOS gave games direct hardware access made more system resources available that otherwise would have gone to Windows. Microsoft offered Windows 3.1 as a paid sub-release in 1993. Windows 3.1 features included support for TrueType fonts and peer-to-peer networking.

1995: Windows 95

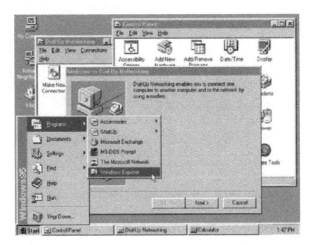

Windows 95 introduced the Windows operating system to a wider audience with a marketing campaign that featured The Rolling Stones song "Start Me Up" to celebrate the Start button's arrival to the masses. Windows 95 facilitated hardware installation with its Plug and Play feature. Microsoft also unveiled 32-bit color depth, enhanced multimedia capabilities and TCP/IP network support.

1998: Windows 98

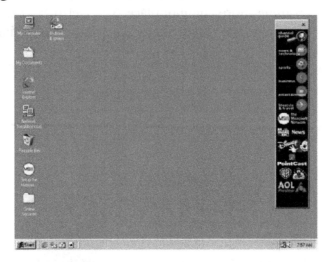

Microsoft improved speed and Plug and Play hardware support in Windows 98. The company also debuted USB support and the Quick Launch bar in this release. DOS gaming began to wane as Windows gaming technology improved. The popularity of the OS made it an attractive target for malware. Microsoft integrated web technology into the Windows user interface and built its own web browser into the desktop. This feature was one of the defining issues in the U.S. Justice Department's antitrust suit against Microsoft in the 1990s.

2000: Windows ME

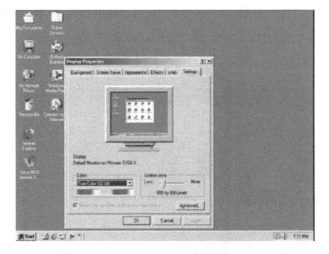

Windows ME (Millennium Edition) was the last use of the Windows 95 codebase. Its most notable new feature was System Restore. Many customers found this release to be unstable, and it was acknowledged as a poor release by Steve Ballmer and Microsoft. Some critics said ME stood for "mistake edition."

Microsoft released the professional desktop OS Windows 2000 the same year. Microsoft based this OS on the more stable Windows NT code. Some home users installed Windows 2000 for its greater reliability. Microsoft updated Plug and Play support, which spurred home users to switch to this OS.

2001: Windows XP

Microsoft delivered Windows XP as the first NT-based system with a version aimed squarely at the home user. Home users and critics rated XP highly. The system improved Windows appearance with colorful themes and provided a more stable platform.

Microsoft virtually ended gaming in DOS with this release. DirectX-enabled features in 3D gaming that OpenGL had difficulties with. XP offered the first Windows support for 64-bit computing, but it was not very well supported, lacking drivers and applications to run.

2006: Windows Vista

Microsoft hyped Windows Vista after the company spent a lot of resources to develop a more polished appearance. Vista had interesting visual effects but the OS was slow to start and run. The 32-bit version, in particular, didn't enable enough RAM for the memory-hungry OS to operate properly.

Microsoft tightened licensing rights and made it more work to activate Windows. The company also peeled back user control of the operating system's internal workings.

Microsoft lost market share to Apple and Linux variants. Vista's flaws - coupled with the fact that many older computers lacked the resources to run the system - led to many home and business users staying with XP.

2009: Windows 7

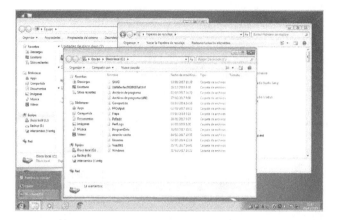

Microsoft built Windows 7 on the Vista kernel. Windows 7 picked up Vista's visual capabilities but featured more stability. To many end users, the biggest changes between Vista and Windows 7 were faster boot times, new user interface and the addition of Internet Explorer 8.

With true 64-bit support and more Direct X features, Windows 7 proved to be a popular release for Windows users.

2012: Windows 8

Microsoft released Windows 8 with a number of enhancements and debuted its tile-based Metro user interface. Windows 8 took better advantage of multicore processing, solid-state drives (SSD), touchscreens and other alternate input methods. Users found the switching from the traditional desktop to the tile-based interface awkward. Even after Microsoft's UI and other updates in 8.1, Windows 8 trailed not just Windows 7 but XP in user numbers into 2014.

Changes in Security

Microsoft did not implement many security methods in its operating systems until Windows NT and XP. For example, the default user on a Windows computer received administrator privileges until Vista.

Consumer editions of early versions of Windows did not have security measures built in since Microsoft designed the OS for single users without network connections. The company integrated security features in Windows NT, but they weren't in the forefront of Microsoft's design. The combination of lack of security and widespread popularity made Windows systems a target for malicious programs, such as viruses or system exploits.

Microsoft began to release monthly patches every second Tuesday of the month, known as Patch Tuesday, in 2003. Patches to update critical issues may be released on a faster schedule, known as out-of-band patches.

Windows Vista added User Account Control, a privilege evaluation feature based on a token system. The token allowed users only the most basic privileges, such as the ability to execute tasks that may modify system data. When an administrator logged on, they received two tokens - one that a standard user would receive and another that allowed administrator-level tasks.

Microsoft released its Windows Defender security application as a beta program for Windows XP in 2005. Windows Defender protects systems from spyware threats. Microsoft included Defender in later versions of Windows, such as Windows 10. Microsoft further buttressed system security with Windows Defender Credential Guard for virtualization-based security, System Guard to protect firmware components and configurations and Application Guard to protect against malware and hacking threats in the Microsoft Edge browser.

Differences in Windows Operating System Editions

Starting with Windows XP, Microsoft separated Windows to give different features to distinct audiences. Windows 10, for example, has multiple editions including Windows 10 Home, Pro and Enterprise editions.

Microsoft makes its consumer operating systems for users in an ordinary household setting. Enterprise operating system is designed for large organizations in a business setting. The enterprise software tends to have more customization abilities and features that an organization can utilize, such as security or language packs.

Microsoft designed Windows 10 Home for consumers and tailored to operate on PCs, tablets and 2-in-1 devices. Microsoft built Windows 10 Pro as a baseline OS for any business, while it developed Windows 10 Enterprise for businesses with higher security needs.

Security features differ from Windows 10 Home, Pro and Enterprise editions. Windows 10 Home includes basic security features such as Windows Defender, Device Encryption and Windows Information Protection. Windows 10 Pro adds more security features such as Bitlocker, Windows Defender System Guard, Windows Defender Exploit Guard and Windows Defender Antivirus. Windows 10 Enterprise is identical in features and functionality to Pro but adds more security features such as Windows Defender Credential Guard, Windows Defender Application Guard and Windows Defender Application Control.

Windows NT

Windows NT is a family of operating systems produced by Microsoft, the first version of which was released on July 27, 1993. It is a processor-independent, multiprocessing and multi-user operating system.

The first version of Windows NT was Windows NT 3.1 and was produced for workstations and server computers. It was intended to complement consumer versions of Windows that were based on MS-DOS (including Windows 1.0 through Windows 3.1x). Gradually, the Windows NT family was expanded into Microsoft's general-purpose operating system product line for all personal computers, deprecating the Windows 9x family.

"NT" formerly expanded to "New Technology" but no longer carries any specific meaning. Starting with Windows 2000, "NT" was removed from the product name and is only included in the product version string.

NT was the first purely 32-bit version of Windows, whereas its consumer-oriented counterparts, Windows 3.1x and Windows 9x, were 16-bit/32-bit hybrids. It is a multi-architecture operating system. Initially, it supported several instruction set architectures, including IA-32, MIPS, and DEC Alpha; support for PowerPC, Itanium, x64, and ARM were added later. The latest versions support x86 (more specifically IA-32 and x64) and ARM. Major features of the Windows NT family include Windows Shell, Windows API, Native API, Active Directory, Group Policy, Hardware Abstraction Layer, NTFS, BitLocker, Windows Store, Windows Update, and Hyper-V.

Major Features

A main design goal of NT was hardware and software portability. Various versions of NT family operating systems have been released for a variety of processor architectures, initially IA-32, MIPS, and DEC Alpha, with PowerPC, Itanium, x86-64 and ARM supported in later releases. The idea was to have a common code base with a custom Hardware Abstraction Layer (HAL) for each platform. However, support for MIPS, Alpha, and PowerPC was later dropped in Windows 2000. Broad software compatibility was achieved with support for several API "personalities", including Windows API, POSIX, and OS/2 APIs – the latter two were phased out starting with Windows XP. Partial MS-DOS compatibility was achieved via an integrated DOS Virtual Machine – although this feature is being phased out in the x86-64 architecture. NT supported per-object (file, function, and role) access control lists allowing a rich set of security permissions to be applied to systems and services. NT supported Windows network protocols, inheriting the previous OS/2 LAN Manager networking, as well as TCP/IP networking (for which Microsoft would implement a TCP/IP stack derived at first from a STREAMS-based stack from Spider Systems, then later rewritten in-house).

Windows NT 3.1 was the first version of Windows to use 32-bit flat virtual memory addressing on 32-bit processors. Its companion product, Windows 3.1, used segmented addressing and switches from 16-bit to 32-bit addressing in pages.

Windows NT 3.1 featured a core kernel providing a system API, running in supervisor mode (ring 0 in x86; referred to in Windows NT as "kernel mode" on all platforms), and a set of user-space environments with their own APIs which included the new Win32 environment, an OS/2 1.3 text-mode environment and a POSIX environment. The full preemptive multitasking kernel could interrupt running tasks to schedule other tasks, without relying on user programs to voluntarily give up control of the CPU, as in Windows 3.1 Windows applications (although MS-DOS applications were preemptively multitasked in Windows starting with Windows/386).

Notably, in Windows NT 3.x, several I/O driver subsystems, such as video and printing, were user-mode subsystems. In Windows NT 4, the video, server, and printer spooler subsystems were moved into kernel mode. Windows NT's first GUI was strongly influenced by (and programmatically compatible with) that from Windows 3.1; Windows NT 4's interface was redesigned to match that of the brand new Windows 95, moving from the Program Manager to the Windows shell design.

NTFS, a journaled, secure file system, was created for NT. Windows NT also allows for other installable file systems; starting with versions 3.1, NT could be installed on FAT or HPFS file systems.

Windows NT introduced its own driver model, the Windows NT driver model, and is incompatible with older driver frameworks. With Windows 2000, the Windows NT driver model was enhanced to become the Windows Driver Model, which was first introduced with Windows 98, but was based on the NT driver model. Windows Vista added native support for the Windows Driver Foundation, which is also available for Windows XP, Windows Server 2003 and to an extent, Windows 2000.

Development

Original Windows NT wordmark.

Microsoft decided to create a portable operating system, compatible with OS/2 and POSIX and supporting multiprocessing, in October 1988. When development started in November 1989, Windows NT was to be known as OS/2 3.0, the third version of the operating system developed jointly by Microsoft and IBM. To ensure portability, initial development was targeted at the Intel i860XR RISC processor, switching to the MIPS R3000 in late 1989, and then the Intel i386 in 1990. Microsoft also continued parallel development of the DOS-based and less resource-demanding Windows environment, resulting in the release of Windows 3.0 in May 1990. Windows 3 was eventually so successful that Microsoft decided to change the primary application programming interface for the still unreleased NT OS/2 (as it was then known) from an extended OS/2 API to an extended Windows API. This decision caused tension between Microsoft and IBM and the collaboration ultimately fell apart. IBM continued OS/2 development alone while Microsoft continued work on the newly renamed Windows NT. Though neither operating system would immediately be as popular as Microsoft's MS-DOS or Windows products, Windows NT would eventually be far more successful than OS/2.

Microsoft hired a group of developers from Digital Equipment Corporation led by Dave Cutler to build Windows NT, and many elements of the design reflect earlier DEC experience with Cutler's VMS and RSX-11, but also an unreleased object-based operating system developed by Dave Cutler for DEC Prism. The team was joined by selected members of the disbanded OS/2 team, including Moshe Dunie. The operating system was designed to run on multiple instruction set architectures and multiple hardware platforms within each architecture. The platform dependencies are largely hidden from the rest of the system by a kernel mode module called the HAL (Hardware Abstraction Layer).

Windows NT's kernel mode code further distinguishes between the "kernel", whose primary purpose is to implement processor- and architecture-dependent functions, and the "executive". This was designed as a modified microkernel, as the Windows NT kernel was influenced by the Mach microkernel developed at Carnegie Mellon University, but does not meet all of the criteria of a pure microkernel. Both the kernel and the executive are linked together into the single loaded module ntoskrnl.exe; from outside this module, there is little distinction between the kernel and the executive. Routines from each are directly accessible, as for example from kernel-mode device drivers.

API sets in the Windows NT family are implemented as subsystems atop the publicly undocument- ed "native" API; this allowed the late adoption of the Windows API (into the Win32 subsystem). Windows NT was one of the earliest operating systems to use Unicode internally.

Programming Language

Windows NT is written in C and C++, with a very small amount written in assembly language. C is mostly used for the kernel code while C++ is mostly used for user-mode code. Assembly language is avoided where possible because it would impede portability.

Supported Platforms

32-bit Platforms

In order to prevent Intel x86-specific code from slipping into the operating system by developers used to developing on x86 chips, Windows NT 3.1 was initially developed using non-x86 develop- ment systems and then ported to the x86 architecture. This work was initially based on the Intel i860-based *Dazzle* system and, later, the MIPS R4000-based *Jazz* platform. Both systems were designed internally at Microsoft.

Windows NT 3.1 was released for Intel x86 PC compatible, PC-98, DEC Alpha, and ARC-compliant MIPS platforms. Windows NT 3.51 added support for the PowerPC processor in 1995, specifically PReP-compliant systems such as the IBM Power Series desktops/laptops and Motorola Power- Stack series; but despite meetings between Michael Spindler and Bill Gates, not on the Power Macintosh as the PReP compliant Power Macintosh project failed to ship.

Intergraph Corporation ported Windows NT to its Clipper architecture and later announced inten- tion to port Windows NT 3.51 to Sun Microsystems' SPARC architecture, but neither version was sold to the public as a retail product.

Only two of the Windows NT 4.0 variants (IA-32 and Alpha) have a full set of service packs avail- able. All of the other ports done by third parties (Motorola, Intergraph, etc.) have few, if any, pub- licly available updates.

Windows NT 4.0 was the last major release to support Alpha, MIPS, or PowerPC, though develop- ment of Windows 2000 for Alpha continued until August 1999, when Compaq stopped support for Windows NT on that architecture; and then three days later Microsoft also canceled their AlphaNT program, even though the Alpha NT 5 (Windows 2000) release had reached RC1 status.

Microsoft announced on January 5, 2011 that the next major version of the Windows NT family will include support for the ARM architecture. Microsoft demonstrated a preliminary version of Win- dows (version 6.2.7867) running on an ARM-based computer at the 2011 Consumer Electronics

Show. This eventually led to the commercial release of the Windows 8-derived Windows RT on October 26, 2012, and the implementation of NT over CE on Windows Phone 8.

According to Microsoft, it is a common misconception that the Xbox and Xbox 360 use a modified Windows 2000 kernel, for the Xbox operating system was built from scratch but implements a subset of Windows APIs.

64-bit Platforms

The 64-bit versions of Windows NT were originally intended to run on Itanium and DEC Alpha; the latter was used internally at Microsoft during early development of 64-bit Windows. This continued for some time after Microsoft publicly announced that it was cancelling plans to ship 64-bit Windows for Alpha. Because of this, Alpha versions of Windows NT are 32-bit only.

While Windows 2000 only supports Intel IA-32 (32-bit), Windows XP, Server 2003, Server 2008 and Server 2008 R2 each have one edition dedicated to Itanium-based systems. In comparison with Itanium, Microsoft adopted x64 on a greater scale: every version of Windows since Windows XP (which has a dedicated x64 edition), has x64 editions.

Hardware Requirements

The minimum hardware specification required to run each release of the professional workstation version of Windows NT has been fairly slow-moving until the 6.0 Vista release, which requires a minimum of 15 GB of free disk space, a 10-fold increase in free disk space alone over the previous version.

Windows NT minimum hardware requirements			
Windows version	CPU	RAM	Free disk space
NT 3.1	i386, 25 MHz	12 MB	90 MB
NT 3.1 Advanced Server		16 MB	
NT 3.5 Workstation		12 MB	
NT 3.5 Server		16 MB	
NT 3.51 Workstation		12 MB	
NT 3.51 Server		16 MB	
NT 4.0 Workstation	i486, 25 MHz	12 MB	124 MB
NT 4.0 Server		16 MB	
2000 Professional	Pentium, 133 MHz	32 MB	650 MB
2000 Server		128 MB	
XP	Pentium, 233 MHz	64 MB	1.5 GB
Server 2003	133 MHz	128 MB	
Vista Home Basic	800 MHz	512 MB	20 GB
Vista (other editions)	1 GHz	1 GB	40 GB
7 for IA-32			16 GB
7 for x64		2 GB	20 GB
8 for IA-32	1 GHz with NX bit, SSE2, PAE	1 GB	16 GB
8 for x64		2 GB	20 GB
8.1 for IA-32		1 GB	16 GB

8.1 for x64	1 GHz with NX bit, SSE2, PAE, CMPX-CHG16b, PrefetchW and LAHF/SAHF	2 GB	20 GB
10 for IA-32	1 GHz with NX bit, SSE2, PAE	1 GB	16 GB
10 for x64	1 GHz with NX bit, SSE2, PAE, CMPX-CHG16b, PrefetchW and LAHF/SAHF	2 GB	20 GB

Architecture of Windows NT

The architecture of Windows NT, a line of operating systems produced and sold by Microsoft, is a layered design that consists of two main components, user mode and kernel mode. It is a pre-emptive, reentrant multitasking operating system, which has been designed to work with uniprocessor and symmetrical multiprocessor (SMP)-based computers. To process input/output (I/O) requests, they use packet-driven I/O, which utilizes I/O request packets (IRPs) and asynchronous I/O. Starting with Windows XP, Microsoft began making 64-bit versions of Windows available; before this, there were only 32-bit versions of these operating systems.

Programs and subsystems in user mode are limited in terms of to what system resources they have access, while the kernel mode has unrestricted access to the system memory and external devices. Kernel mode in Windows NT has full access to the hardware and system resources of the computer. The Windows NT kernel is a hybrid kernel; the architecture comprises a simple kernel, hardware abstraction layer (HAL), drivers, and a range of services (collectively named Executive), which all exist in kernel mode.

User mode in Windows NT is made of subsystems capable of passing I/O requests to the appropriate kernel mode device drivers by using the I/O manager. The user mode layer of Windows NT is made up of the "Environment subsystems", which run applications written for many different types of operating systems, and the "Integral subsystem", which operates system-specific functions on behalf of environment subsystems. The kernel mode stops user mode services and applications from accessing critical areas of the operating system that they should not have access to.

The Executive interfaces, with all the user mode subsystems, deal with I/O, object management, security and process management. The kernel sits between the hardware abstraction layer and the Executive to provide *multiprocessor synchronization*, thread and interrupt scheduling and dispatching, and trap handling and exception dispatching. The kernel is also responsible for initializing device drivers at bootup. Kernel mode drivers exist in three levels: highest level drivers, intermediate drivers and low-level drivers. Windows Driver Model (WDM) exists in the intermediate layer and was mainly designed to be binary and source compatible between Windows 98 and Windows 2000. The lowest level drivers are either legacy Windows NT device drivers that control a device directly or can be a plug and play (PnP) hardware bus.

User mode

User mode is made up of various system-defined processes and DLLs.

The interface between user mode applications and operating system kernel functions is called an "environment subsystem." Windows NT can have more than one of these, each implementing a different API set. This mechanism was designed to support applications written for many different types of operating systems. None of the environment subsystems can directly access hardware; access to hardware functions is done by calling into kernel mode routines.

There are four main environment subsystems: the Win32 subsystem, an OS/2 subsystem, the Windows Subsystem for Linux and a POSIX subsystem.

- The Win32 environment subsystem can run 32-bit Windows applications. It contains the console as well as text window support, shutdown and hard-error handling for all other environment subsystems. It also supports Virtual DOS Machines (VDMs), which allow MS-DOS and 16-bit Windows (Win16) applications to run on Windows NT. There is a specific MS-DOS VDM that runs in its own address space and which emulates an Intel 80486 running MS-DOS 5.0. Win16 programs, however, run in a Win16 VDM. Each program, by default, runs in the same process, thus using the same address space, and the Win16 VDM gives each program its own thread on which to run. However, Windows NT does allow users to run a Win16 program in a separate Win16 VDM, which allows the program to be preemptively multitasked, as Windows NT will pre-empt the whole VDM process, which only contains one running application. The Win32 environment subsystem process (csrss.exe) also includes the window management functionality, sometimes called a "window manager". It handles input events (such as from the keyboard and mouse), then passes messages to the applications that need to receive this input. Each application is responsible for drawing or refreshing its own windows and menus, in response to these messages.

- The OS/2 environment subsystem supports 16-bit character-based OS/2 applications and emulates OS/2 1.x, but not 32-bit or graphical OS/2 applications as used with OS/2 2.x or later, on x86 machines only. To run graphical OS/2 1.x programs, the Windows NT Add-On Subsystem for Presentation Manager must be installed. The last version of Windows NT to have an OS/2 subsystem was Windows 2000; it was removed as of Windows XP.

- The POSIX environment subsystem supports applications that are strictly written to either the POSIX.1 standard or the related ISO/IEC standards. This subsystem has been replaced by Interix, which is a part of Windows Services for UNIX. This was in turn replaced by the Windows Subsystem for Linux.

The security subsystem deals with security tokens, grants or denies access to user accounts based on resource permissions, handles login requests and initiates login authentication, and determines which system resources need to be audited by Windows NT. It also looks after Active Directory. The workstation service implements the network redirector, which is the client side of Windows file and print sharing; it implements local requests to remote files and printers by "redirecting" them to the appropriate servers on the network. Conversely, the server service allows other computers on the network to access file shares and shared printers offered by the local system.

Kernel Mode

Windows NT kernel mode has full access to the hardware and system resources of the computer and runs code in a protected memory area. It controls access to scheduling, thread prioritization, memory management and the interaction with hardware. The kernel mode stops user mode services and applications from accessing critical areas of the operating system that they should not have access to; user mode processes must ask the kernel mode to perform such operations on their behalf.

While the x86 architecture supports four different privilege levels (numbered 0 to 3), only the two extreme privilege levels are used. Usermode programs are run with CPL 3, and the kernel runs with CPL 0. These two levels are often referred to as "ring 3" and "ring 0", respectively. Such a design decision had been done to achieve code portability to RISC platforms that only support two privilege levels, though this breaks compatibility with OS/2 applications that contain I/O privilege segments that attempt to directly access hardware.

Code running in kernel mode includes: the executive, which is itself made up of many modules that do specific tasks; the kernel, which provides low-level services used by the Executive; the Hardware Abstraction Layer (HAL); and *kernel drivers*.

Executive

The Windows Executive services make up the low-level kernel-mode portion, and are contained in the file NTOSKRNL.EXE. It deals with I/O, object management, security and process management. These are divided into several *subsystems*, among which are *Cache Manager*, *Configuration Manager*, *I/O Manager*, *Local Procedure Call (LPC)*, *Memory Manager*, *Object Manager*, *Process Structure* and *Security Reference Monitor (SRM)*. Grouped together, the components can be called *Executive services* (internal name *Ex*). *System Services* (internal name *Nt*), i.e., system calls, are implemented at this level, too, except very few that call directly into the kernel layer for better performance.

The term "service" in this context generally refers to a callable routine, or set of callable routines. This is distinct from the concept of a "service process", which is a user mode component somewhat analogous to a daemon in Unix-like operating systems.

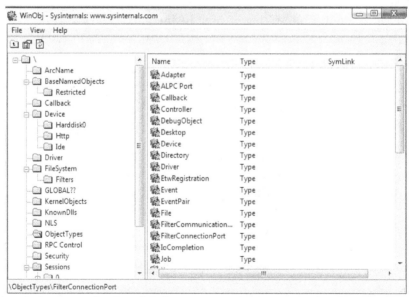

Each object in Windows NT exists in a global namespace. This is a screenshot from Sysinternals WinObj.

Object Manager

The *Object Manager* (internal name *Ob*) is an executive subsystem that all other executive subsystems, especially system calls, must pass through to gain access to Windows NT resources— essentially making it a resource management infrastructure service. The object manager is used to reduce the duplication of object resource management functionality in other executive subsystems, which could potentially lead to bugs and make development of Windows NT harder. To the object manager, each resource is an object, whether that resource is a physical resource (such as a file system or peripheral) or a logical resource (such as a file). Each object has a structure or *object type* that the object manager must know about.

Object creation is a process in two phases, *creation* and *insertion*. *Creation* causes the allocation of an empty object and the reservation of any resources required by the object manager, such as an (optional) name in the namespace. If creation was successful, the subsystem responsible for the creation fills in the empty object. Finally, if the subsystem deems the initialization successful, it instructs the object manager to *insert* the object, which makes it accessible through its (optional) name or a cookie called a *handle*. From then on, the lifetime of the object is handled by the object manager, and it's up to the subsystem to keep the object in a working condition until being signaled by the object manager to dispose of it.

Handles are identifiers that represent a reference to a kernel resource through an opaque value. Similarly, opening an object through its name is subject to security checks, but acting through an existing, open handle is only limited to the level of access requested when the object was opened or created.

Object types define the object procedures and any data specific to the object. In this way, the object manager allows Windows NT to be an object-oriented operating system, as object types can be thought of as polymorphic classes that define objects. Most subsystems, though, with a notable exception in the I/O Manager, rely on the default implementation for all object type procedures.

Each instance of an object that is created stores its name, parameters that are passed to the object creation function, security attributes and a pointer to its object type. The object also contains an object close procedure and a reference count to tell the object manager how many other objects in the system reference that object and thereby determines whether the object can be destroyed when a close request is sent to it. Every named object exists in a hierarchical object namespace.

Cache Controller

Closely coordinates with the Memory Manager, I/O Manager and I/O drivers to provide a common cache for regular file I/O. The Windows Cache Manager operates on file blocks (rather than device blocks), for consistent operation between local and remote files, and ensures a certain degree of coherency with memory-mapped views of files, since cache blocks are a special case of memory-mapped views and cache misses a special case of page faults.

Configuration Manager

Implements the Windows Registry.

I/O Manager

Allows devices to communicate with user-mode subsystems. It translates user-mode read and write commands into read or write IRPs which it passes to device drivers. It accepts file system I/O requests and translates them into device specific calls, and can incorporate low-level device drivers that directly manipulate hardware to either read input or write output. It also includes a cache manager to improve disk performance by caching read requests and write to the disk in the background.

Local Procedure Call (LPC)

Provides inter-process communication ports with connection semantics. LPC ports are used by user-mode subsystems to communicate with their clients, by Executive subsystems to communicate with user-mode subsystems, and as the basis for the local transport for Microsoft RPC.

Memory Manager

Manages virtual memory, controlling memory protection and the paging of memory in and out of physical memory to secondary storage, and implements a general-purpose allocator of physical memory. It also implements a parser of PE executables that lets an executable be mapped or unmapped in a single, atomic step.

Starting from Windows NT Server 4.0, Terminal Server Edition, the memory manager implements a so-called *session space*, a range of kernel-mode memory that is subject to context switching just like user-mode memory. This lets multiple instances of the kernel-mode Win32 subsystem and GDI drivers run side-by-side, despite shortcomings in their initial design. Each session space is shared by several processes, collectively referred to as a "session".

To ensure a degree of isolation between sessions without introducing a new object type, the association between processes and sessions is handled by the Security Reference Monitor, as an attribute of a security subject (token), and it can only be changed while holding special privileges.

The relatively unsophisticated and ad-hoc nature of sessions is due to the fact they weren't part of the initial design, and had to be developed, with minimal disruption to the main line, by a third party (Citrix Systems) as a prerequisite for their terminal server product for Windows NT, called WinFrame. Starting with Windows Vista, though, sessions finally became a proper aspect of the Windows architecture. No longer a memory manager construct that creeps into user mode indirectly through Win32, they were expanded into a pervasive abstraction affecting most Executive subsystems. As a matter of fact, regular use of Windows Vista always results in a multi-session environment.

Process Structure

Handles process and thread creation and termination, and it implements the concept of *Job*, a group of processes that can be terminated as a whole, or be placed under shared restrictions (such a total maximum of allocated memory, or CPU time). Job objects were introduced in Windows 2000.

PnP Manager

Handles plug and play and supports device detection and installation at boot time. It also has the responsibility to stop and start devices on demand—this can happen when a bus (such as USB or IEEE 1394 FireWire) gains a new device and needs to have a device driver loaded to support it.

Its bulk is actually implemented in user mode, in the *Plug and Play Service*, which handles the often complex tasks of installing the appropriate drivers, notifying services and applications of the arrival of new devices, and displaying GUI to the user.

Power Manager

Deals with power events (power-off, stand-by, hibernate, etc.) and notifies affected drivers with special IRPs (*Power IRPs*).

Security Reference Monitor (SRM)

The primary authority for enforcing the security rules of the security integral subsystem. It determines whether an object or resource can be accessed, via the use of access control lists (ACLs), which are themselves made up of access control entries (ACEs). ACEs contain a Security Identifier (SID) and a list of operations that the ACE gives a select group of trustees—a user account, group account, or login session—permission (allow, deny, or audit) to that resource.

GDI

The Graphics Device Interface is responsible for tasks such as drawing lines and curves, rendering fonts and handling palettes. The Windows NT 3.x series of releases had placed the GDI component in the user-mode Client/Server Runtime Subsystem, but this was moved into kernel mode with Windows NT 4.0 to improve graphics performance.

Kernel

The kernel sits between the HAL and the Executive and provides multiprocessor synchronization, thread and interrupt scheduling and dispatching, and trap handling and exception dispatching; it is also responsible for initializing device drivers at bootup that are necessary to get the operating system up and running. That is, the kernel performs almost all the tasks of a traditional microkernel; the strict distinction between Executive and Kernel is the most prominent remnant of the original microkernel design, and historical design documentation consistently refers to the kernel component as "the microkernel".

The kernel often interfaces with the process manager. The level of abstraction is such that the kernel never calls into the process manager, only the other way around (save for a handful of corner cases, still never to the point of a functional dependence).

Kernel-mode Drivers

Windows NT uses kernel-mode device drivers to enable it to interact with hardware devices. Each of the drivers has well defined system routines and internal routines that it exports to the rest of the operating system. All devices are seen by user mode code as a file object in the I/O manager, though to the I/O manager itself the devices are seen as device objects, which it defines as either file, device or driver objects. Kernel mode drivers exist in three levels: highest level drivers, intermediate drivers and low level drivers. The highest level drivers, such as file system drivers for FAT and NTFS, rely on intermediate drivers. Intermediate drivers consist of function drivers—or main driver for a device—that are optionally sandwiched between lower and higher level filter drivers. The function driver then relies on a bus driver—or a driver that services a bus controller, adapter, or bridge—which can have an optional bus filter driver that sits between itself and the function driver. Intermediate drivers rely on the lowest level drivers to function. The Windows Driver Model (WDM) exists in the intermediate layer. The lowest level drivers are either legacy Windows NT device drivers that control a device directly or can be a PnP hardware bus. These lower level drivers directly control hardware and do not rely on any other drivers.

Hardware Abstraction Layer

The Windows NT hardware abstraction layer, or HAL, is a layer between the physical hardware of the computer and the rest of the operating system. It was designed to hide differences in hardware and provide a consistent platform on which the kernel is run. The HAL includes hardware-specific code that controls I/O interfaces, interrupt controllers and multiple processors.

However, despite its purpose and designated place within the architecture, the HAL isn't a layer that sits entirely below the kernel, the way the kernel sits below the Executive: All known HAL implementations depend in some measure on the kernel, or even the Executive. In practice, this means that kernel and HAL variants come in matching sets that are specifically constructed to work together.

In particular hardware abstraction does *not* involve abstracting the instruction set, which generally falls under the wider concept of portability. Abstracting the instruction set, when necessary (such as for handling the several revisions to the x86 instruction set, or emulating a missing math coprocessor), is performed by the kernel, or via hardware virtualization.

Windows XP

Windows XP is a personal computer operating system produced by Microsoft as part of the Windows NT family of operating systems. It was released to manufacturing on August 24, 2001, and broadly released for retail sale on October 25, 2001.

Development of Windows XP began in the late 1990s as "Neptune", an operating system (OS) built on the Windows NT kernel which was intended specifically for mainstream consumer use. An updated version of Windows 2000 was also originally planned for the business market; however, in January 2000, both projects were scrapped in favor of a single OS codenamed "Whistler", which would serve as a single OS platform for both consumer and business markets. As such, Windows XP was the first consumer edition of Windows not to be based on MS-DOS.

Upon its release, Windows XP received critical acclaim, with critics noting increased performance and stability (especially in comparison to Windows Me, the previous version of Windows aimed at home users), a more intuitive user interface, improved hardware support, and expanded multimedia capabilities. However, some industry reviewers were concerned by the new licensing model and product activation system.

Extended support for Windows XP ended on April 8, 2014, after which the operating system ceased receiving further support or security updates (with exceptional security updates being made e.g. in 2019, to address potential ransomware threats) to most users. By August 2019, Microsoft (and others) had ended support for games on Windows XP. As of August 2019, 1.65% of Windows PCs run Windows XP. At least one country has double digit use, Armenia where it's highest ranked at 44.6%, and China is also exceptionally high at 5.38%.

On August 11, 2019, researchers reported that Windows 10 users may be at risk for "critical" system compromise due to design flaws of hardware device drivers from multiple providers. Also in August 2019, computer experts reported that the BlueKeep security vulnerability, CVE- 2019-0708, that potentially affects older unpatched Microsoft Windows versions via the program's Remote Desktop Protocol, allowing for the possibility of remote code execution, may now include related flaws, collectively named *DejaBlue*, affecting newer Windows versions (i.e., Windows 7 and all recent versions) as well. In addition, experts reported a Microsoft security vulnerability, CVE-2019-1162, based on legacy code involving Microsoft CTF and ctfmon (ctfmon.exe), that affects all Windows versions from the older Windows XP version to the most recent Windows 10 versions; a patch to correct the flaw is currently available.

Development

In the late 1990s, initial development of what would become Windows XP was focused on two individual products; "Odyssey", which was reportedly intended to succeed the future Windows 2000, and "Neptune", which was reportedly a consumer-oriented operating system using the Windows NT architecture, succeeding the MS-DOS-based Windows 98.

However, the projects proved to be too ambitious. In January 2000, shortly prior to the official release of Windows 2000, technology writer Paul Thurrott reported that Microsoft had shelved both Neptune and Odyssey in favor of a new product codenamed "Whistler", after Whistler, British Columbia, as many Microsoft employees skied at the Whistler-Blackcomb ski resort. The goal of Whistler was to unify both the consumer and business-oriented Windows lines under a single, Windows NT platform: Thurrott stated that Neptune had become "a black hole when all the features that were cut from [Windows Me] were simply re-tagged as Neptune features. And since Neptune and Odyssey would be based on the same code-base anyway, it made sense to combine them into a single project".

At PDC on July 13, 2000, Microsoft announced that Whistler would be released during the second half of 2001, and also unveiled the first preview build, 2250. The build notably introduced an early version of Windows XP's visual styles system.

Microsoft released the first beta build of Whistler, build 2296, on October 31, 2000. Subsequent builds gradually introduced features that users of the release version of Windows XP would recognise, such as Internet Explorer 6.0, the Microsoft Product Activation system and the *Bliss* desktop background.

On February 5, 2001, Microsoft announced that Whistler would be officially known as Windows XP, where XP stands for "eXPerience".

Release

In June 2001, Microsoft indicated that it was planning to, in conjunction with Intel and other PC makers, spend at least 1 billion US dollars on marketing and promoting Windows XP. The theme of the campaign, "Yes You Can", was designed to emphasize the platform's overall capabilities.

Microsoft had originally planned to use the slogan "Prepare to Fly", but it was replaced due to sensitivity issues in the wake of the September 11 attacks.

On August 24, 2001, Windows XP build 2600 was released to manufacturing. During a ceremonial media event at Microsoft Redmond Campus, copies of the RTM build were given to representatives of several major PC manufacturers in briefcases, who then flew off on decorated helicopters. While PC manufacturers would be able to release devices running XP beginning on September 24, 2001, XP was expected to reach general, retail availability on October 25, 2001. On the same day, Microsoft also announced the final retail pricing of XP's two main editions, "Home" and "Professional".

New and Updated Features

User Interface

Updated start menu in the Royale theme, now featuring two columns.

While retaining some similarities to previous versions, Windows XP's interface was overhauled with a new visual appearance, with an increased use of alpha compositing effects, drop shadows, and "visual styles", which completely changed the appearance of the operating system. The number of effects enabled are determined by the operating system based on the computer's processing power, and can be enabled or disabled on a case-by-case basis. XP also added ClearType, a new subpixel rendering system designed to improve the appearance of fonts on liquid-crystal displays. A new set of system icons was also introduced. The default wallpaper, *Bliss*, is a photo of a landscape in the Napa Valley outside Napa, California, with rolling green hills and a blue sky with stratocumulus and cirrus clouds.

The Start menu received its first major overhaul in XP, switching to a two-column layout with the ability to list, pin, and display frequently used applications, recently opened documents, and the traditional cascading "All Programs" menu. The taskbar can now group windows opened by a single application into one taskbar button, with a popup menu listing the individual windows. The notification area also hides "inactive" icons by default. A "common tasks" list was added, and Windows Explorer's sidebar was updated to use a new task-based design with lists of common actions; the tasks displayed are contextually relevant to the type of content in a folder (e.g. a folder with music displays offers to play all the files in the folder, or burn them to a CD).

Fast user switching allows additional users to log into a Windows XP machine without existing users having to close their programs and logging out. Although only one user at the time can use the console (i.e. monitor, keyboard and mouse), previous users can resume their session once they regain control of the console.

Infrastructure

Windows XP uses prefetching to improve startup and application launch times. It also became possible to revert the installation of an updated device driver, should the updated driver produce undesirable results.

A copy protection system known as Windows Product Activation was introduced with Windows XP and its server counterpart, Windows Server 2003. All Windows licenses must be tied to a unique ID generated using information from the computer hardware, transmitted either via the internet or a telephone hotline. If Windows is not activated within 30 days of installation, the OS will cease to function until it is activated. Windows also periodically verifies the hardware to check for changes. If significant hardware changes are detected, the activation is voided, and Windows must be re-activated.

Networking and Internet Functionality

Windows XP was originally bundled with Internet Explorer 6, Outlook Express 6, Windows Messenger, and MSN Explorer. New networking features were also added, including Internet Connection Firewall, Internet Connection Sharing integration with UPnP, NAT traversal APIs, Quality of Service features, IPv6 and Teredo tunneling, Background Intelligent Transfer Service, extended fax features, network bridging, peer to peer networking, support for most DSL modems, IEEE 802.11 (Wi-Fi) connections with auto configuration and roaming, TAPI 3.1, and networking over FireWire. Remote Assistance and Remote Desktop were also added, which allow users to connect to a computer running Windows XP from across a network or the Internet and access their applications, files, printers, and devices or request help. Improvements were also made to *IntelliMirror* features such as Offline Files, Roaming user profiles and Folder redirection.

Other Features

- Improved application compatibility and shims compared to Windows 2000.
- DirectX 8.1, upgradeable to DirectX 9.0c.
- A number of new features in Windows Explorer including task panes, thumbnails, and the option to view photos as a slideshow.
- Improved imaging features such as *Windows Picture and Fax Viewer*.
- Faster start-up, (due to improved Prefetch functions) logon, logoff, hibernation, and application launch sequences.

- Numerous improvements to increase the system reliability such as improved System Re-store, Automated System Recovery,, and driver reliability improvements through Device Driver Rollback.

- Hardware support improvements such as FireWire 800, and improvements to multi-mon-itor support under the name "DualView".

- Fast user switching.

- The ClearType font rendering mechanism, which is designed to improve text readability on liquid-crystal display (LCD) and similar monitors, especially laptops.

- Side-by-side assemblies and registration-free COM.

- General improvements to international support such as more locales, languages and scripts, MUI support in Terminal Services, improved Input Method Editors, and National Language Support.

Removed Features

Some of the programs and features that were part of the previous versions of Windows did not make it to Windows XP. Various MS-DOS commands available in its Windows 9x predecessor were removed, as were the POSIX & OS/2 subsystems.

In networking, NetBEUI and NetDDE were deprecated and not installed by default. Plug-and-play–incompatible communication devices (like modems and network interface cards) were no longer supported.

Service Pack 2 and Service Pack 3 also removed features from Windows XP but to a less noticeable extent. For instance, support for TCP half-open connections was removed in Service Pack 2, and the address bar on the taskbar was removed in Service Pack 3.

Editions

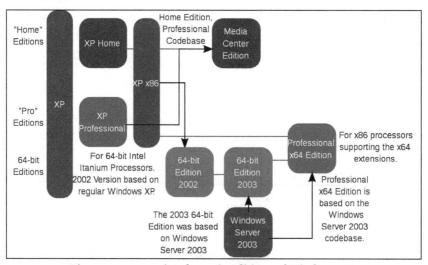

Diagram representing the main editions of Windows XP.
It is based on the category of the edition (grey) and codebase (black arrow).

Windows XP was released in two major editions on launch: *Home Edition* and *Professional Edition*. Both editions were made available at retail as pre-loaded software on new computers and as boxed copies. Boxed copies were sold as "Upgrade" or "Full" licenses; the "Upgrade" versions were slightly cheaper, but require an existing version of Windows to install. The "Full" version can be installed on systems without an operating system or existing version of Windows. The two editions of XP were aimed at different markets: *Home Edition* is explicitly intended for consumer use and disables or removes certain advanced and enterprise-oriented features present on *Professional*, such as the ability to join a Windows domain, Internet Information Services, and Multilingual User Interface. Windows 98 or Me can be upgraded to either version, but Windows NT 4.0 and Windows 2000 can only be upgraded to *Professional*. Windows' software license agreement for pre-loaded licenses allows the software to be "returned" to the OEM for a refund if the user does not wish to use it. Despite the refusal of some manufacturers to honor the entitlement, it has been enforced by courts in some countries.

Two specialized variants of XP were introduced in 2002 for certain types of hardware, exclusively through OEM channels as pre-loaded software. Windows XP Media Center Edition was initially designed for high-end home theater PCs with TV tuners (marketed under the term "Media Center PC"), offering expanded multimedia functionality, an electronic program guide, and digital video recorder (DVR) support through the Windows Media Center application. Microsoft also unveiled Windows XP Tablet PC Edition, which contains additional pen input features, and is optimized for mobile devices meeting its Tablet PC specifications. Two different 64-bit editions of XP were made available; the first, Windows XP 64-Bit Edition, was intended for IA-64 (Itanium) systems; as IA-64 usage declined on workstations in favor of AMD's x86-64 architecture (which was supported by the later Windows XP Professional x64 Edition), the Itanium version was discontinued in 2005.

Microsoft also targeted emerging markets with the 2004 introduction of Windows XP Starter Edition, a special variant of Home Edition intended for low-cost PCs. The OS is primarily aimed at first-time computer owners, containing heavy localization (including wallpapers and screen savers incorporating images of local landmarks), and a "My Support" area which contains video tutorials on basic computing tasks. It also removes certain "complex" features, and does not allow users to run more than three applications at a time. After a pilot program in India and Thailand, Starter was released in other emerging markets throughout 2005. In 2006, Microsoft also unveiled the FlexGo initiative, which would also target emerging markets with subsidized PCs on a pre-paid, subscription basis.

As the result of unfair competition lawsuits in Europe and South Korea, which both alleged that Microsoft had improperly leveraged its status in the PC market to favor its own bundled software, Microsoft was ordered to release special versions of XP in these markets that excluded certain applications. In March 2004, after the European Commission fined Microsoft €497 million (US$603 million), Microsoft was ordered to release "N" versions of XP that excluded Windows Media Player, encouraging users to pick and download their own media player software. As it was sold at the same price as the version with Windows Media Player included, certain OEMs (such as Dell, who offered it for a short period, along with Hewlett-Packard, Lenovo and Fujitsu Siemens) chose not to offer it. Consumer interest was minuscule, with roughly 1,500 units shipped to OEMs, and no reported sales to consumers. In December 2005, the Korean Fair Trade Commission ordered Microsoft to make available editions of Windows XP and Windows Server 2003 that do not contain Windows Media Player or Windows Messenger. The "K" and "KN" editions of Windows XP were released in August 2006, and are only available in English and Korean, and also contain links to third-party instant messenger and media player software.

Service Packs

A service pack is cumulative update package that is a superset of all updates, and even service packs, that have been released before it. Three service packs have been released for Windows XP. Service Pack 3 is slightly different, in that it needs at least Service Pack 1 to have been installed, in order to update a live OS. However, Service Pack 3 can still be embedded into a Windows installation disc; SP1 is not reported as a prerequisite for doing so.

Service Pack 1

Service Pack 1 (SP1) for Windows XP was released on September 9, 2002. It contained over 300 minor, post-RTM bug fixes, along with all security patches released since the original release of XP. SP1 also added USB 2.0 support, the Microsoft Java Virtual Machine, .NET Framework support, and support for technologies used by the then-upcoming Media Center and Tablet PC editions of XP. The most significant change on SP1 was the addition of Set Program Access and Defaults, a settings page which allows programs to be set as default for certain types of activities (such as media players or web browsers) and for access to bundled, Microsoft programs (such as Internet Explorer or Windows Media Player) to be disabled. This feature was added to comply with the settlement of United States v. Microsoft Corp., which required Microsoft to offer the ability for OEMs to bundle third-party competitors to software it bundles with Windows (such as Internet Explorer and Windows Media Player), and give them the same level of prominence as those normally bundled with the OS.

On February 3, 2003, Microsoft released Service Pack 1a (SP1a). It was the same as SP1, except that the Microsoft Java Virtual Machine was removed.

Service Pack 2

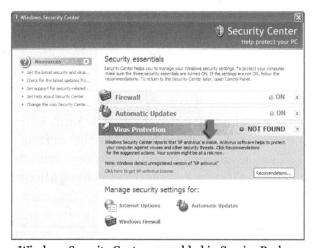

Windows Security Center was added in Service Pack 2.

Service Pack 2 (SP2) was released on August 25, 2004. Headline features included WPA encryption compatibility for Wi-Fi and usability improvements to the Wi-Fi networking user interface, partial Bluetooth support, and various improvements to security systems.

The security improvements (codenamed "Springboard", as these features were intended to under-pin additional changes in Longhorn), included a major revision to the included firewall (renamed Windows Firewall, and now enabled by default), and an update to Data Execution Prevention, which gained hardware support in the NX bit that can stop some forms of buffer overflow attacks. Raw socket support is removed (which supposedly limits the damage done by zombie machines) and the Windows Messenger service (which had been abused to cause pop-up advertisements to be displayed as system messages without a web browser or any additional software) became disabled by default. Additionally, security-related improvements were made to e-mail and web browsing. Service Pack 2 also added Security Center, an interface which provides a general overview of the system's security status, including the state of the firewall and automatic updates. Third-party firewall and antivirus software can also be monitored from Security Center.

In August 2006, Microsoft released updated installation media for Windows XP and Windows Server 2003 SP2 (SP2b), in order to incorporate a patch requiring ActiveX controls in Internet Explorer to be manually activated before a user may interact with them. This was done so that the browser would not violate a patent owned by Eolas. Microsoft has since licensed the patent, and released a patch reverting the change in April 2008. In September 2007, another minor revision known as SP2c was released for XP Professional, extending the number of available product keys for the operating system to "support the continued availability of Windows XP Professional through the scheduled system builder channel end-of-life (EOL) date of January 31, 2009."

Service Pack 3

The third and final Service Pack, SP3, was released to manufacturing on April 21, 2008, and to the public via both the Microsoft Download Center and Windows Update on May 6, 2008. Service Pack 3 is not available for Windows XP x64 Edition, which is based on the Windows Server 2003 kernel.

It began being automatically pushed out to *Automatic Updates* users on July 10, 2008. A feature set overview which details new features available separately as stand-alone updates to Windows XP, as well as backported features from Windows Vista, has been posted by Microsoft. A total of 1,174 fixes are included in SP3. Service Pack 3 can be installed on systems with Internet Explorer versions 6, 7, or 8; Internet Explorer 7 is not included as part of SP3.

Service Pack 3 included security enhancements over and above those of SP2, including APIs allow-ing developers to enable Data Execution Prevention for their code, independent of system-wide compatibility enforcement settings, the Security Support Provider Interface, improvements to WPA2 security, and an updated version of the Microsoft Enhanced Cryptographic Provider Mod-ule that is FIPS 140-2 certified.

In incorporating all previously released updates not included in SP2, Service Pack 3 included many other key features. Windows Imaging Component allowed camera vendors to integrate their own proprietary image codecs with the operating system's features, such as thumbnails and slideshows. In enterprise features, Remote Desktop Protocol 6.1 included support for ClearType and 32-bit color depth over RDP, while improvements made to Windows Management Instrumentation in Windows Vista to reduce the possibility of corruption of the WMI repository were backported to XP SP3.

In addition, SP3 contains updates to the operating system components of Windows XP Media Cen-ter Edition (MCE) and Windows XP Tablet PC Edition, and security updates for .NET Framework version 1.0, which is included in these editions. However, it does not include update rollups for the Windows Media Center application in Windows XP MCE 2005. SP3 also omits security updates for Windows Media Player 10, although the player is included in Windows XP MCE 2005. The Address Bar DeskBand on the Taskbar is no longer included due to antitrust violation concerns.

System Requirements

System requirements for Windows XP are as follows:

	Minimum	Recommended
Home/Professional Edition		
CPU	Pentium or compatible, 233 MHz BIOS or compatible firmware	Pentium or compatible, 300 MHz BIOS or compatible firmware
Memory	64 MB	128 MB
Hard drive	1.5 GB Master boot record used	+661 MB for Service Pack 1 and 1a +1.8 GB for Service Pack 2 +900 MB for Service Pack 3
Media	CD-ROM drive or compatible	
Display	Super VGA (800 × 600)	
Sound hardware	N/A	Sound card plus speakers/headphones
Input device(s)	Keyboard, mouse	
Professional x64 Edition		
CPU	x86-64 or compatible BIOS or compatible firmware	
Memory	256 MB	
Hard drive	1.5 GB Master boot record used	
Media	CD-ROM drive or compatible	
Display	Super VGA (800 × 600)	
Sound hardware	N/A	Sound card plus speakers/headphones
Input device(s)	Keyboard, mouse	
64-Bit Edition		
CPU	Itanium 733 MHz	Itanium 800 MHz
Memory	1 GB	
Hard drive	6 GB	
Media	CD-ROM drive or compatible	
Display	Super VGA (800 × 600)	
Input device(s)	Keyboard, mouse	

Physical Memory Limits

The maximum amount of RAM that Windows XP can support varies depending on the product edition and the processor architecture, as shown in the following table.

Physical memory limits of Windows XP	
Edition	Maximum
Starter	512 MB

Home	4 GB
Media Center	
Tablet PC	
Professional	
Professional x64	128 GB
64-bit (Itanium)	

Processor Limits

Windows XP Professional supports up to two physical processors; Windows XP Home Edition is limited to one.

However, XP supports a greater number of logical processors: 32-bit editions support up to 32 logical processors, whereas 64-bit editions support up to 64 logical processors.

Support Lifecycle

Support for Windows XP without a service pack ended on September 30, 2005. Windows XP Service Packs 1 and 1a were retired on October 10, 2006, and Service Pack 2 reached end of support on July 13, 2010, almost six years after its general availability. The company stopped general licensing of Windows XP to OEMs and terminated retail sales of the operating system on June 30, 2008, 17 months after the release of Windows Vista. However, an exception was announced on April 3, 2008, for OEMs producing what it defined as "ultra low-cost personal computers", particularly netbooks, until one year after the availability of Windows 7 on October 22, 2010. Analysts felt that the move was primarily intended to compete against Linux-based netbooks, although Microsoft's Kevin Hutz stated that the decision was due to apparent market demand for low-end computers with Windows.

Variants of Windows XP for embedded systems have different support policies: Windows XP Embedded SP3 and Windows Embedded for Point of Service SP3 were supported until January and April 2016, respectively. Windows Embedded Standard 2009 and Windows Embedded POSReady 2009 were supported until January and April 2019, respectively. These updates, while intended for the embedded versions, can also be downloaded on standard Windows XP with a registry hack, which enables unofficial patches until April 2019. However, Microsoft advises against Windows XP users installing these fixes.

End of Support

On April 14, 2009, Windows XP exited mainstream support and entered the extended support phase; Microsoft continued to provide security updates every month for Windows XP, however, free technical support, warranty claims, and design changes were no longer being offered. Extended support ended on April 8, 2014, over 12 years since the release of XP; normally Microsoft products have a support life cycle of only 10 years. Beyond the final security updates released on April 8, no more security patches or support information are provided for XP free-of-charge; "critical patches" will still be created, and made available only to customers subscribing to a paid "Custom Support" plan. As it is a Windows component, all versions of Internet Explorer for Windows XP also became unsupported.

In January 2014, it was estimated that more than 95% of the 3 million automated teller machines in the world were still running Windows XP (which largely replaced IBM's OS/2 as the predominant operating system on ATMs); ATMs have an average lifecycle of between seven and ten years, but some have had lifecycles as long as 15. Plans were being made by several ATM vendors and their customers to migrate to Windows 7-based systems over the course of 2014, while vendors have also considered the possibility of using Linux-based platforms in the future to give them more flexibility for support lifecycles, and the ATM Industry Association (ATMIA) has since endorsed Windows 10 as a further replacement. However, ATMs typically run the embedded variant of Windows XP, which was supported through January 2016. As of May 2017, around 60% of the 220,000 ATMs in India still run Windows XP.

Furthermore, at least 49% of all computers in China still ran XP at the beginning of 2014. These holdouts were influenced by several factors; prices of genuine copies of Windows in the country are high, while Ni Guangnan of the Chinese Academy of Sciences warned that Windows 8 could allegedly expose users to surveillance by the United States government, and the Chinese government would ban the purchase of Windows 8 products for government use in May 2014 in protest of Microsoft's inability to provide "guaranteed" support. The government also had concerns that the impending end of support could affect their anti-piracy initiatives with Microsoft, as users would simply pirate newer versions rather than purchasing them legally. As such, government officials formally requested that Microsoft extend the support period for XP for these reasons. While Microsoft did not comply with their requests, a number of major Chinese software developers, such as Lenovo, Kingsoft and Tencent, will provide free support and resources for Chinese users migrating from XP. Several governments, in particular those of the Netherlands and the United Kingdom, elected to negotiate "Custom Support" plans with Microsoft for their continued, internal use of Windows XP; the British government's deal lasted for a year, and also covered support for Office 2003 (which reached end-of-life the same day) and cost £5.5 million.

On March 8, 2014, Microsoft deployed an update for XP that, on the 8th of each month, displays a pop-up notification to remind users about the end of support; however, these notifications may be disabled by the user. Microsoft also partnered with Laplink to provide a special "express" version of its PCmover software to help users migrate files and settings from XP to a computer with a newer version of Windows.

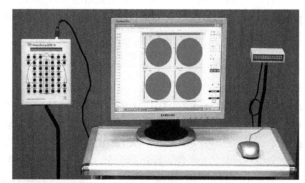

An electroencephalograph running on Windows XP. The medical industry continues to utilise
Windows XP, partly due to medical applications being incompatible with later versions of Windows.

Despite the approaching end of support, there were still notable holdouts that had not migrated past XP; many users elected to remain on XP because of the poor reception of Windows Vista, sales of newer PCs with newer versions of Windows declined due to the Great Recession and the effects of Vista, and deployments of new versions of Windows in enterprise environments require a large amount of planning, which includes testing applications for compatibility (especially those that are dependent on Internet Explorer 6, which is not compatible with newer versions of Windows). Major security software vendors (including Microsoft itself) planned to continue offering support and definitions for Windows XP past the end of support to varying extents, along with the developers of Google Chrome, Mozilla Firefox, and Opera web browsers; despite these measures, critics similarly argued that users should eventually migrate from XP to a supported platform. The United States' Computer Emergency Readiness Team released an alert in March 2014 advising users of the impending end of support, and informing them that using XP after April 8 may prevent them from meeting US government information security requirements. Microsoft continued to provide Security Essentials virus definitions and updates for its Malicious Software Removal Tool (MSRT) for XP until July 14, 2015. As the end of extended support approached, Microsoft began to increasingly urge XP customers to migrate to newer versions such as Windows 7 or 8 in the interest of security, suggesting that attackers could reverse engineer security patches for newer versions of Windows and use them to target equivalent vulnerabilities in XP. Windows XP is remotely exploitable by numerous security holes that were discovered after Microsoft stopped supporting it.

Similarly, specialized devices that run XP, particularly medical devices, must have any revisions to their software—even security updates for the underlying operating system—approved by relevant regulators before they can be released. For this reason, manufacturers often did not allow any updates to devices' operating systems, leaving them open to security exploits and malware.

Despite the end of support for Windows XP, Microsoft has released three emergency security updates for the operating system to patch major security vulnerabilities:

- A patch released in May 2014 to address recently discovered vulnerabilities in Internet Explorer 6 through 11 on all versions of Windows.

- A patch released in May 2017 to address a vulnerability that was being leveraged by the WannaCry ransomware attack.

- A patch released in May 2019 to address a critical code execution vulnerability in Remote Desktop Services which can be exploited in a similar way as the WannaCry vulnerability.

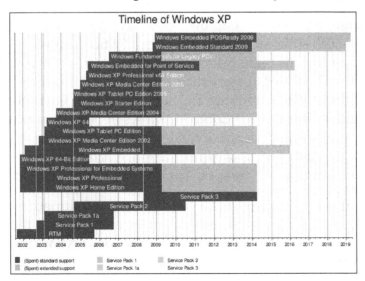

Microsoft announced in July 2019 that the Microsoft Internet Games services on Windows XP and Windows ME would end on July 31, 2019 (and for Windows 7 on January 22, 2020). Others, such as Steam, had done the same, ending support for Windows XP and Windows Vista in January.

Windows Vista

Windows Vista is an operating system that was produced by Microsoft for use on personal computers, including home and business desktops, laptops, tablet PCs and media center PCs. Development was completed on November 8, 2006, and over the following three months, it was released in stages to computer hardware and software manufacturers, business customers and retail channels. On January 30, 2007, it was released worldwide and was made available for purchase and download from the Windows Marketplace; it is the first release of Windows to be made available through a digital distribution platform. The release of Windows Vista came more than five years after the introduction of its predecessor, Windows XP, the longest time span between successive releases of Microsoft Windows desktop operating systems.

New features of Windows Vista include an updated graphical user interface and visual style dubbed Aero, a new search component called Windows Search, redesigned networking, audio, print and display sub-systems, and new multimedia tools such as Windows DVD Maker. Vista aimed to increase the level of communication between machines on a home network, using peer-to-peer technology to simplify sharing files and media between computers and devices. Windows Vista included version 3.0 of the .NET Framework, allowing software developers to write applications without traditional Windows APIs.

Microsoft's primary stated objective with Windows Vista was to improve the state of security in the Windows operating system. One common criticism of Windows XP and its predecessors was their commonly exploited security vulnerabilities and overall susceptibility to malware, viruses and buffer overflows. In light of this, Microsoft chairman Bill Gates announced in early 2002 a company-wide "Trustworthy Computing initiative", which aimed to incorporate security into every aspect of software development at the company. Microsoft stated that it prioritized improving the security of Windows XP and Windows Server 2003 above finishing Windows Vista, thus delaying its completion.

While these new features and security improvements have garnered positive reviews, Vista has also been the target of much criticism and negative press. Criticism of Windows Vista has targeted its high system requirements, its more restrictive licensing terms, the inclusion of a number of then-new DRM technologies aimed at restricting the copying of protected digital media, lack of compatibility with some pre-Vista hardware and software, longer boot time, and the number of authorization prompts for User Account Control. As a result of these and other issues, Windows Vista had seen initial adoption and satisfaction rates lower than Windows XP. However, with an estimated 330 million Internet users as of January 2009, it had been announced that Vista usage had surpassed Microsoft's pre-launch two-year-out expectations of achieving 200 million users.

At the release of Windows 7 (October 2009), Windows Vista (with approximately 400 million Internet users) was the second most widely used operating system on the Internet with an approximately 19% market share, the most widely used being Windows XP with an approximately 63% market share. In May 2010, Windows Vista's market share had an estimated range from 15% to

26%. On October 22, 2010, Microsoft ceased sales of retail copies of Windows Vista, and the OEM sales for Vista ceased a year later. As of August 2019, Vista's market share has declined to 0.6% of Windows' total market share.

In August 2019, computer experts reported that the BlueKeep security vulnerability, CVE- 2019-0708, that potentially affects older unpatched Microsoft Windows versions via the program's Remote Desktop Protocol, allowing for the possibility of remote code execution, may now include related flaws, collectively named *DejaBlue*, affecting newer Windows versions (i.e., Windows 7 and all recent versions) as well. In addition, experts reported a Microsoft security vulnerability, CVE-2019-1162, based on legacy code involving Microsoft CTF and ctfmon (ctfmon.exe), that affects all Windows versions from the older Windows XP version to the most recent Windows 10 versions; a patch to correct the flaw is currently available.

Development

As Longhorn

Desktop screenshot of Microsoft Windows Code Name *Longhorn* build 6.0.4074 (Milestone 7), showing Start menu, early version of Windows Desktop Sidebar, My Computer window, and Slate visual style theme.

Microsoft began work on Windows Vista, known at the time by its codename Longhorn, in May 2001, five months before the release of Windows XP. It was originally expected to ship sometime late in 2003 as a minor step between Windows XP and Blackcomb, which was planned to be the company's next major operating system release. Gradually, "Longhorn" assimilated many of the important new features and technologies slated for Blackcomb, resulting in the release date being pushed back several times in 3 years. In some builds of Longhorn, their license agreement said "For the Microsoft product codenamed "Whistler"". Many of Microsoft's developers were also re-tasked to build updates to Windows XP and Windows Server 2003 to strengthen security. Faced with ongoing delays and concerns about feature creep, Microsoft announced on August 27, 2004, that it had revised its plans. For this reason, Longhorn was reset to start work on componentizing the Windows Server 2003 Service Pack 1 codebase, and over time re-incorporating the features that would be intended for an actual operating system release. However, some previously announced features such as WinFS were dropped or postponed, and a new software development methodology called the Security Development Lifecycle was incorporated in an effort to address concerns with the security of the Windows codebase, which is programmed in C, C++ and assembly. Longhorn became known as Vista in 2005.

The early development stages of Longhorn were generally characterized by incremental improvements and updates to Windows XP. During this period, Microsoft was fairly quiet about what was being worked on, as their marketing and public relations focus was more strongly focused on Windows XP, and Windows Server 2003, which was released in April 2003. Occasional builds of Longhorn were leaked onto popular file sharing networks such as IRC, BitTorrent, eDonkey and various newsgroups, and so most of what is known about builds prior to the first sanctioned development release of Longhorn in May 2003, is derived from these builds.

After several months of relatively little news or activity from Microsoft with Longhorn, Microsoft released Build 4008, which had made an appearance on the Internet around February 28, 2003. It was also privately handed out to a select group of software developers. As an evolutionary release over build 3683, it contained a number of small improvements, including a modified blue "Plex" theme and a new, simplified Windows Image-based installer that operates in graphical mode from the outset, and completed an install of the operating system in approximately one third the time of Windows XP on the same hardware. An optional "new taskbar" was introduced that was thinner than the previous build and displayed the time differently.

The most notable visual and functional difference, however, came with Windows Explorer. The incorporation of the Plex theme made blue the dominant color of the entire application. The Windows XP-style task pane was almost completely replaced with a large horizontal pane that appeared under the toolbars. A new search interface allowed for filtering of results, searching of Windows help, and natural-language queries that would be used to integrate with WinFS. The animated search characters were also removed. The "view modes" were also replaced with a single slider that would resize the icons in real-time, in list, thumbnail, or details mode, depending on where the slider was. File metadata was also made more visible and more easily editable, with more active encouragement to fill out missing pieces of information. Also of note was the conversion of Windows Explorer to being a .NET application.

Most builds of Longhorn and Vista were identified by a label that was always displayed in the bottom-right corner of the desktop. A typical build label would look like "Longhorn Build 3663. Lab06_N.020728-1728". Higher build numbers did not automatically mean that the latest features from every development team at Microsoft was included. Typically, a team working on a certain feature or subsystem would generate their own working builds which developers would test with, and when the code was deemed stable, all the changes would be incorporated back into the main development tree at once. At Microsoft, a number of "Build labs" exist where the compilation of the entirety of Windows can be performed by a team. The name of the lab in which any given build originated is shown as part of the build label, and the date and time of the build follows that. Some builds (such as Beta 1 and Beta 2) only display the build label in the version information dialog (Winver). The icons used in these builds are from Windows XP.

At the Windows Hardware Engineering Conference (WinHEC) in May 2003, Microsoft gave their first public demonstrations of the new Desktop Window Manager and Aero. The demonstrations were done on a revised build 4015 which was never released. A number of sessions for developers and hardware engineers at the conference focused on these new features, as well as the Next-Generation

Secure Computing Base (previously known as "Palladium"), which at the time was Microsoft's proposed solution for creating a secure computing environment whereby any given component of the system could be deemed "trusted". Also at this conference, Microsoft reiterated their roadmap for delivering Longhorn, pointing to an "early 2005" release date.

Development Reset

By 2004, it had become obvious to the Windows team at Microsoft that they were losing sight of what needed to be done to complete the next version of Windows and ship it to customers. Internally, some Microsoft employees were describing the Longhorn project as "another Cairo" or "Cairo.NET", referring to the Cairo development project that the company embarked on through the first half of the 1990s, which never resulted in a shipping operating system (though nearly all the technologies developed in that time did end up in Windows 95 and Windows NT). Microsoft was shocked in 2005 by Apple's release of Mac OS X Tiger. It offered only a limited subset of features planned for Longhorn, in particular fast file searching and integrated graphics and sound processing, but appeared to have impressive reliability and performance compared to contemporary Longhorn builds. Most Longhorn builds had major Explorer.exe system leaks which prevented the OS from performing well, and added more confusion to the development teams in later builds with more and more code being developed which failed to reach stability.

In a September 23, 2005 front-page article in *The Wall Street Journal*, Microsoft co-president Jim Allchin, who had overall responsibility for the development and delivery of Windows, explained how development of Longhorn had been "crashing into the ground" due in large part to the haphazard methods by which features were introduced and integrated into the core of the operating system, without a clear focus on an end-product. Allchin went on to explain how in December 2003, he enlisted the help of two other senior executives, Brian Valentine and Amitabh Srivastava, the former being experienced with shipping software at Microsoft, most notably Windows Server 2003, and the latter having spent his career at Microsoft researching and developing methods of producing high-quality testing systems. Srivastava employed a team of core architects to visually map out the entirety of the Windows operating system, and to proactively work towards a development process that would enforce high levels of code quality, reduce interdependencies between components, and in general, "not make things worse with Vista". Since Microsoft decided that Longhorn needed to be further componentized, work started on the Omega-13 series builds where they would componentize existing Windows Server 2003 source code, and over time add back functionality as development progressed. Future Longhorn builds would start from Windows Server 2003 Service Pack 1 and continue from there.

This change, announced internally to Microsoft employees on August 26, 2004, began in earnest in September, though it would take several more months before the new development process and build methodology would be used by all of the development teams. A number of complaints came from individual developers, and Bill Gates himself, that the new development process was going to be prohibitively difficult to work within.

As Windows Vista

By approximately November 2004, the company had considered several names for the final release, ranging from simple to fanciful and inventive. In the end, Microsoft chose Windows Vista as confirmed on July 22, 2005, believing it to be a "wonderful intersection of what the product really does, what Windows stands for, and what resonates with customers, and their needs". Group Project Manager Greg Sullivan told Paul Thurrott "You want the PC to adapt to you and help you cut through the clutter to focus on what's important to you. That's what Windows Vista is all about: "bringing clarity to your world" (a reference to the three marketing points of Vista—Clear, Connected, Confident), so you can focus on what matters to you". Microsoft co-president Jim Allchin also loved the name, saying that "Vista" creates the right imagery for the new product capabilities and inspires the imagination with all the possibilities of what can be done with Windows—making people's passions come alive."

After Longhorn was named Windows Vista in November 2004, an unprecedented beta-test program was started, involving hundreds of thousands of volunteers and companies. In September of that year, Microsoft started releasing regular Community Technology Previews (CTP) to beta testers from July 2005 to February 2006. The first of these was distributed at the 2005 Microsoft Professional Developers Conference, and was subsequently released to beta testers and Microsoft Developer Network subscribers. The builds that followed incorporated most of the planned features for the final product, as well as a number of changes to the user interface, based largely on feedback from beta testers. Windows Vista was deemed feature-complete with the release of the "February CTP," released on February 22, 2006, and much of the remainder of the work between that build and the final release of the product focused on stability, performance, application and driver compatibility, and documentation. Beta 2, released in late May, was the first build to be made available to the general public through Microsoft's Customer Preview Program. It was downloaded by over five million people. Two release candidates followed in September and October, both of which were made available to a large number of users.

At the Intel Developer Forum on March 9, 2006, Microsoft announced a change in their plans to support EFI in Windows Vista. The UEFI 2.0 specification (which replaced EFI 1.10) was not completed until early 2006, and at the time of Microsoft's announcement, no firmware manufacturers had completed a production implementation which could be used for testing. As a result, the decision was made to postpone the introduction of UEFI support to Windows; support for UEFI on 64-bit platforms was postponed until Vista Service Pack 1 and Windows Server 2008 and 32-bit UEFI would not be supported, as Microsoft did not expect many such systems to be built because the market was quickly moving to 64-bit processors.

While Microsoft had originally hoped to have the consumer versions of the operating system available worldwide in time for the 2006 holiday shopping season, it announced in March 2006 that the release date would be pushed back to January 2007 in order to give the company—and the hardware and software companies that Microsoft depends on for providing device drivers—additional time to prepare. Because a release to manufacturing (RTM) build is the final version of code shipped to retailers and other distributors, the purpose of a pre-RTM build is to eliminate any last "show-stopper" bugs that may prevent the code from responsibly being shipped to customers, as well as anything else that consumers may find annoying. Thus, it is unlikely that any major new features would be introduced; instead, work would focus on Vista's fit and finish. In just a few days, developers had managed to drop Vista's bug count from over 2470 on September 22 to just over 1400 by the time RC2 shipped in early October. However, they still had a way to go before Vista was ready to RTM. Microsoft's internal processes required Vista's bug count to drop to 500 or fewer before the product could go into escrow for RTM. For most of the pre-RTM builds, those 32-bit editions are only released.

On June 14, 2006, Windows developer Philip Su posted a blog entry which decried the development process of Windows Vista, stating that "The code is way too complicated, and that the pace of coding has been tremendously slowed down by overbearing process." The same post also described Windows Vista as having approximately 50 million lines of code, with about 2,000 developers working on the product. During a demonstration of the speech recognition feature new to Windows Vista at Microsoft's Financial Analyst Meeting on July 27, 2006, the software recognized the phrase "Dear mom" as *"Dear aunt"*. After several failed attempts to correct the error, the sentence eventually became *"Dear aunt, let's set so double the killer delete select all"*. A developer with Vista's speech recognition team later explained that there was a bug with the build of Vista that was causing the microphone gain level to be set very high, resulting in the audio being received by the speech recognition software being "incredibly distorted".

Windows Vista build 5824 (October 17, 2006) was supposed to be the RTM release, but a bug, which destroyed any system that was upgraded from Windows XP, prevented this, damaging development and lowering the chance that it would hit its January 2007 deadline.

Development of Windows Vista came to an end when Microsoft announced that it had been finalized on November 8, 2006, and was concluded by co-president of Windows development, Jim Allchin. The RTM's build number had also jumped to 6000 to reflect Vista's internal version number, NT 6.0. Jumping RTM build numbers is common practice among consumer-oriented Windows versions, like Windows 98 (build 1998), Windows 98 SE (build 2222), Windows Me (build 3000) or Windows XP (build 2600), as compared to the business-oriented versions like Windows 2000 (build 2195) or Server 2003 (build 3790). On November 16, 2006, Microsoft made the final build available to MSDN and Technet Plus subscribers. A business-oriented Enterprise edition was made available to volume license customers on November 30. Windows Vista was launched for general customer availability on January 30, 2007.

New or Changed Features

Windows Vista introduced several features and functionality not present in its predecessors.

End-user

- Windows Aero: The new graphical user interface is named *Windows Aero*, which Jim Allchin stated is an acronym for *Authentic, Energetic, Reflective, and Open*. Microsoft intended the new interface to be cleaner and more aesthetically pleasing than those of previous Windows versions, featuring new transparencies, live thumbnails, live icons, and animations, thus providing a new level of eye candy. Laptop users report, however, that enabling Aero shortens battery life and reduces performance.

- Windows shell: The new Windows shell offers a new range of organization, navigation, and search capabilities: Task panes in Windows Explorer are removed, integrating the relevant task options into the toolbar. A "Favorite links" pane has been added, enabling one-click access to common directories. A search box appears in every Explorer window. The address bar has been replaced with a breadcrumb navigation bar. Icons of certain file types in Windows Explorer are "live" and can be scaled in size up to 256 × 256 pixels. The preview pane allows users to see thumbnails of various files and view the contents of documents. The details pane shows information such as file size and type, and allows viewing and editing of embedded tags in supported file formats. The Start menu has changed as well; incorporating an instant search box, and the *All Programs* list uses a horizontal scroll bar instead of the cascading flyout menu seen in Windows XP. The word "Start" itself has been removed in favor of a blue orb that bears the Windows logo.

- Windows Search: A new search component of Windows Vista, it features instant search (also known as *search as you type*), which provides instant search results, thus finding files more quickly than the search features found in previous versions of Windows and can search the contents of recognized file types. Users can search for certain metadata such as name, extension, size, date or attributes.

- Windows Sidebar: A transparent panel, anchored to the right side of the screen, wherein a user can place Desktop Gadgets, which are small applets designed for a specialized purpose (such as displaying the weather or sports scores). Gadgets can also be placed on the desktop.

- Windows Internet Explorer 7: New user interface, tabbed browsing, RSS, a search box, improved printing, Page Zoom, Quick Tabs (thumbnails of all open tabs), Anti-Phishing filter, a number of new security protection features, Internationalized Domain Name support (IDN), and improved web standards support. IE7 in Windows Vista runs in isolation from other applications in the operating system (protected mode); exploits and malicious software are restricted from writing to any location beyond Temporary Internet Files without explicit user consent.

- Windows Media Player 11, a major revamp of Microsoft's program for playing and organizing music and video. New features in this version include word wheeling (incremental search or "search as you type"), a new GUI for the media library, photo display and organization, the ability to share music libraries over a network with other Windows Vista machines, Xbox 360 integration, and support for other Media Center Extenders.

- Windows Defender: An antispyware program with several real-time protection agents. It includes a software explorer feature, which provides access to startup programs, and allows one to view currently running software, network connected applications, and Winsock providers (Winsock LSPs).

- Backup and Restore Center: Includes a backup and restore application that gives users the ability to schedule periodic backups of files on their computer, as well as recovery from previous backups. Backups are incremental, storing only the changes made each time, minimizing disk usage. It also features Complete PC Backup (available only in the Ultimate, Business, and Enterprise versions), which backs up an entire computer as an image onto a hard disk or DVD. Complete PC Backup can automatically recreate a machine setup onto new hardware or hard disk in case of any hardware failures. Complete PC Restore can be initiated from within Windows Vista or from the Windows Vista installation CD in the event that a PC is so corrupt that it cannot start normally from the hard disk.

- Windows Mail: A replacement for Outlook Express that includes a new mail store that improves stability, and features integrated instant search. It has the Phishing Filter like Internet Explorer 7 and Junk mail filtering that is enhanced through regular updates via Windows Update.

- Windows Calendar is a new calendar and task application which integrates with Windows Contacts and Windows Mail. It is compatible with various calendar file types, such as the popular iCalendar.

- Windows Photo Gallery, a photo and movie library management application. It can import from digital cameras, tag and rate individual items, adjust colors and exposure, create and display slideshows (with pan and fade effects) through Direct3D and burn slideshows to a DVD.

- Windows DVD Maker, a companion program to Windows Movie Maker that provides the ability to create video DVDs based on a user's content. Users can design a DVD with title, menus, video, soundtrack, pan and zoom motion effects on pictures or slides.

- Windows Media Center, which was previously exclusively bundled in a separate version of Windows XP, known as Windows XP Media Center Edition, has been incorporated into the Home Premium and Ultimate editions of Windows Vista.

- Games: Most of the standard computer games included in previous versions of Windows have been redesigned to showcase Vista's new graphical capabilities. New games available in Windows Vista are Chess Titans (3D Chess game), Mahjong Titans (3D Mahjong game), and Purble Place (a small collection of games, oriented towards younger children, including a matching game, a cake-creator game, and a dress-up puzzle game). Purble Place is the only one of the new games available in the Windows Vista Home Basic edition. InkBall is available for Home Premium (or better) users.

- Games Explorer: A new special folder called "Games" exposes installed video games and information about them. These metadata may be updated from the Internet.

- Windows Mobility Center is a control panel that centralizes the most relevant information related to mobile computing (brightness, sound, battery level / power scheme selection, wireless network, screen orientation, presentation settings, etc.).

- Windows Fax and Scan Allows computers with fax modems to send and receive fax documents, as well as scan documents. It is not available in the Home versions of Windows Vista, but is available in the Business, Enterprise and Ultimate editions.

- Windows Meeting Space replaces NetMeeting. Users can share applications (or their entire desktop) with other users on the local network, or over the Internet using peer-to-peer technology (higher versions than Starter and Home Basic can take advantage of hosting capabilities, Starter and Home Basic editions are limited to "join" mode only).

- Windows HotStart enables compatible computers to start applications directly from operating system startup or resume by the press of a button—this enables what Microsoft has described as appliance-like availability, which allows computers to function in a manner similar to a consumer electronics device such as a DVD player; the feature was also designed to provide the instant-on feature availability that is traditionally associated with mobile devices. While Microsoft has emphasized multimedia scenarios with Windows Hot-Start, a user can configure this feature so that a button launches a preferred application.

- Shadow Copy automatically creates daily backup copies of files and folders. Users can also create "shadow copies" by setting a System Protection Point using the System Protection tab in the System control panel. The user can view multiple versions of a file throughout a limited history and be allowed to restore, delete, or copy those versions. This feature is available only in the Business, Enterprise, and Ultimate editions of Windows Vista and is inherited from Windows Server 2003.

- Windows Update: Software and security updates have been simplified, now operating solely via a control panel instead of as a web application. Windows Mail's spam filter and Windows Defender's definitions are updated automatically via Windows Update. Users who choose the recommended setting for Automatic Updates will have the latest drivers installed and available when they add a new device.

- Parental controls: Allows administrators to monitor and restrict user activity, as well as control which websites, programs and games each Standard user can use and install. This feature is not included in the Business or Enterprise editions of Vista.

- Windows SideShow: Enables the auxiliary displays on newer laptops or on supported Windows Mobile devices. It is meant to be used to display device gadgets while the computer is on or off.

- Speech recognition is integrated into Vista. It features a redesigned user interface and configurable command-and-control commands. Unlike the Office 2003 version, which works only in Office and WordPad, Speech Recognition in Windows Vista works for any accessible application. In addition, it currently supports several languages: British and American English, Spanish, French, German, Chinese (Traditional and Simplified) and Japanese.

- New fonts, including several designed for screen reading, and improved Chinese (Yahei, JhengHei), Japanese (Meiryo), and Korean (Malgun) fonts. ClearType has also been enhanced and enabled by default.

- Improved audio controls allow the system-wide volume or volume of individual audio devices and even individual applications to be controlled separately. New audio functionalities such as room correction, bass management, speaker fill, and headphone virtualization have also been incorporated.

- Problem Reports and Solutions, a feature that allows users to check for solutions to problems or view previously sent problems for any solutions or additional information, if available.

- Windows System Assessment Tool is a tool used to benchmark system performance. Software such as games can retrieve this rating and modify its own behavior at runtime to improve performance. The benchmark tests CPU, RAM, 2-D and 3-D graphics acceleration, graphics memory and hard disk space.

- Windows Ultimate Extras: The Ultimate edition of Windows Vista provides, via Windows Update, access to some additional features. These are a collection of additional MUI language packs, Texas Hold 'Em (a Poker game) and Microsoft Tinker (a strategy game where the character is a robot), BitLocker and EFS enhancements that allow users to back up their encryption key online in a Digital Locker, and Windows Dreamscene, which enables the use of videos in MPEG and WMV formats as the desktop background. On April 21, 2008, Microsoft launched two more Ultimate Extras; three new Windows sound schemes, and a content pack for Dreamscene. Various DreamScene Content Packs have been released since the final version of DreamScene was released.

- Reliability and Performance Monitor includes various tools for tuning and monitoring system performance and resources activities of CPU, disks, network, memory and other resources. It shows the operations on files, the opened connections, etc.

- Disk Management: The Logical Disk Manager in Windows Vista supports shrinking and expanding volumes on-the-fly.

- Windows Anytime Upgrade: is a program that allows a user to upgrade their computer running Vista to a higher edition. For example, a computer running Windows Vista Home Basic can be upgraded to Home Premium or better. Anytime Upgrade permits users to upgrade without having their programs and data erased, and is cheaper than replacing the existing installation of Windows. Anytime Upgrade is no longer available for Vista.

- Digital Locker Assistant: A program that facilitated access to downloads and purchases from the Windows Marketplace digital distribution platform. Apps purchased from Windows Marketplace are managed by Microsoft Account credentials, which are used to access a user's digital locker that stores the app and its associated information (e.g., licenses) off-site.

Core

Vista includes technologies such as ReadyBoost and ReadyDrive, which employ fast flash memory (located on USB flash drives and hybrid hard disk drives) to improve system performance by caching commonly used programs and data. This manifests itself in improved battery life on notebook computers as well, since a hybrid drive can be spun down when not in use. Another new technology called SuperFetch utilizes machine learning techniques to analyze usage patterns to allow Windows Vista to make intelligent decisions about what content should be present in system memory at any given time. It uses almost all the extra RAM as disk cache. In conjunction with SuperFetch, an automatic built-in Windows Disk Defragmenter makes sure that those applications are strategically positioned on the hard disk where they can be loaded into memory very quickly with the least amount of physical movement of the hard disk's read-write heads.

As part of the redesign of the networking architecture, IPv6 has been fully incorporated into the operating system and a number of performance improvements have been introduced, such as TCP window scaling. Earlier versions of Windows typically needed third-party wireless networking software to work properly, but this is not the case with Vista, which includes more comprehensive wireless networking support.

For graphics, Vista introduces a new Windows Display Driver Model and a major revision to Direct3D. The new driver model facilitates the new Desktop Window Manager, which provides the tearing-free desktop and special effects that are the cornerstones of Windows Aero. Direct3D 10, developed in conjunction with major graphics card manufacturers, is a new architecture with more advanced shader support, and allows the graphics processing unit to render more complex scenes without assistance from the CPU. It features improved load balancing between CPU and GPU and also optimizes data transfer between them. WDDM also provides video content playback that rivals typical consumer electronics devices. It does this by making it easy to connect to external monitors, providing for protected HD video playback and increasing overall video playback quality. For the first time in Windows, graphics processing unit (GPU) multitasking is possible, enabling users to run more than one GPU-intensive application simultaneously.

At the core of the operating system, many improvements have been made to the memory manager, process scheduler and I/O scheduler. The Heap Manager implements additional features such as integrity checking in order to improve robustness and defend against buffer overflow security exploits, although this comes at the price of breaking backward compatibility with some legacy applications. A Kernel Transaction Manager has been implemented that enables applications to work with the file system and Registry using atomic transaction operations.

Security-related

Improved security was a primary design goal for Vista. Microsoft's Trustworthy Computing initiative, which aims to improve public trust in its products, has had a direct effect on its development. This effort has resulted in a number of new security and safety features and an Evaluation Assurance Level rating of 4+.

User Account Control, or UAC is perhaps the most significant and visible of these changes. UAC is a security technology that makes it possible for users to use their computer with fewer privileges by default, with a view to stopping malware from making unauthorized changes to the system. This was often difficult in previous versions of Windows, as the previous "limited" user accounts proved too restrictive and incompatible with a large proportion of application software, and even prevented some basic operations such as looking at the calendar from the notification tray. In Windows Vista, when an action is performed that requires administrative rights (such as installing/uninstalling software or making system-wide configuration changes), the user is first prompted for an administrator name and password; in cases where the user is already an administrator, the user is still prompted to confirm the pending privileged action. Regular use of the computer such as running programs, printing, or surfing the Internet does not trigger UAC prompts. User Account Control asks for credentials in a Secure Desktop mode, in which the entire screen is dimmed, and only the authorization window is active and highlighted. The intent is to stop a malicious program misleading the user by interfering with the authorization window, and to hint to the user the importance of the prompt.

Testing by Symantec Corporation has proven the effectiveness of UAC. Symantec used over 2,000 active malware samples, consisting of backdoors, keyloggers, rootkits, mass mailers, trojan horses, spyware, adware, and various other samples. Each was executed on a default Windows Vista installation within a standard user account. UAC effectively blocked over 50 percent of each threat, excluding rootkits. 5 percent or less of the malware that evaded UAC survived a reboot.

Internet Explorer 7's new security and safety features include a phishing filter, IDN with anti-spoofing capabilities, and integration with system-wide parental controls. For added security, ActiveX controls are disabled by default. Also, Internet Explorer operates in a protected mode, which operates with lower permissions than the user and runs in isolation from other applications in the operating system, preventing it from accessing or modifying anything besides the Temporary Internet Files directory. Microsoft's anti-spyware product, *Windows Defender*, has been incorporated into Windows, providing protection against malware and other threats. Changes to various system configuration settings (such as new auto-starting applications) are blocked unless the user gives consent.

Whereas prior releases of Windows supported per-file encryption using Encrypting File System, the Enterprise and Ultimate editions of Vista include BitLocker Drive Encryption, which can protect entire volumes, notably the operating system volume. However, BitLocker requires approximately a 1.5-gigabyte partition to be permanently not encrypted and to contain system files in order for Windows to boot. In normal circumstances, the only time this partition is accessed is when the computer is booting, or when there is a Windows update that changes files in this area, which is a legitimate reason to access this section of the drive. The area can be a potential security issue, because a hexadecimal editor (such as dskprobe.exe), or malicious software running with administrator and/or kernel level privileges would be able to write to this "Ghost Partition" and allow a piece of malicious software to compromise the system, or disable the encryption. BitLocker can work in conjunction with a Trusted Platform Module (TPM) cryptoprocessor (version 1.2) embedded in a computer's motherboard, or with a USB key. However, as with other full disk encryption technologies, BitLocker is vulnerable to a cold boot attack, especially where TPM is used as a key protector without a boot PIN being required too.

A variety of other privilege-restriction techniques are also built into Vista. An example is the concept of "integrity levels" in user processes, whereby a process with a lower integrity level cannot interact with processes of a higher integrity level and cannot perform DLL–injection to a processes of a higher integrity level. The security restrictions of Windows services are more fine-grained, so that services (especially those listening on the network) have no ability to interact with parts of the operating system they do not need to. Obfuscation techniques such as address space layout randomization are used to increase the amount of effort required of malware before successful infiltration of a system. Code integrity verifies that system binaries have not been tampered with by malicious code.

As part of the redesign of the network stack, Windows Firewall has been upgraded, with new support for filtering both incoming and outgoing traffic. Advanced packet filter rules can be created that can grant or deny communications to specific services.

The 64-bit versions of Vista require that all device drivers be digitally signed, so that the creator of the driver can be identified.

System Management

While much of the focus of Vista's new capabilities highlighted the new user-interface, security technologies, and improvements to the core operating system, Microsoft also adding new deployment and maintenance features:

- The Windows Imaging Format (WIM) provides the cornerstone of Microsoft's new deployment and packaging system. WIM files, which contain a HAL-independent image of Windows Vista, can be maintained and patched without having to rebuild new images.

Windows Images can be delivered via Systems Management Server or Business Desktop Deployment technologies. Images can be customized and configured with applications then deployed to corporate client personal computers using little to no touch by a system administrator. ImageX is the Microsoft tool used to create and customize images.

- Windows Deployment Services replaces Remote Installation Services for deploying Vista and prior versions of Windows.

- Approximately 700 new Group Policy settings have been added, covering most aspects of the new features in the operating system, as well as significantly expanding the configurability of wireless networks, removable storage devices, and user desktop experience. Vista also introduced an XML-based format (ADMX) to display registry-based policy settings, making it easier to manage networks that span geographic locations and different languages.

- Services for UNIX, renamed as "Subsystem for UNIX-based Applications", comes with the Enterprise and Ultimate editions of Vista. Network File System (NFS) client support is also included.

- Multilingual User Interface–Unlike previous versions of Windows (which required the loading of language packs to provide local-language support), Windows Vista Ultimate and Enterprise editions support the ability to dynamically change languages based on the logged-on user's preference.

- Wireless Projector support.

Developer

Windows Vista includes a large number of new application programming interfaces. Chief among them is the inclusion of version 3.0 of the .NET Framework, which consists of a class library and Common Language Runtime and OS/2 environment just like its NT predecessors. Version 3.0 includes four new major components:

- Windows Presentation Foundation is a user interface subsystem and framework based vector graphics, which makes use of 3D computer graphics hardware and Direct3D technologies. It provides the foundation for building applications and blending together application UI, documents, and media content. It is the successor to Windows Forms.

- Windows Communication Foundation is a service-oriented messaging subsystem that enables applications and systems to interoperate locally or remotely using Web services.

- Windows Workflow Foundation provides task automation and integrated transactions using workflows. It is the programming model, engine and tools for building workflow-enabled applications on Windows.

- Windows CardSpace is a component that securely stores digital identities of a person, and provides a unified interface for choosing the identity for a particular transaction, such as logging into a website.

These technologies are also available for Windows XP and Windows Server 2003 to facilitate their introduction to and usage by developers and end users.

There are also significant new development APIs in the core of the operating system, notably the completely re-designed audio, networking, print, and video interfaces, major changes to the security infrastructure, improvements to the deployment and installation of applications ("ClickOnce" and Windows Installer 4.0), new device driver development model ("Windows Driver Foundation"), Transactional NTFS, mobile computing API advancements (power management, Tablet PC Ink support, SideShow) and major updates to (or complete replacements of) many core subsystems such as Winlogon and CAPI.

There are some issues for software developers using some of the graphics APIs in Vista. Games or programs built solely on the Windows Vista-exclusive version of DirectX, version 10, cannot work on prior versions of Windows, as DirectX 10 is not available for previous Windows versions. Also, games that require the features of D3D9Ex, the updated implementation of DirectX 9 in Windows Vista are also incompatible with previous Windows versions. According to a Microsoft blog, there are three choices for OpenGL implementation on Vista. An application can use the default implementation, which translates OpenGL calls into the Direct3D API and is frozen at OpenGL version 1.4, or an application can use an Installable Client Driver (ICD), which comes in two flavors: legacy and Vista-compatible. A legacy ICD disables the Desktop Window Manager, a Vista-compatible ICD takes advantage of a new API, and is fully compatible with the Desktop Window Manager. At least two primary vendors, ATI and NVIDIA provided full Vista-compatible ICDs. However, hardware overlay is not supported, because it is considered as an obsolete feature in Vista. ATI and NVIDIA strongly recommend using compositing desktop/Framebuffer Objects for same functionality.

Installation

Windows Vista is the first Microsoft operating system:

- To use DVD-ROM media for installation;

- Can be installed only on a partition formatted with the NTFS file system;

- Provides support for loading drivers for SCSI, SATA and RAID controllers from any source other than floppy disks prior to its installation.

Removed Features

Some notable Windows XP features and components have been replaced or removed in Windows Vista, including several shell and Windows Explorer features, multimedia features, networking related functionality, Windows Messenger, NTBackup, the network Windows Messenger service, HyperTerminal, MSN Explorer, Active Desktop, and the replacement of NetMeeting with Windows Meeting Space. Windows Vista also does not include the Windows XP "Luna" visual theme, or most of the classic color schemes that have been part of Windows since the Windows 3.x era. The "Hardware profiles" startup feature has also been removed, along with support for older motherboard technologies like the EISA bus, APM and game port support (though on the 32-bit version game port support can be enabled by applying an older driver). IP over FireWire (TCP/IP over IEEE 1394) has been removed as well. The IPX/SPX protocol has also been removed, although it can be enabled by a third-party plug-in.

Editions

Windows Vista shipped in six different editions. These are roughly divided into two target markets, consumer and business, with editions varying to cater for specific sub-markets. For consumers, there are three editions, with two available for economically more developed countries. Windows Vista Starter edition is aimed for low powered computers with availability only in emerging markets. Windows Vista Home Basic is intended for budget users. Windows Vista Home Premium covers the majority of the consumer market, and contains applications for creating and using multimedia. The home editions cannot join a Windows Server domain. For businesses, there are three editions as well. Windows Vista Business is specifically designed for small and medium-sized enterprises, while Windows Vista Enterprise is only available to customers participating in Microsoft's Software Assurance program. Windows Vista Ultimate contains the complete feature-set of both the Home and Business (combination of both Home Premium and Enterprise) editions, as well as a set of Windows Ultimate Extras, and is aimed at enthusiasts.

All editions except Windows Vista Starter support both 32-bit (x32) and 64-bit (x64) processor architectures.

In the European Union, Home Basic N and Business N versions are also available. These come without Windows Media Player, due to EU sanctions brought against Microsoft for violating anti-trust laws. Similar sanctions exist in South Korea.

Visual Styles

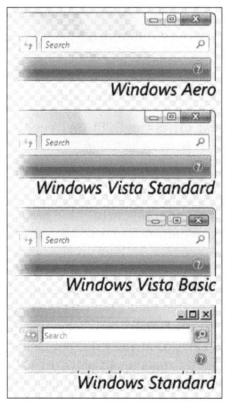

A comparison of the four visual styles included in Windows Vista.

Windows Vista has four distinct visual styles:

- Windows Aero: Vista's default visual style, Windows Aero, is built on a new desktop composition engine called Desktop Window Manager. Windows Aero introduces support for translucency effects (Glass), live thumbnails, window animations, and other visual effects (for example Windows Flip 3D), and is intended for mainstream and high-end video cards. To enable these features, the contents of every open window are stored in video memory to facilitate tearing-free movement of windows. As such, Windows Aero has significantly higher hardware requirements than its predecessors. The minimum requirement is for 128 MB of graphics memory, depending on resolution used. Windows Aero (including Windows Flip 3D) is not included in the Starter and Home Basic editions.

- Windows Vista Standard: This style is a variation of Windows Aero without the glass effects, window animations, and other advanced graphical effects such as Windows Flip 3D. Like Windows Aero, it uses the Desktop Window Manager, and has generally the same video hardware requirements as Windows Aero. This visual style is included with Home Basic edition only as a "cheap" replacement of Windows Aero style.

- Windows Vista Basic: This style has aspects that are similar to Windows XP's "Luna" visual style with the addition of subtle animations such as those found on progress bars. It does not employ the Desktop Window Manager, as such, it does not feature transparency or translucency, window animation, Windows Flip 3D or any of the functions provided by the DWM. The Basic mode does not require the new Windows Display Driver Model (WDDM) for display drivers, and has similar video card requirements to Windows XP. For computers with video cards that are not powerful enough to support Windows Aero, this is the default graphics mode. Prior to Service Pack 1, a machine that failed Windows Genuine Advantage validation would also default to this visual style.

- Windows Standard: The Windows Standard (or Windows Classic) visual style is similar to that of Windows 9x, Windows 2000 and Microsoft's Windows Server line of operating systems. It does not use the Desktop Window Manager, and does not require a WDDM driver. As with previous versions of Windows, this visual style supports color schemes, which are collections of color settings. Windows Vista includes six color schemes: four high-contrast color schemes and the default color schemes from Windows 98 (titled "Windows Classic") and Windows 2000/Windows Me (titled "Windows Standard").

Hardware Requirements

Computers capable of running Windows Vista are classified as Vista Capable and Vista Premium Ready. A Vista Capable or equivalent PC is capable of running all editions of Windows Vista although some of the special features and high-end graphics options may require additional or more advanced hardware. A Vista Premium Ready PC can take advantage of Vista's high-end features.

Windows Vista's Basic and Classic interfaces work with virtually any graphics hardware that supports Windows XP or 2000; accordingly, most discussion around Vista's graphics requirements centers on those for the Windows Aero interface. As of Windows Vista Beta 2, the NVIDIA GeForce

6 series and later, the ATI Radeon 9500 and later, Intel's GMA 950 and later integrated graphics, and a handful of VIA chipsets and S3 Graphics discrete chips are supported. Although originally supported, the GeForce FX 5 series has been dropped from newer drivers from NVIDIA. The last driver from NVIDIA to support the GeForce FX series on Vista was 96.85. Microsoft offered a tool called the Windows Vista Upgrade Advisor to assist Windows XP and Vista users in determining what versions of Windows their machine is capable of running. The required server connections for this utility are no longer available. Although the installation media included in retail packages is a 32-bit DVD, customers needing a CD-ROM or customers who wish for a 64-bit install media are able to acquire this media through the Windows Vista Alternate Media program. The Ultimate edition includes both 32-bit and 64-bit media. The digitally downloaded version of Ultimate includes only one version, either 32-bit or 64-bit, from Windows Marketplace.

Windows Vista system requirements		
Component of PC	Minimum required	Recommended
Processor	800 MHz	1 GHz
Memory	512 MB (384 MB for Starter edition)	1 GB
Graphics card	Super VGA	WDDM 1.0-compliant 32 bits per pixel DirectX 9.0 support Pixel Shader 2.0 support
Graphics memory	N/A	128 MB
Total HDD capacity	20 GB	40 GB
Free HDD space	15 GB	15 GB
Optical drives	CD-ROM drive	DVD-ROM drive
Others	N/A	TV tuner card (Premium, Ultimate) Touchscreen (Premium, Business, Ultimate) USB flash drive (Ultimate) Trusted Platform Module (Ultimate)

Physical Memory Limits

The maximum amount of RAM that Windows Vista can support varies, depending on both its edition and its processor architecture, as shown in the table.

Edition	Processor architecture	
	IA-32	x64
Ultimate	4 GB	128 GB
Enterprise		
Business		
Home Premium		16 GB
Home Basic		8 GB
Starter	1 GB	N/A

Processor Limits

The maximum number of logical processors in a PC that Windows Vista supports is: 32 for 32-bit; 64 for 64-bit.

The maximum number of physical processors in a PC that Windows Vista supports is: 2 for Business, Enterprise, and Ultimate, and 1 for Starter, Home Basic, and Home Premium.

Updates

Microsoft occasionally releases updates such as service packs for its Windows operating systems to fix bugs, improve performance and add new features.

Service Pack 1

Windows Vista Service Pack 1 (SP1) was released on February 4, 2008, alongside Windows Server 2008 to OEM partners, after a five-month beta test period. The initial deployment of the service pack caused a number of machines to continually reboot, rendering the machines unusable. This temporarily caused Microsoft to suspend automatic deployment of the service pack until the problem was resolved. The synchronized release date of the two operating systems reflected the merging of the workstation and server kernels back into a single code base for the first time since Windows 2000. MSDN subscribers were able to download SP1 on February 15, 2008. SP1 became available to current Windows Vista users on Windows Update and the Download Center on March 18, 2008. Initially, the service pack only supported five languages – English, French, Spanish, German and Japanese. Support for the remaining 31 languages was released on April 14, 2008.

A white paper, published by Microsoft on August 29, 2007, outlined the scope and intent of the service pack, identifying three major areas of improvement: reliability and performance, administration experience, and support for newer hardware and standards.

One area of particular note is performance. Areas of improvement include file copy operations, hibernation, logging off on domain-joined machines, JavaScript parsing in Internet Explorer, network file share browsing, Windows Explorer ZIP file handling, and Windows Disk Defragmenter. The ability to choose individual drives to defragment is being reintroduced as well.

Service Pack 1 introduced support for some new hardware and software standards, notably the exFAT file system, 802.11n wireless networking, IPv6 over VPN connections, and the Secure Socket Tunneling Protocol.

Booting a system using Extensible Firmware Interface on x64 systems was also introduced; this feature had originally been slated for the initial release of Vista but was delayed due to a lack of compatible hardware at the time. Booting from a GUID Partition Table–based hard drive greater than 2.19 TB is supported (x64 only).

Two areas have seen changes in SP1 that have come as the result of concerns from software vendors. One of these is desktop search; users will be able to change the default desktop search program to one provided by a third party instead of the Microsoft desktop search program that comes with Windows Vista, and desktop search programs will be able to seamlessly tie in their services into the operating system. These changes come in part due to complaints from Google, whose Google Desktop Search application was hindered by the presence of Vista's built-in desktop search. In June 2007, Google claimed that the changes being introduced for SP1 "are a step in the right direction, but they should be improved further to give consumers greater access to alternate desktop search providers". The other area of note is a set of new security APIs being introduced for the benefit of antivirus software that currently relies on the unsupported practice of patching the kernel.

An update to DirectX 10, named DirectX 10.1, marked mandatory several features that were previously optional in Direct3D 10 hardware. Graphics cards will be required to support DirectX 10.1. SP1 includes a kernel (6001.18000) that matches the version shipped with Windows Server 2008.

The Group Policy Management Console (GPMC) was replaced by the Group Policy Object Editor. An updated downloadable version of the Group Policy Management Console was released soon after the service pack.

SP1 enables support for hotpatching, a reboot-reduction servicing technology designed to maximize uptime. It works by allowing Windows components to be updated (or "patched") while they are still in use by a running process. Hotpatch-enabled update packages are installed via the same methods as traditional update packages, and will not trigger a system reboot.

Service Pack 2

Service Pack 2 for Windows Vista was released to manufacturing on April 28, 2009, and released to Microsoft Download Center and Windows Update on May 26, 2009. In addition to a number of security and other fixes, a number of new features have been added. However, it did not include Internet Explorer 8. Windows Vista Service Pack 2 build number is 6002.18005.090410-1830.

- Windows Search 4 (available for SP1 systems as a standalone update);

- Feature Pack for Wireless adds support for Bluetooth 2.1;

- Windows Feature Pack for Storage enables the data recording onto Blu-ray media;

- Windows Connect Now (WCN) to simplify Wi-Fi configuration;

- Improved support for resuming with active Wi-Fi connections;

- Improved support for eSATA drives;

- The limit of 10 half open, outgoing TCP connections introduced in Windows XP SP2 was removed;

- Enables the exFAT file system to support UTC timestamps, which allows correct file synchronization across time zones;

- Support for ICCD/CCID smart cards;

- Support for VIA 64-bit CPUs;

- Improved performance and responsiveness with the RSS feeds sidebar;

- Improves audio and video performance for streaming high-definition content;

- Improves Windows Media Center (WMC) in content protection for TV;

- Provides an improved power management policy that is approximately 10% more efficient than the original with the default policies.

Windows Vista and Windows Server 2008 share a single service pack binary, reflecting the fact that their code bases were joined with the release of Server 2008. Service Pack 2 is not a cumulative update meaning that Service Pack 1 must be installed first.

Platform Update

The Platform Update for Windows Vista was released on October 27, 2009. It includes major new components that shipped with Windows 7, as well as updated runtime libraries. It requires Service Pack 2 of Windows Vista or Windows Server 2008 and is listed on Windows Update as a Recommended download.

The Platform Update allows application developers to target both Windows Vista and Windows 7. It consists of the following components:

- Windows Graphics runtime: Direct2D, DirectWrite, Direct3D 11, DXGI 1.1, and WARP;

- Updates to Windows Imaging Component;

- Updates to XPS Print API, XPS Document API and XPS Rasterization Service;

- Windows Automation API (updates to MSAA and UI Automation);

- Windows Portable Devices Platform (adds support for MTP over Bluetooth and MTP Device Services);

- Windows Ribbon API;

- Windows Animation Manager library.

Some updates are available as separate releases for both Windows XP and Windows Vista:

- Windows Management Framework: Windows PowerShell 2.0, Windows Remote Management 2.0, BITS 4.0;

- Remote Desktop Connection 7.0 (RDP7) client.

Although extensive, the Platform Update does not bring Windows Vista to the level of features and performance offered by Windows 7. For example, even though Direct3D 11 runtime will be able to run on D3D9-class hardware and WDDM drivers using "feature levels" first introduced in Direct3D 10.1, Desktop Window Manager has not been updated to use Direct3D 10.1.

In July 2011, Microsoft released the Platform Update Supplement for Windows Vista and Windows Server 2008, which contains several bug fixes and performance improvements.

Criticism

Windows Vista has received a number of negative assessments. Criticism targets include protracted development time (5–6 years), more restrictive licensing terms, the inclusion of a number of technologies aimed at restricting the copying of protected digital media, and the usability of the new User Account Control security technology. Moreover, some concerns have been raised about many PCs meeting "Vista Premium Ready" hardware requirements and Vista's pricing.

Hardware Requirements

While in 2005 Microsoft claimed "nearly all PCs on the market today will run Windows Vista", the higher requirements of some of the "premium" features, such as the Aero interface, affected many upgraders. According to the UK newspaper *The Times* in May 2006, the full set of features "would be available to less than 5 percent of Britain's PC market"; however, this prediction was made several months before Vista was released. This continuing lack of clarity eventually led to a class action against Microsoft as people found themselves with new computers that were unable to use the new software to its full potential despite the assurance of "Vista Capable" designations. The court case has made public internal Microsoft communications that indicate that senior executives have also had difficulty with this issue. For example, Mike Nash (Corporate Vice President, Windows Product Management) commented, "now we have a $2,100 e-mail machine" because his laptop's lack of an appropriate graphics chip so hobbled Vista.

Licensing

Criticism of upgrade licenses pertaining to Windows Vista Starter through Home Premium was expressed by *Ars Technica*'s Ken Fisher, who noted that the new requirement of having a prior operating system already installed was going to cause irritation for users who reinstall Windows on a regular basis. It has been revealed that an Upgrade copy of Windows Vista can be installed clean without first installing a previous version of Windows. On the first install, Windows will refuse to activate. The user must then reinstall that same copy of Vista. Vista will then activate on the reinstall, thus allowing a user to install an Upgrade of Windows Vista without owning a previous operating system. As with Windows XP, separate rules still apply to OEM versions of Vista installed on new PCs: Microsoft asserts that these versions are not legally transferable (although whether this conflicts with the right of first sale has yet to be clearly decided legally).

Cost

Initially, the cost of Windows Vista was also a source of concern and commentary. A majority of users in a poll said that the prices of various Windows Vista editions posted on the Microsoft Canada website in August 2006 make the product too expensive. A BBC News report on the day of Vista's release suggested that, "there may be a backlash from consumers over its pricing plans—with the cost of Vista versions in the US roughly half the price of equivalent versions in the UK." Since the release of Vista in 2006, Microsoft has reduced the retail, and upgrade price point of Vista. Originally, Vista Ultimate was priced at $399, and Home Premium Vista at $239. These prices have since been reduced to $319 and $199 respectively.

Digital Rights Management

Windows Vista supports additional forms of DRM restrictions. One aspect of this is the Protected Video Path, which is designed so that "premium content" from HD DVD or Blu-ray Discs may mandate that the connections between PC components be encrypted. Depending on what the content demands, the devices may not pass premium content over non-encrypted outputs, or they must artificially degrade the quality of the signal on such outputs or not display it at all. Drivers for such hardware must be approved by Microsoft; a revocation mechanism is also included, which allows Microsoft to disable drivers of devices in end-user PCs over the Internet. Peter Gutmann, security researcher and author of the open source cryptlib library, claims that these mechanisms violate fundamental rights of the user (such as fair use), unnecessarily increase the cost of hardware, and make systems less reliable (the "tilt bit" being a particular worry; if triggered, the entire graphic subsystem performs a reset) and vulnerable to denial-of-service attacks. However, despite several requests for evidence supporting such claims Peter Gutmann has never supported his claims with any researched evidence. Proponents have claimed that Microsoft had no choice but to follow the demands of the movie studios, and that the technology will not actually be enabled until after 2010; Microsoft also noted that content protection mechanisms have existed in Windows as far back as Windows ME, and that the new protections will not apply to any existing content (only future content).

User Account Control

Although User Account Control (UAC) is an important part of Vista's security infrastructure, as it blocks software from silently gaining administrator privileges without the user's knowledge, it has been widely criticized for generating too many prompts. This has led many Vista UAC users to consider it troublesome, with some consequently either turning the feature off or (for Windows Vista Enterprise or Windows Vista Ultimate users) putting it in auto-approval mode. Responding to this criticism, Microsoft altered the implementation to reduce the number of prompts with SP1. Though the changes have resulted in some improvement, it has not alleviated the concerns completely.

Downgrade Rights

For Windows 8 licenses acquired through an OEM, a user may downgrade to the equivalent edition of Windows Vista. Customers licensed for use of Windows 8 Enterprise are generally licensed for Windows 8 Pro, which may be downgraded to Windows Vista Business. End users of licenses of Windows 7 acquired through OEM or volume licensing may downgrade to the equivalent edition of Windows Vista. Downgrade rights are not offered for Starter, Home Basic or Home Premium editions of Windows 7.

Windows 7

Windows 7 is a personal computer operating system that was produced by Microsoft as part of the Windows NT family of operating systems. It was released to manufacturing on July 22, 2009 and became generally available on October 22, 2009, less than three years after the release of its predecessor, Windows Vista. Windows 7's server counterpart, Windows Server 2008 R2, was released at the same time.

Windows 7 was primarily intended to be an incremental upgrade to Microsoft Windows, intended to address Windows Vista's poor critical reception while maintaining hardware and software compatibility. Windows 7 continued improvements on Windows Aero (the user interface introduced in Windows Vista) with the addition of a redesigned taskbar that allows applications to be "pinned" to it, and new window management features. Other new features were added to the operating system, including libraries, the new file sharing system HomeGroup, and support for multitouch input. A new "Action Center" interface was also added to provide an overview of system security and maintenance information, and tweaks were made to the User Account Control system to make it less intrusive. Windows 7 also shipped with updated versions of several stock applications, including Internet Explorer 8, Windows Media Player, and Windows Media Center.

In contrast to Windows Vista, Windows 7 was generally praised by critics, who considered the operating system to be a major improvement over its predecessor due to its increased performance, its more intuitive interface (with particular praise devoted to the new taskbar), fewer User Account Control popups, and other improvements made across the platform. Windows 7 was a major success for Microsoft; even prior to its official release, pre-order sales for 7 on the online retailer Amazon.com had surpassed previous records. In just six months, over 100 million copies had been sold worldwide, increasing to over 630 million licenses by July 2012. As of July 2019, 31.24% of computers running Windows are running Windows 7, which still has over 50% market share in a number of countries such as in China at 51.21%, and is the most used version in many countries, mostly those in Africa. Windows 10 is by now most popular on all continents, after overtaking Windows 7 in Africa.

On August 11, 2019, researchers reported that Windows 10 users may be at risk for "critical" system compromise due to design flaws of hardware device drivers from multiple providers. Also in August 2019, computer experts reported that the BlueKeep security vulnerability, CVE- 2019-0708, that potentially affects older unpatched Microsoft Windows versions via the program's Remote Desktop Protocol, allowing for the possibility of remote code execution, may now include related flaws, collectively named DejaBlue, affecting newer Windows versions (i.e., Windows 7 and all recent versions) as well. In addition, experts reported a Microsoft security vulnerability, CVE-2019-1162, based on legacy code involving Microsoft CTF and ctfmon (ctfmon.exe), that affects all Windows versions from the older Windows XP version to the most recent Windows 10 versions; a patch to correct the flaw is currently available.

Development

Originally, a version of Windows codenamed "Blackcomb" was planned as the successor to Windows XP and Windows Server 2003 in 2000. Major features were planned for Blackcomb, including an emphasis on searching and querying data and an advanced storage system named WinFS to enable such scenarios. However, an interim, minor release, codenamed "Longhorn," was announced for 2003, delaying the development of Blackcomb. By the middle of 2003, however, Longhorn had acquired some of the features originally intended for Blackcomb. After three major malware outbreaks—the Blaster, Nachi, and Sobig worms—exploited flaws in Windows operating systems within a short time period in August 2003, Microsoft changed its development priorities, putting some of Longhorn's major development work on hold while developing new service packs for Windows XP and Windows Server 2003. Development of Longhorn (Windows Vista) was also restarted, and thus delayed, in August 2004. A number of features were cut from Longhorn. Blackcomb was renamed Vienna in early 2006.

When released, Windows Vista was criticized for its long development time, performance issues, spotty compatibility with existing hardware and software on launch, changes affecting the compatibility of certain PC games, and unclear assurances by Microsoft that certain computers shipping with XP prior to launch would be "Vista Capable" (which led to a class action lawsuit), among other critiques. As such, adoption of Vista in comparison to XP remained somewhat low. In July 2007, six months following the public release of Vista, it was reported that the next version of Windows would then be codenamed Windows 7, with plans for a final release within three years. Bill Gates, in an interview with Newsweek, suggested that Windows 7 would be more "user-centric". Gates later said that Windows 7 would also focus on performance improvements. Steven Sinofsky later expanded on this point, explaining in the Engineering Windows 7 blog that the company was using a variety of new tracing tools to measure the performance of many areas of the operating system on an ongoing basis, to help locate inefficient code paths and to help prevent performance regressions. Senior Vice President Bill Veghte stated that Windows Vista users migrating to Windows 7 would not find the kind of device compatibility issues they encountered migrating from Windows XP. An estimated 1,000 developers worked on Windows 7. These were broadly divided into "core operating system" and "Windows client experience", in turn organized into 25 teams of around 40 developers on average.

In October 2008, it was announced that Windows 7 would also be the official name of the operating system. There has been some confusion over naming the product Windows 7, while versioning it as 6.1 to indicate its similar build to Vista and increase compatibility with applications that only check major version numbers, similar to Windows 2000 and Windows XP both having 5.x version numbers. The first external release to select Microsoft partners came in January 2008 with Milestone 1, build 6519. Speaking about Windows 7 on October 16, 2008, Microsoft CEO Steve Ballmer confirmed compatibility between Windows Vista and Windows 7, indicating that Windows 7 would be a refined version of Windows Vista.

At PDC 2008, Microsoft demonstrated Windows 7 with its reworked taskbar. On December 27, 2008, the Windows 7 Beta was leaked onto the Internet via BitTorrent. According to a performance test by ZDNet, Windows 7 Beta beat both Windows XP and Vista in several key areas, including boot and shutdown time and working with files, such as loading documents. Other areas did not beat XP, including PC Pro benchmarks for typical office activities and video editing, which remain identical to Vista and slower than XP. On January 7, 2009, the x64 version of the Windows 7 Beta (build 7000) was leaked onto the web, with some torrents being infected with a trojan. At CES 2009, Microsoft CEO Steve Ballmer announced the Windows 7 Beta, build 7000, had been made available for download to MSDN and TechNet subscribers in the format of an ISO image. The stock wallpaper of the beta version contained a digital image of the Betta fish.

The release candidate, build 7100, became available for MSDN and TechNet subscribers, and Connect Program participants on April 30, 2009. On May 5, 2009, it became available to the general public, although it had also been leaked onto the Internet via BitTorrent. The release candidate was available in five languages and expired on June 1, 2010, with shutdowns every two hours starting March 1, 2010. Microsoft stated that Windows 7 would be released to the general public on October 22, 2009. Microsoft released Windows 7 to MSDN and Technet subscribers on August 6, 2009, at 10:00 am PDT. Microsoft announced that Windows 7, along with Windows Server 2008 R2, was released to manufacturing on July 22, 2009. Windows 7 RTM is build 7600.16385.090713-1255, which was compiled on July 13, 2009, and was declared the final RTM build after passing all Microsoft's tests internally.

Features

New and Changed

Among Windows 7's new features are advances in touch and handwriting recognition, support for virtual hard disks, improved performance on multi-core processors, improved boot performance, DirectAccess, and kernel improvements. Windows 7 adds support for systems using multiple heterogeneous graphics cards from different vendors (Heterogeneous Multi-adapter), a new version of Windows Media Center, a Gadget for Windows Media Center, improved media features, XPS Essentials Pack and Windows PowerShell being included, and a redesigned Calculator with multiline capabilities including *Programmer* and *Statistics* modes along with unit conversion for length, weight, temperature, and several others. Many new items have been added to the Control Panel, including ClearType Text Tuner Display Color Calibration Wizard, Gadgets, Recovery, Troubleshooting, Workspaces Center, Location and Other Sensors, Credential Manager, Biometric Devices, System Icons, and Display. Windows Security Center has been renamed to Windows Action Center (Windows Health Center and Windows Solution Center in earlier builds), which encompasses both security and maintenance of the computer. ReadyBoost on 32-bit editions now supports up to 256 gigabytes of extra allocation. Windows 7 also supports images in RAW image format through the addition of Windows Imaging Component-enabled image decoders, which enables raw image thumbnails, previewing and metadata display in Windows Explorer, plus full-size viewing and slideshows in Windows Photo Viewer and Windows Media Center. Windows 7 also has a native TFTP client with the ability to transfer files to or from a TFTP server.

Windows 7 live thumbnails, showing Internet Explorer 11 tabs.

The taskbar has seen the biggest visual changes, where the old Quick Launch toolbar has been replaced with the ability to pin applications to taskbar. Buttons for pinned applications are integrated with the task buttons. These buttons also enable Jump Lists to allow easy access to common tasks. The revamped taskbar also allows the reordering of taskbar buttons. To the far right of the system clock is a small rectangular button that serves as the Show desktop icon. By default, hovering over this button makes all visible windows transparent for a quick look at the desktop. In touch-enabled displays such as touch screens, tablet PCs, etc., this button is slightly (8 pixels) wider in order to accommodate being pressed by a finger. Clicking this button minimizes all windows, and clicking it a second time restores them.

Window management in Windows 7 has several new features: Snap maximizes a window when it is dragged to the top of the screen. Dragging windows to the left or right edges of the screen allows users to snap software windows to either side of the screen, such that the windows take up half the screen. When a user moves windows that were snapped or maximized using Snap, the system restores their previous state. Snap functions can also be triggered with keyboard shortcuts. Shake hides all inactive windows when the active window's title bar is dragged back and forth rapidly (metaphorically shaken).

Windows 7 includes 13 additional sound schemes, titled Afternoon, Calligraphy, Characters, Cityscape,

Delta, Festival, Garden, Heritage, Landscape, Quirky, Raga, Savanna, and Sonata. Internet Spades, Internet Backgammon and Internet Checkers, which were removed from Windows Vista, were restored in Windows 7. Users are able to disable or customize many more Windows components than was possible in Windows Vista. New additions to this list of components include Internet Explorer 8, Windows Media Player 12, Windows Media Center, Windows Search, and Windows Gadget Platform. A new version of Microsoft Virtual PC, newly renamed as Windows Virtual PC was made available for Windows 7 Professional, Enterprise, and Ultimate editions. It allows multiple Windows environments, including *Windows XP Mode*, to run on the same machine. Windows XP Mode runs Windows XP in a virtual machine, and displays applications within separate windows on the Windows 7 desktop. Furthermore, Windows 7 supports the mounting of a virtual hard disk (VHD) as a normal data storage, and the bootloader delivered with Windows 7 can boot the Windows system from a VHD; however, this ability is only available in the Enterprise and Ultimate editions. The Remote Desktop Protocol (RDP) of Windows 7 is also enhanced to support real-time multimedia application including video playback and 3D games, thus allowing use of DirectX 10 in remote desktop environments. The three application limit, previously present in the Windows Vista and Windows XP Starter Editions, has been removed from Windows 7. All editions include some new and improved features, such as Windows Search, Security features, and some features new to Windows 7, that originated within Vista. Optional BitLocker Drive Encryption is included with Windows 7 Ultimate and Enterprise. Windows Defender is included; Microsoft Security Essentials antivirus software is a free download. All editions include Shadow Copy, which—every day or so—System Restore uses to take an automatic "previous version" snapshot of user files that have changed. Backup and restore have also been improved, and the Windows Recovery Environment—installed by default—replaces the optional Recovery Console of Windows XP.

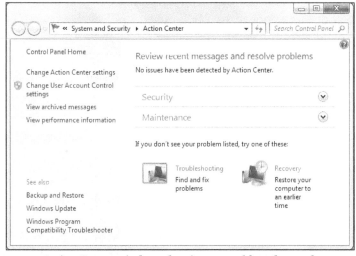

Action Center window, showing no problem detected.

A new system known as "Libraries" was added for file management; users can aggregate files from multiple folders into a "Library". By default, libraries for categories such as Documents, Pictures, Music, and Video are created, consisting of the user's personal folder and the Public folder for each. The system is also used as part of a new home networking system known as HomeGroup; devices are added to the network with a password, and files and folders can be shared with all other devices in the HomeGroup, or with specific users. The default libraries, along with printers, are shared by default, but the personal folder is set to read-only access by other users, and the Public folder can be accessed by anyone.

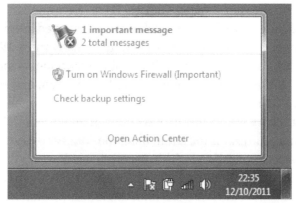

When the Action Center flag is clicked on, it lists all security and maintenance issues in a small popup window.

Windows 7 includes improved globalization support through a new Extended Linguistic Services API to provide multilingual support (particularly in Ultimate and Enterprise editions). Microsoft has also implemented better support for solid-state drives, including the new TRIM command, and Windows 7 is able to identify a solid-state drive uniquely. Native support for USB 3.0 is not included due to delays in the finalization of the standard. At WinHEC 2008 Microsoft announced that color depths of 30-bit and 48-bit would be supported in Windows 7 along with the wide color gamut scRGB (which for HDMI 1.3 can be converted and output as xvYCC). The video modes supported in Windows 7 are 16-bit sRGB, 24-bit sRGB, 30-bit sRGB, 30-bit with extended color gamut sRGB, and 48-bit scRGB.

For developers, Windows 7 includes a new networking API with support for building SOAP-based web services in native code (as opposed to .NET-based WCF web services), new features to simplify development of installation packages and shorten application install times. Windows 7, by default, generates fewer User Account Control (UAC) prompts because it allows digitally signed Windows components to gain elevated privileges without a prompt. Additionally, users can now adjust the level at which UAC operates using a sliding scale.

Removed

Certain capabilities and programs that were a part of Windows Vista are no longer present or have been changed, resulting in the removal of certain functionalities; these include the classic Start Menu user interface, some taskbar features, Windows Explorer features, Windows Media Player features, Windows Ultimate Extras, Search button, and InkBall. Four applications bundled with Windows Vista—Windows Photo Gallery, Windows Movie Maker, Windows Calendar and Windows Mail—are not included with Windows 7 and were replaced by Windows Live-branded versions as part of the Windows Live Essentials suite.

Editions

Windows 7 is available in six different editions, of which the Home Premium, Professional, and Ultimate were available at retail in most countries, and as pre-loaded software on new computers. Home Premium and Professional were aimed at home users and small businesses respectively, while Ultimate was aimed at enthusiasts. Each edition of Windows 7 includes all of the capabilities and features of the edition below it, and adds additional features oriented towards their market segments; for example, Professional adds additional networking and security features such as Encrypting File System and the ability to join a domain. Ultimate contained a superset of the features from Home Premium and Professional, along with other advanced features oriented towards power users, such as BitLocker drive encryption; unlike Windows Vista, there were no "Ultimate Extras" add-ons created for Windows 7 Ultimate. Retail copies were available in "upgrade" and higher-cost "full" version licenses; "upgrade" licenses require an existing version of Windows to install, while "full" licenses can be installed on computers with no existing operating system.

The remaining three editions were not available at retail, of which two were available exclusively through OEM channels as pre-loaded software. The Starter edition is a stripped-down version of Windows 7 meant for low-cost devices such as netbooks. In comparison to Home Premium, Starter has reduced multimedia functionality, does not allow users to change their desktop wallpaper or theme, disables the "Aero Glass" theme, does not have support for multiple monitors, and can only address 2GB of RAM. Home Basic was sold only in emerging markets, and was positioned in between Home Premium and Starter. The highest edition, Enterprise, is functionally similar to Ultimate, but is only sold through volume licensing via Microsoft's Software Assurance program.

All editions aside from Starter support both IA-32 and x86-64 architectures; Starter only supports 32-bit systems. Retail copies of Windows 7 are distributed on two DVDs: one for the IA-32 version and the other for x86-64. OEM copies include one DVD, depending on the processor architecture licensed. The installation media for consumer versions of Windows 7 are identical; the product key and corresponding license determines the edition that is installed. The Windows Anytime Upgrade service can be used to purchase an upgrade that unlocks the functionality of a higher edition, such as going from Starter to Home Premium, and Home Premium to Ultimate. Most copies of Windows 7 only contained one license; in certain markets, a "Family Pack" version of Windows 7 Home Premium was also released for a limited time, which allowed upgrades on up to three computers. In certain regions, copies of Windows 7 were only sold in, and could only be activated in a designated region.

Support Lifecycle

Support for Windows 7 without Service Pack 1 ended on April 9, 2013, requiring users to update in order to continue receiving updates and support. Microsoft ended the sale of new retail copies of Windows 7 in October 2014, and the sale of new OEM licenses for Windows 7 Home Basic, Home Premium, and Ultimate ended on October 31, 2014. Professional currently remains available to OEMs, primarily as part of downgrade rights for Windows 8 and 10 licenses. OEM sales of PCs with Windows 7 Professional preinstalled ended on October 31, 2016. The sale of non-Professional OEM licences was stopped on October 31, 2014.

Mainstream support for Windows 7 ended on January 13, 2015. Extended support for Windows 7 will end on January 14, 2020.

On September 7, 2018, Microsoft announced a paid "Extended Security Updates" service that will offer additional updates for Windows 7 Professional and Enterprise for three years after the end of extended support.

In March 2019, Microsoft announced that it would display notifications to users informing users of the upcoming end of support, and direct users to a website urging them to purchase a Windows 10 upgrade or a new device.

System Requirements

Minimum hardware requirements for Windows 7		
Component	Operating system architecture	
	32-bit	64-bit
Processor	1 GHz IA-32 processor	1 GHz x86-64 processor
Memory (RAM)	1 GB	2 GB
Graphics card	DirectX 9 graphics processor with WDDM driver model 1.0	
Free hard drive space	16 GB	20 GB
Installation media	DVD drive or USB drive	

Additional requirements to use certain features:

- Windows XP Mode (Professional, Ultimate and Enterprise): Requires an additional 1 GB of RAM and additional 15 GB of available hard disk space. The requirement for a processor capable of hardware virtualization has been lifted.

- Windows Media Center (included in Home Premium, Professional, Ultimate and Enterprise), requires a TV tuner to receive and record TV.

Extent of Hardware Support

Physical Memory

The maximum amount of RAM that Windows 7 supports varies depending on the product edition and on the processor architecture, as shown in the following table.

Physical memory limits of Windows 7		
Edition	Processor architecture	
	IA-32 (32-bit)	x64 (64-bit)
Ultimate		
Enterprise		192 GB
Professional	4 GB	
Home Premium		16 GB
Home Basic		8 GB
Starter	2 GB	N/A

Processor Limits

Windows 7 Professional and up support up to 2 physical processors (CPU sockets), whereas Windows 7 Starter, Home Basic, and Home Premium editions support only 1. Physical processors with either multiple cores, or hyper-threading, or both, implement more than one logical processor per physical processor. The x86 editions of Windows 7 support up to 32 logical processors; x64 editions support up to 256 (4 x 64).

In January 2016, Microsoft announced that it would no longer support Windows platforms older than Windows 10 on any future Intel-compatible processor lines, citing difficulties in reliably allowing the operating system to operate on newer hardware. Microsoft stated that effective July

17, 2017, devices with Intel Skylake CPUs were only to receive the "most critical" updates for Windows 7 and 8.1, and only if they have been judged not to affect the reliability of Windows 7 on older hardware. For enterprise customers, Microsoft issued a list of Skylake-based devices "certified" for Windows 7 and 8.1 in addition to Windows 10, to assist them in migrating to newer hardware that can eventually be upgraded to 10 once they are ready to transition. Microsoft and their hardware partners provide special testing and support for these devices on 7 and 8.1 until the July 2017 date.

On March 18, 2016, in response to criticism from enterprise customers, Microsoft delayed the end of support and non-critical updates for Skylake systems to July 17, 2018, but stated that they would also continue to receive security updates through the end of extended support. In August 2016, citing a "strong partnership with our OEM partners and Intel", Microsoft retracted the decision and stated that it would continue to support Windows 7 and 8.1 on Skylake hardware through the end of their extended support lifecycle. However, the restrictions on newer CPU microarchitectures remain in force.

In March 2017, a Microsoft knowledge base article was discovered which implies that devices using Intel Kaby Lake, AMD Bristol Ridge, or AMD Ryzen, would be blocked from using Windows Update entirely. In addition, official Windows 7 device drivers are not available for the Kaby Lake and Ryzen platforms.

Security updates released since March 2018 contain bugs which affect processors that do not support SSE2 extensions, including all Pentium III processors. Microsoft initially stated that it would attempt to resolve the issue, and prevented installation of the affected patches on these systems. However, on June 15, 2018, Microsoft retroactively modified its support documents to remove the promise that this bug would be resolved, replacing it with a statement suggesting that users obtain a newer processor. This effectively ends future patch support for Windows 7 on these systems.

Updates

Service Pack 1

Windows 7 Service Pack 1 (SP1) was announced on March 18, 2010. A beta was released on July 12, 2010. The final version was released to the public on February 22, 2011. At the time of release, it was not made mandatory. It was available via Windows Update, direct download, or by ordering the Windows 7 SP1 DVD. The service pack is on a much smaller scale than those released for previous versions of Windows, particularly Windows Vista.

Windows 7 Service Pack 1 adds support for Advanced Vector Extensions (AVX), a 256-bit instruction set extension for processors, and improves IKEv2 by adding additional identification fields such as E-mail ID to it. In addition, it adds support for Advanced Format 512e as well as additional Identity Federation Services. Windows 7 Service Pack 1 also resolves a bug related to HDMI audio and another related to printing XPS documents.

In Europe, the automatic nature of the BrowserChoice.eu feature was dropped in Windows 7 Service Pack 1 in February 2011 and remained absent for 14 months despite Microsoft reporting that it was still present, subsequently described by Microsoft as a "technical error". As a result, in March 2013 the European Commission fined Microsoft €561 million to deter companies from reneging on settlement promises.

Platform Update

The Platform Update for Windows 7 SP1 and Windows Server 2008 R2 SP1 was released on February 26, 2013 after a pre-release version had been released on November 5, 2012. It is also included with Internet Explorer 10 for Windows 7.

It includes enhancements to Direct2D, DirectWrite, Direct3D, Windows Imaging Component (WIC), Windows Advanced Rasterization Platform (WARP), Windows Animation Manager (WAM), XPS Document API, H.264 Video Decoder and JPEG XR decoder. However support for Direct3D 11.1 is limited as the update does not include DXGI/WDDM 1.2 from Windows 8, making unavailable many related APIs and significant features such as stereoscopic frame buffer, feature level 11_1 and optional features for levels 10_0, 10_1 and 11_0.

Disk Cleanup Update

In October 2013, a Disk Cleanup Wizard addon was released that lets users delete outdated Windows updates on Windows 7 SP1, thus reducing the size of the WinSxS directory. This update backports some features found in Windows 8.

Windows Management Framework 5.0

Windows Management Framework 5.0 includes updates to Windows PowerShell, Windows PowerShell Desired State Configuration (DSC), Windows Remote Management (WinRM), Windows Management Instrumentation (WMI). It was released on February 24, 2016 and was eventually superseded by Windows Management Framework 5.1.

Convenience Rollup

In May 2016, Microsoft released a "Convenience rollup update for Windows 7 SP1 and Windows Server 2008 R2 SP1", which contains all patches released between the release of SP1 and April 2016. The rollup is not available via Windows Update, and must be downloaded manually. This package can also be integrated into a Windows 7 installation image.

Since October 2016, all security and reliability updates are cumulative. Downloading and installing updates that address individual problems is no longer possible, but the number of updates that must be downloaded to fully update the OS is significantly reduced.

Windows 8

Windows 8 is a personal computer operating system that was produced by Microsoft as part of the Windows NT family of operating systems. The operating system was released to manufacturing on August 1, 2012, with general availability on October 26, 2012.

Windows 8 introduced major changes to the operating system's platform and user interface to improve its user experience on tablets, where Windows was now competing with mobile operating systems, including Android and iOS. In particular, these changes included a touch-optimized Windows shell based on Microsoft's "Metro" design language, the Start screen (which displays programs and dynamically updated content on a grid of tiles), a new platform for developing "apps" with an emphasis on touchscreen input, integration with online services (including the ability to synchronize apps and settings between devices), and Windows Store, an online store for downloading and purchasing new software. Windows 8 added support for USB 3.0, Advanced Format hard drives, near field communications, and cloud computing. Additional security features were introduced, such as built-in antivirus software, integration with Microsoft SmartScreen phishing filtering service and support for UEFI Secure Boot on supported devices with UEFI firmware, to prevent malware from infecting the boot process.

Windows 8 was released to a mixed critical reception. Although reaction towards its performance improvements, security enhancements, and improved support for touchscreen devices was positive, the new user interface of the operating system was widely criticized for being potentially confusing and difficult to learn, especially when used with a keyboard and mouse instead of a touchscreen. Despite these shortcomings, 60 million Windows 8 licenses were sold through January 2013, a number that included both upgrades and sales to OEMs for new PCs.

On October 17, 2013, Microsoft released Windows 8.1. It addressed some aspects of Windows 8 that were criticized by reviewers and early adopters and incorporated additional improvements to various aspects of the operating system. Windows 8 was ultimately succeeded by Windows 10 in July 2015. Microsoft stopped providing support and updates for Windows 8 RTM on January 12, 2016, and Windows 8.1 must be installed to maintain support and receive further updates per Microsoft lifecycle policies regarding service packs.

On August 11, 2019, researchers reported that Windows 10 users may be at risk for "critical" system compromise due to design flaws of hardware device drivers from multiple providers. Also in August 2019, computer experts reported that the BlueKeep security vulnerability, CVE- 2019-0708, that potentially affects older unpatched Microsoft Windows versions via the program's Remote Desktop Protocol, allowing for the possibility of remote code execution, may now include related flaws, collectively named DejaBlue, affecting newer Windows versions (i.e., Windows 7 and all recent versions) as well. In addition, experts reported a Microsoft security vulnerability, CVE-2019-1162, based on legacy code involving Microsoft CTF and ctfmon (ctfmon.exe), that affects all Windows versions from the older Windows XP version to the most recent Windows 10 versions; a patch to correct the flaw is currently available.

Development

Windows 8 development started before Windows 7 had shipped in 2009. At the Consumer Electronics Show in January 2011, it was announced that the next version of Windows would add support for ARM system-on-chips alongside the existing x86 processors produced by vendors, especially AMD and Intel. Windows division president Steven Sinofsky demonstrated an early build of the port on prototype devices, while Microsoft CEO Steve Ballmer announced the company's goal for Windows to be "everywhere on every kind of device without compromise." Details also began to surface about a new application framework for Windows 8 codenamed "Jupiter", which would be used to make "immersive" applications using XAML (similarly to Windows Phone and Silverlight) that could be distributed via a new packaging system and a rumored application store.

Three milestone releases of Windows 8 leaked to the general public. Milestone 1, Build 7850, was leaked on April 12, 2011. It was the first build where the text of a window was written centered instead of aligned to the left. It was also probably the first appearance of the Metro-style font, and its wallpaper had the text shhh let's not leak our hard work. However, its detailed build number reveals that the build was created on September 22, 2010. The leaked copy was Enterprise edition. The OS still reads as "Windows 7". Milestone 2, Build 7955, was leaked on April 25, 2011. The traditional Blue Screen of Death (BSoD) was replaced by a new black screen, although this was later scrapped. This build introduced a new ribbon in Windows Explorer. Build 7959, with minor changes but the first 64-bit version was leaked on May 1, 2011. The "Windows 7" logo was temporarily replaced with text displaying "Microsoft Confidential". On June 17, 2011, build 7989 64-bit edition was leaked. It introduced a new boot screen featuring the same fish as the default Windows 7 Beta wallpaper, which was later scrapped, and the circling dots as featured in the final (although the final version comes with smaller circling dots throbber). It also had the text Welcome below them, although this was also scrapped.

On June 1, 2011, Microsoft unveiled Windows 8's new user interface, as well as additional features at both Computex Taipei and the D9: All Things Digital conference in California.

The "Building Windows 8" blog launched on August 15, 2011, featuring details surrounding Windows 8's features and its development process.

A screenshot of Windows 8 Developer Preview running on
a multi-monitor system, showcasing some features.

Microsoft unveiled more Windows 8 features and improvements on the first day of the Build conference on September 13, 2011. Microsoft released the first public beta build of Windows 8, Windows Developer Preview (build 8102) at the event. A Samsung tablet running the build was also distributed to conference attendees.

The build was released for download later in the day in standard 32-bit and 64-bit versions, plus a special 64-bit version which included SDKs and developer tools (Visual Studio Express and Expression Blend) for developing Metro-style apps. The Windows Store was announced during the presentation, but was not available in this build. According to Microsoft, there were about 535,000 downloads of the developer preview within the first 12 hours of its release. Originally set to expire on March 11, 2012, in February 2012 the Developer Preview's expiry date was changed to January 15, 2013.

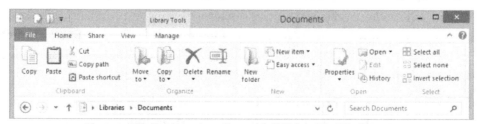

The new File Explorer interface with "Ribbon" in Windows 8.

On February 19, 2012, Microsoft unveiled a new logo to be adopted for Windows 8. Designed by Pentagram partner Paula Scher, the Windows logo was changed to resemble a set of four window panes. Additionally, the entire logo is now rendered in a single solid color.

On February 29, 2012, Microsoft released Windows 8 Consumer Preview, the beta version of Windows 8, build 8250. Alongside other changes, the build removed the Start button from the taskbar for the first time since its debut on Windows 95; according to Windows manager Chaitanya Sareen, the Start button was removed to reflect their view that on Windows 8, the desktop was an "app" itself, and not the primary interface of the operating system. Windows president Steven Sinofsky said more than 100,000 changes had been made since the developer version went public. The day after its release, Windows 8 Consumer Preview had been downloaded over one million times. Like the Developer Preview, the Consumer Preview expired on January 15, 2013.

Many other builds were released until the Japan's Developers Day conference, when Steven Sinofsky announced that Windows 8 Release Preview (build 8400) would be released during the first week of June. On May 28, 2012, Windows 8 Release Preview (Standard Simplified Chinese x64 edition, not China-specific version, build 8400) was leaked online on various Chinese and BitTorrent websites. On May 31, 2012, Windows 8 Release Preview was released to the public by Microsoft. Major items in the Release Preview included the addition of Sports, Travel, and News apps, along with an integrated version of Adobe Flash Player in Internet Explorer. Like the Developer Preview and the Consumer Preview, the release preview expired on January 15, 2013.

Release

Windows 8 launch event at Pier 57 in New York City.

On August 1, 2012, Windows 8 (build 9200) was released to manufacturing with the build number 6.2.9200.16384 . Microsoft planned to hold a launch event on October 25, 2012 and release Windows 8 for general availability on the next day. However, only a day after its release to manufacturing, a copy of the final version of Windows 8 Enterprise N (a version for European markets which lacks bundled media players to comply with an antitrust ruling) leaked online, followed by leaks of the final versions of Windows 8 Pro and Enterprise a few days later. On August 15, 2012, Windows 8 was made available to download for MSDN and TechNet subscribers. Windows 8 was made available to Software Assurance customers on August 16, 2012. Windows 8 was made available for students with a DreamSpark Premium subscription on August 22, 2012, earlier than advertised.

Relatively few changes were made from the Release Preview to the final version; these included updated versions of its pre-loaded apps, the renaming of Windows Explorer to File Explorer, the replacement of the Aero Glass theme from Windows Vista and 7 with a new flat and solid-colored theme, and the addition of new background options for the Start screen, lock screen, and desktop. Prior to its general availability on October 26, 2012, updates were released for some of Windows 8's bundled apps, and a "General Availability Cumulative Update" (which included fixes to improve performance, compatibility, and battery life) was released on Tuesday, October 9, 2012. Microsoft indicated that due to improvements to its testing infrastructure, general improvements of this nature are to be released more frequently through Windows Update instead of being relegated to OEMs and service packs only.

Microsoft began an advertising campaign centered around Windows 8 and its Surface tablet in October 2012, starting with its first television advertisement premiering on October 14, 2012. Microsoft's advertising budget of US$1.5–1.8 billion was significantly larger than the US$200 million campaign used to promote Windows 95. As part of its campaign, Microsoft set up 34 pop-up stores inside malls to showcase the Surface product line, provided training for retail employees in partnership with Intel, and collaborated with the electronics store chain Best Buy to design expanded spaces to showcase devices. In an effort to make retail displays of Windows 8 devices more "personal", Microsoft also developed a character known in English-speaking markets as "Allison Brown", whose fictional profile (including personal photos, contacts, and emails) is also featured on demonstration units of Windows 8 devices.

Windows 8 Pro DVD case, containing a 32-bit and a 64-bit installation disc.

In May 2013, Microsoft launched a new television campaign for Windows 8 illustrating the capabilities and pricing of Windows 8 tablets in comparison to the iPad, which featured the voice of Siri remarking on the iPad's limitations in a parody of Apple's "Get a Mac" advertisements. On June 12, 2013 during game 1 of the 2013 Stanley Cup Finals, Microsoft premiered the first ad in its "Windows Everywhere" campaign, which promoted Windows 8, Windows Phone 8, and the company's suite of online services as an interconnected platform.

New and Changed Features

New features and functionality in Windows 8 include a faster startup through UEFI integration and the new "Hybrid Boot" mode (which hibernates the Windows kernel on shutdown to speed up the subsequent boot), a new lock screen with a clock and notifications, and the ability for enterprise users to create live USB versions of Windows (known as Windows To Go). Windows 8 also adds native support for USB 3.0 devices, which allow for faster data transfers and improved power management with compatible devices, and hard disk 4KB Advanced Format support, as well as support for near field communication to facilitate sharing and communication between devices.

Windows Explorer, which has been renamed File Explorer, now includes a ribbon in place of the command bar. File operation dialog boxes have been updated to provide more detailed statistics, the ability to pause file transfers, and improvements in the ability to manage conflicts when copying files. A new "File History" function allows incremental revisions of files to be backed up to and restored from a secondary storage device, while Storage Spaces allows users to combine different sized hard disks into virtual drives and specify mirroring, parity, or no redundancy on a folder-by-folder basis. For easier management of files and folders, Windows 8 introduces the ability to move selected files or folders via drag and drop from a parent folder into a subfolder listed within the breadcrumb hierarchy of the address bar in File Explorer.

Task Manager has been redesigned, including a new processes tab with the option to display fewer or more details of running applications and background processes, a heat map using different colors indicating the level of resource usage, network and disk counters, grouping by process type (e.g. applications, background processes and Windows processes), friendly names for processes and a new option which allows users to search the web to find information about obscure processes. Additionally, the Blue Screen of Death has been updated with a simpler and modern design with less technical information displayed.

Safety and Security

New security features in Windows 8 include two new authentication methods tailored towards touchscreens (PINs and picture passwords), the addition of antivirus capabilities to Windows Defender (bringing it in parity with Microsoft Security Essentials). SmartScreen filtering integrated into Windows, Family Safety offers Parental controls, which allows parents to monitor and manage their children's activities on a device with activity reports and safety controls. Windows 8 also provides integrated system recovery through the new "Refresh" and "Reset" functions, including system recovery from USB drive. Windows 8's first security patches would be released on November 13, 2012; it would contain three fixes deemed "critical" by the company.

Windows 8 supports a feature of the UEFI specification known as "Secure boot", which uses a public-key infrastructure to verify the integrity of the operating system and prevent unauthorized programs such as bootkits from infecting the device's boot process. Some pre-built devices may be described as "certified" by Microsoft; these must have secure boot enabled by default, and provide ways for users to disable or re-configure the feature. ARM-based Windows RT devices must have secure boot permanently enabled.

Online Services and Functionality

Windows 8 provides heavier integration with online services from Microsoft and others. A user can now log into Windows with a Microsoft account, which can be used to access services and synchronize applications and settings between devices. Windows 8 also ships with a client app for

Microsoft's SkyDrive cloud storage service, which also allows apps to save files directly to SkyDrive. A SkyDrive client for the desktop and File Explorer is not included in Windows 8, and must be downloaded separately. Bundled multimedia apps are provided under the Xbox brand, including Xbox Music, Xbox Video, and the Xbox SmartGlass companion for use with an Xbox 360 console. Games can integrate into an Xbox Live hub app, which also allows users to view their profile and gamerscore. Other bundled apps provide the ability to link Flickr and Facebook. Due to Facebook Connect service changes, Facebook support is disabled in all bundled apps effective June 8, 2015.

Internet Explorer 10 is included as both a desktop program and a touch-optimized app, and includes increased support for HTML5, CSS3, and hardware acceleration. The Internet Explorer app does not support plugins or ActiveX components, but includes a version of Adobe Flash Player that is optimized for touch and low power usage. Initially, Adobe Flash would only work on sites included on a "Compatibility View" whitelist; however, after feedback from users and additional compatibility tests, an update in March 2013 changed this behavior to use a smaller blacklist of sites with known compatibility issues instead, allowing Flash to be used on most sites by default. The desktop version does not contain these limitations.

Windows 8 also incorporates improved support for mobile broadband; the operating system can now detect the insertion of a SIM card and automatically configure connection settings (including APNs and carrier branding), and reduce its Internet usage in order to conserve bandwidth on metered networks. Windows 8 also adds an integrated airplane mode setting to globally disable all wireless connectivity as well. Carriers can also offer account management systems through Windows Store apps, which can be automatically installed as a part of the connection process and offer usage statistics on their respective tile.

Windows Store Apps

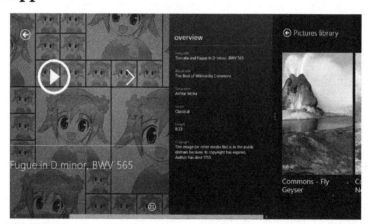

Snap feature: Xbox Music, alongside Photos snapped into a sidebar to the right side of the screen.

Windows 8 introduces a new style of application, Windows Store apps. According to Microsoft developer Jensen Harris, these apps are to be optimized for touchscreen environments and are more specialized than current desktop applications. Apps can run either in a full-screen mode or be snapped to the side of a screen. Apps can provide toast notifications on screen or animate their tiles on the Start screen with dynamic content. Apps can use "contracts"; a collection of hooks to provide common functionality that can integrate with other apps, including search and sharing. Apps can also provide integration with other services; for example, the People app can connect to a variety of different social networks and services (such as Facebook, Skype, and People service), while the Photos app can aggregate photos from services such as Facebook and Flickr.

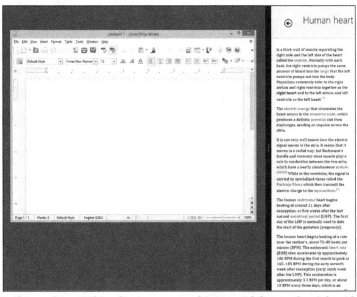

Snap feature: Desktop, along Wikipedia App snapped into a sidebar to the right side of the screen.
In Windows 8, desktop and everything on it is treated as one Metro-style app.

Windows Store apps run within a new set of APIs known as Windows Runtime, which supports programming languages such as C, C++, Visual Basic .NET, C#, along with HTML5 and JavaScript. If written in some "high-level" languages, apps written for Windows Runtime can be compatible with both Intel and ARM versions of Windows, otherwise they are not binary code compatible. Components may be compiled as Windows Runtime Components, permitting consumption by all compatible languages. To ensure stability and security, apps run within a sandboxed environment, and require permissions to access certain functionality, such as accessing the Internet or a camera.

Retail versions of Windows 8 are only able to install these apps through Windows Store — a namesake distribution platform that offers both apps, and listings for desktop programs certified for comparability with Windows 8. A method to sideload apps from outside Windows Store is available to devices running Windows 8 Enterprise and joined to a domain; Windows 8 Pro and Windows RT devices that are not part of a domain can also sideload apps, but only after special product keys are obtained through volume licensing.

The term "Immersive app" had been used internally by Microsoft developers to refer to the apps prior to the first official presentation of Windows 8, after which they were referred to as "Metro-style apps" in reference to the Metro design language. The term was phased out in August 2012; a Microsoft spokesperson denied rumors that the change was related to a potential trademark issue, and stated that "Metro" was only a codename that would be replaced prior to Windows 8's release. Following these reports, the terms "Modern UI-style apps", "Windows 8-style apps" and "Windows Store apps" began to be used by various Microsoft documents and material to refer to the new apps. In an interview on September 12, 2012, Soma Somasegar (vice president of Microsoft's development software division) confirmed that "Windows Store apps" would be the official term for the apps. An MSDN page explaining the Metro design language uses the term "Modern design" to refer to the language as a whole.

Web Browsers

Exceptions to the restrictions faced by Windows Store apps are given to web browsers. The user's default browser can distribute a Metro-style web browser in the same package as the desktop version, which has access to functionality unavailable to other apps, such as being able to permanently run in the background, use multiple background processes, and use Windows API code instead of WinRT (allowing for code to be re-used with the desktop version, while still taking advantage of features available to Windows Store apps, such as charms). Microsoft advertises this exception privilege "New experience enabled" (formerly "Metro-style enabled").

The developers of both Chrome and Firefox committed to developing Metro-style versions of their browsers; while Chrome's "Windows 8 mode" (discontinued on Chrome version 49) uses a full-screen version of the existing desktop interface, Firefox's version (which was first made available on the "Aurora" release channel in September 2013) uses a touch-optimized interface inspired by the Android version of Firefox. In October 2013, Chrome's app was changed to mimic the desktop environment used by Chrome OS. Development of the Firefox app for Windows 8 has since been cancelled, citing a lack of user adoption for the beta versions.

Interface and Desktop

Windows 8 introduces significant changes to the operating system's user interface, many of which are aimed at improving its experience on tablet computers and other touchscreen devices. The new user interface is based on Microsoft's Metro design language and uses a Start screen similar to that of Windows Phone 7 as the primary means of launching applications. The Start screen displays a customizable array of tiles linking to various apps and desktop programs, some of which can display constantly updated information and content through "live tiles". As a form of multi-tasking, apps can be snapped to the side of a screen. Alongside the traditional Control Panel, a new simplified and touch-optimized settings app known as "PC Settings" is used for basic configuration and user settings. It does not include many of the advanced options still accessible from the normal Control Panel.

A vertical toolbar known as the charms (accessed by swiping from the right edge of a touchscreen, swiping from the right edge of a trackpad, or pointing the cursor at hotspots in the right corners of a screen) provides access to system and app-related functions, such as search, sharing, device management, settings, and a Start button. The traditional desktop environment for running desktop applications is accessed via a tile on the Start screen. The Start button on the taskbar from previous versions of Windows has been converted into a hotspot in the lower-left corner of the screen, which displays a large tooltip displaying a thumbnail of the Start screen. However, Windows 8.1 added the start button back to the taskbar after many complaints. Swiping from the left edge of a touchscreen or clicking in the top-left corner of the screen allows one to switch between apps and Desktop. Pointing the cursor in the top-left corner of the screen and moving down reveals a thumbnail list of active apps. Aside from the removal of the Start button and the replacement of the Aero Glass theme with a flatter and solid-colored design, the desktop interface on Windows 8 is similar to that of Windows 7.

Removed Features

Several notable features have been removed in Windows 8; support for playing DVD-Video was removed from Windows Media Player due to the cost of licensing the necessary decoders (especially for devices which do not include optical disc drives at all) and the prevalence of online streaming services. For the same reasons, Windows Media Center is not included by default on Windows 8, but Windows Media Center and DVD playback support can be purchased in the "Pro Pack" (which upgrades the system to Windows 8 Pro) or "Media Center Pack" add-on for Windows 8 Pro. As with prior versions, third-party DVD player software can still be used to enable DVD playback.

Backup and Restore, the backup component of Windows, is deprecated. It still ships with Windows 8 and continues to work on preset schedules, but is pushed to the background and can only be accessed through a Control Panel applet called "Windows 7 File Recovery". Shadow Copy, a component of Windows Explorer that once saved previous versions of changed files, no longer protects local files and folders. It can only access previous versions of shared files stored on a Windows Server computer. The subsystem on which these components worked, however, is still available for other software to use.

Hardware Requirements

PCs

The minimum system requirements for Windows 8 are slightly higher than those of Windows 7. The CPU must support the Physical Address Extension (PAE), NX bit, and SSE2. Windows Store apps require a screen resolution of 1024×768 or higher to run; a resolution of 1366×768 or higher is required to use the snap functionality. To receive certification, Microsoft requires candidate x86 systems to resume from standby in 2 seconds or less.

Minimum hardware requirements for Windows 8		
Component	Minimum	Recommended
Processor	1 GHz clock rate IA-32 or x64 architecture Support for PAE, NX and SSE2	x64 architecture Second Level Address Translation (SLAT) support for Hyper-V
Memory (RAM)	IA-32 edition: 1 GB x64 edition: 2 GB	4 GB
Graphics Card	DirectX 9 graphics device WDDM 1.0 or higher driver	DirectX 10 graphics device
Display screen	N/A	1024×768 pixels
Input device	Keyboard and mouse	multi-touch display screen
Hard disk space	IA-32 edition: 16 GB x64 edition: 20 GB	N/A
Other	N/A	UEFI v2.3.1 Errata B with Microsoft Windows Certification Authority in its database Trusted Platform Module (TPM) Internet connectivity

Microsoft's Connected Standby specification, which hardware vendors may optionally comply with, sets new power consumption requirements that extend above the above minimum specifications. Included in this standard are a number of security-specific requirements designed to improve physical security, notably against Cold Boot Attacks.

32-bit SKUs of Windows 8 only support a maximum of 4 GB of RAM. 64-bit SKUs, however support more: Windows 8 x64 supports 128 GB while Windows 8 Pro and Enterprise x64 support 512 GB.

In January 2016, Microsoft announced that it would no longer support Windows 8.1 or 7 on devices using Intel's Skylake CPU family effective July 17, 2018, and that all future CPU microarchitectures, as well as Skylake systems after this date, would only be supported on Windows 10. After the deadline, only critical security updates were to be released for users on these platforms. After this new policy faced criticism from users and enterprise customers, Microsoft partially retracted the change and stated that both operating systems would remain supported on Skylake hardware through the end of their Extended support lifecycle. Windows 8.1 remains officially unsupported on all newer CPU families, and neither AMD or Intel will provide official chipset drivers for Windows operating systems other than Windows 10. However, on August 2016, Microsoft again extended the Skylake support policy until the end of support for Windows 7 and 8.1 (2020 and 2023, respectively).

Tablets and Convertibles

Microsoft released minimum hardware requirements for tablet and laplet devices to be "certified" for Windows 8 and defined a convertible form factor as a standalone device that combines the PC, display, and rechargeable power source with a mechanically attached keyboard and pointing device in a single chassis. A convertible can be transformed into a tablet where the attached input devices are hidden or removed leaving the display as the only input mechanism. On March 12, 2013, Microsoft amended its certification requirements to only require that screens on tablets have a minimum resolution of 1024×768 (down from the previous 1366×768). The amended requirement is intended to allow "greater design flexibility" for future products.

Hardware certification requirements for Windows tablets	
Graphics card	DirectX 10 graphics device with WDDM 1.2 or higher driver
Storage	10 GB free space, after the out-of-box experience completes
Standard buttons	Power, Rotation lock, Windows key, Volume up, Volume down
Screen	Touch screen supporting a minimum of 5-point digitizers and resolution of at least 1024×768. The physical dimensions of the display panel must match the aspect ratio of the native resolution. The native resolution of the panel can be greater than 1024 (horizontally) and 768 (vertically). Minimum native color depth is 32-bits. If the display is under 1366×768, disclaimers must be included in documentation to notify users that the Snap function is not available.
Camera	Minimum 720p
Accelerometer	3 axes with data rates at or above 50 Hz
USB 2.0	At least one controller and exposed port.
Connect	Wi-Fi and Bluetooth 4.0 + LE (low energy)
Other	Speaker, microphone, magnetometer and gyroscope. If a mobile broadband device is integrated into a tablet or convertible system, then an assisted GPS radio is required. Devices supporting near field communication need to have visual marks to help users locate and use the proximity technology. The new button combination for Ctrl + Alt + Del is Windows Key + Power.

Updated certification requirements were implemented to coincide with Windows 8.1. As of 2014, all certified devices with integrated displays must contain a 720p webcam and higher quality speakers and microphones, while all certified devices that support Wi-Fi must support Bluetooth as well. As of 2015, all certified devices must contain Trusted Platform Module 2.0 chips.

Editions

Windows 8 is available in three different editions, of which the lowest version, branded simply as Windows 8, and Windows 8 Pro, were sold at retail in most countries, and as pre-loaded software on new computers. Each edition of Windows 8 includes all of the capabilities and features of the edition below it, and add additional features oriented towards their market segments. For example, Pro added BitLocker, Hyper-V, the ability to join a domain, and the ability to install Windows Media Center as a paid add-on. Users of Windows 8 can purchase a "Pro Pack" license that upgrades their system to Windows 8 Pro through Add features to Windows. This license also includes Windows Media Center. Windows 8 Enterprise contains additional features aimed towards business environments, and is only available through volume licensing. A port of Windows 8 for ARM architecture, Windows RT, is marketed as an edition of Windows 8, but was only included as pre-loaded software on devices specifically developed for it.

Windows 8 was distributed as a retail box product on DVD, and through a digital download that could be converted into DVD or USB install media. As part of a launch promotion, Microsoft offered Windows 8 Pro upgrades at a discounted price of US$39.99 online, or $69.99 for retail box from its launch until January 31, 2013; afterward the Windows 8 price has been $119.99 and the Pro price $199.99. Those who purchased new PCs pre-loaded with Windows 7 Home Basic, Home Premium, Professional, or Ultimate between June 2, 2012 and January 31, 2013 could digitally purchase a Windows 8 Pro upgrade for US$14.99. Several PC manufacturers offered rebates and refunds on Windows 8 upgrades obtained through the promotion on select models, such as Hewlett-Packard (in the U.S. and Canada on select models), and Acer (in Europe on selected Ultrabook models). During these promotions, the Windows Media Center add-on for Windows 8 Pro was also offered for free.

Unlike previous versions of Windows, Windows 8 was distributed at retail in "Upgrade" licenses only, which require an existing version of Windows to install. The "full version software" SKU, which was more expensive but could be installed on computers without an eligible OS or none at all, was discontinued. In lieu of full version, a specialized "System Builder" SKU was introduced. The "System Builder" SKU replaced the original equipment manufacturer (OEM) SKU, which was only allowed to be used on PCs meant for resale but added a "Personal Use License" exemption that officially allowed its purchase and personal use by users on homebuilt computers.

Retail distribution of Windows 8 has since been discontinued in favor of Windows 8.1. Unlike 8, 8.1 is available as "full version software" at both retail and online for download that does not require a previous version of Windows in order to be installed. Pricing for these new copies remain identical. With the retail release returning to full version software for Windows 8.1, the "Personal Use License" exemption was removed from the OEM SKU, meaning that end users building their own PCs for personal use must use the full retail version in order to satisfy the Windows 8.1 licensing requirements. *Windows 8.1 with Bing* is a special OEM-specific SKU of *Windows 8.1* subsidized by Microsoft's Bing search engine.

Software Compatibility

The three desktop editions of Windows 8 support 32-bit and 64-bit architectures; retail copies of Windows 8 include install DVDs for both architectures, while the online installer automatically installs the version corresponding with the architecture of the system's existing Windows installation. The 32-bit version runs on CPUs compatible with x86 architecture 3rd generation (known as IA-32) or newer, and can run 32-bit and 16-bit applications, although 16-bit support must be enabled first. (16-bit applications are developed for CPUs compatible with x86 2nd generation, first conceived in 1978. Microsoft started moving away from this architecture after Windows 95.)

The 64-bit version runs on CPUs compatible with x86 8th generation (known as x86-64, or x64) or newer, and can run 32-bit and 64-bit programs. 32-bit programs and operating system are restricted to supporting only 4 gigabytes of memory while 64-bit systems can theoretically support 2048 gigabytes of memory. 64-bit operating systems require a different set of device drivers than those of 32-bit operating systems.

Windows RT, the only edition of Windows 8 for systems with ARM processors, only supports applications included with the system (such as a special version of Office 2013), supplied through Windows Update, or Windows Store apps, to ensure that the system only runs applications that are optimized for the architecture. Windows RT does not support running IA-32 or x64 applications. Windows Store apps can either support both the x86 and ARM architectures, or compiled to support a specific architecture.

Windows 8.1

A feature update to Windows 8 known as Windows 8.1 was officially announced by Microsoft on May 14, 2013. Following a presentation devoted to it at Build 2013, a public beta version of the upgrade was released on June 26, 2013. Windows 8.1 was released to OEM hardware partners on August 27, 2013, and released publicly as a free download through Windows Store on October 17, 2013. Volume license customers and subscribers to MSDN Plus and TechNet Plus were initially unable to obtain the RTM version upon its release; a spokesperson said the policy was changed to allow Microsoft to work with OEMs "to ensure a quality experience at general availability." However, after criticism, Microsoft reversed its decision and released the RTM build on MSDN and TechNet on September 9, 2013.

Windows 8.1 addressed a number of criticisms faced by Windows 8 upon its release, with additional customization options for the Start screen, the restoration of a visible Start button on the desktop, the ability to snap up to four apps on a single display, and the ability to boot to the desktop instead of the Start screen. Windows 8's stock apps were also updated, a new Bing-based unified search system was added, SkyDrive was given deeper integration with the operating system, and a number of new stock apps, along with a tutorial, were added. Windows 8.1 also added support for 3D printing, Miracast media streaming, NFC printing, and Wi-Fi Direct.

Microsoft marketed Windows 8.1 as an "update" rather than as a "service pack", as it had done with such revisions on previous versions of Windows. Nonetheless, Microsoft's support lifecycle policy treats Windows 8.1 similarly to previous Windows service packs: upgrading to 8.1 has been required to maintain access to mainstream support and updates after January 12, 2016. Although Windows 8 RTM is unsupported, Microsoft released an emergency security patch in May 2017 for Windows 8 RTM, as well as other unsupported versions of Windows (including Windows XP and Windows Server 2003), to address a vulnerability that was being leveraged by the WannaCry ransomware attack. Updates to apps published on Windows Store after July 1, 2019 will not be available to Windows 8 RTM users.

Retail and OEM installations of Windows 8, Windows 8 *Pro*, and Windows RT can be upgraded through Windows Store free of charge. However, volume license customers, TechNet or MSDN subscribers and users of Windows 8 Enterprise must acquire a standalone installation media for 8.1 and install through the traditional Windows setup process, either as an in-place upgrade or clean install. This requires an 8.1-specific product key.

Windows 10

Windows 10 is a Microsoft operating system for personal computers, tablets, embedded devices and internet of things devices.

Microsoft released Windows 10 in July 2015 as a follow-up to Windows 8. The company has said it will update Windows 10 in perpetuity rather than release a new, full-fledged operating system as a successor.

Windows 10 features built-in capabilities that allow corporate IT departments to use mobile device management (MDM) software to secure and control devices running the operating system. In addition, organizations can use traditional desktop management software such as Microsoft System Center Configuration Manager.

Windows 10 Mobile is a version of the operating system Microsoft designed specifically for smartphones.

Windows 10 Features

The familiar Start Menu, which Microsoft replaced with Live Tiles in Windows 8, returned in Windows 10. Users can still access Live Tiles and the touch-centric Metro interface from a panel on the right side of the Start Menu, however.

Windows 10 tablet start screen.

Microsoft Windows 10 Continuum allows users to toggle between touchscreen and keyboard interfaces on devices that offer both. Continuum automatically detects the presence of a keyboard and orients the interface to match.

Windows 10's integrated search feature allows users to search all local locations, as well as the web simultaneously.

Microsoft Edge debuted with Windows 10 and replaces Internet Explorer as the default web browser. Edge includes tools such as Web Notes, which allows users to mark up web sites, and Reading View, which allows users to view certain websites without the clutter of ads. The browser integrates directly with Cortana, Microsoft's digital assistant, which is also embedded within Windows 10.

Cortana integrates directly with the Bing search engine and supports both text and voice input. It tracks and analyzes location services, communication history, email and text messages, speech and input personalization, services and applications, and browsing and search history in an effort to customize the OS experience to best suit users' needs. IT professionals can disable Cortana and some of its features with Group Policy settings.

Windows 10 Security

Microsoft Windows 10 integrated support for multifactor authentication technologies, such as smartcards and tokens. In addition, Windows Hello brought biometric authentication to Windows 10, allowing users to log in with a fingerprint scan, iris scan or facial recognition technology.

The operating system also includes virtualization-based security tools such as Isolated User Mode, Windows Defender Device Guard and Windows Defender Credential Guard. These Windows 10 features keep data, processes and user credentials isolated in an attempt to limit the damage from any attacks.

Windows 10 also expanded support for BitLocker encryption to protect data in motion between users' devices, storage hardware, emails and cloud services.

Windows 10 System Requirements

The minimum Windows 10 hardware requirements for a PC or 2-in-1 device are:

- Processor: 1 gigahertz (GHz) or faster processor or system-on-a-chip (SoC).
- RAM: 1 gigabyte (GB) for 32-bit or 2 GB for 64-bit.
- Hard disk space: 16 GB for 32-bit OS 20 GB for 64-bit OS.
- Graphics card: DirectX 9 or later with Windows Display Driver Model 1.0.
- Display: 800x600.

The minimum Windows 10 Mobile hardware requirements for a smartphone are 1 GB RAM, 8 GB flash storage, a Trusted Platform Module, Unified Extensible Firmware Interface, 32 bits of color per pixel, and 720p screen resolution. Smartphones also require a Snapdragon SoC from Qualcomm Technologies.

Windows 10 Updates

There are four licensing structures, called branches, that dictate how and when Windows 10 devices receive updates.

The Insider Preview Branch is limited to members of the Microsoft Insiders Program. With this branch, IT professionals get access to the latest Windows 10 updates before they are made available to the general public, which gives them more time to test out the newest features and evaluate compatibility.

Current Branch, which is designed for consumer devices, delivers updates automatically to any device running Windows 10 that is connected to the internet and has Windows Update on.

Current Branch for Business is an enterprise-focused option that is available for the Professional, Enterprise and Education editions of Windows 10. It gives IT four months to preview the latest update and eight months to apply it. IT must apply the updates within the eight-month timeframe or it loses Microsoft support.

The Long Term Servicing Branch (LTSB), which is geared toward systems that cannot afford downtime for regular updates such as emergency room devices and automatic teller machines, gives IT the most control. With the LTSB, IT receives full OS updates every two to three years. IT can delay the update for up to 10 years. If IT does not update within 10 years it loses Microsoft support.

No matter which update branch an organization uses, security and stability updates, which patch security holes, protect against threats and make sure the OS continues to run smoothly, still come on a monthly basis.

Windows 10 Privacy Concerns

Microsoft collects a range of data from Windows 10 users, including information on security settings and crashes, as well as contact lists, passwords, user names, IP addresses and website visits.

IT and users can put limits on the data Microsoft collects. There are three settings that determine how much telemetry data Windows 10 sends back to Microsoft: Basic, Full and Enhanced. Enhanced is the default and sends the most data back, but IT or users can easily select one of the other two options. Windows 10 Enterprise and Education users can turn telemetry data off too.

Microsoft does not actually read the contents of users' communications, however, and anonymizes all the data. The company's privacy statement says the purpose of the data collection is to improve performance and provide a positive user experience.

Another way IT professionals and end users can limit data collection is by disabling data sharing through privacy settings. IT can also use Group Policy settings to tighten up what information leaves devices.

UNIX

Unix is a family of multitasking, multiuser computer operating systems that derive from the original AT&T Unix, development starting in the 1970s at the Bell Labs research center by Ken Thompson, Dennis Ritchie, and others.

Initially intended for use inside the Bell System, AT&T licensed Unix to outside parties in the late 1970s, leading to a variety of both academic and commercial Unix variants from vendors including University of California, Berkeley (BSD), Microsoft (Xenix), IBM (AIX), and Sun Microsystems (Solaris). In the early 1990s, AT&T sold its rights in Unix to Novell, which then sold its Unix business to the Santa Cruz Operation (SCO) in 1995. The UNIX trademark passed to The Open Group, a neutral industry consortium, which allows the use of the mark for certified operating systems that comply with the Single UNIX Specification (SUS). As of 2014, the Unix version with the largest installed base is Apple's macOS.

Unix systems are characterized by a modular design that is sometimes called the "Unix philosophy". This concept entails that the operating system provides a set of simple tools that each performs a limited, well-defined function, with a unified filesystem (the Unix filesystem) as the main means of communication, and a shell scripting and command language (the Unix shell) to combine the tools to perform complex workflows. Unix distinguishes itself from its predecessors as the first portable operating system: almost the entire operating system is written in the C programming language, thus allowing Unix to reach numerous platforms.

Version 7 Unix, the Research Unix ancestor of all modern Unix systems.

Unix was originally meant to be a convenient platform for programmers developing software to be run on it and on other systems, rather than for non-programmers. The system grew larger as the operating system started spreading in academic circles, as users added their own tools to the system and shared them with colleagues.

At first, Unix was not designed to be portable or multi-tasking. Later, Unix gradually gained portability, multi-tasking and multi-user capabilities in a time-sharing configuration. Unix systems are characterized by various concepts: the use of plain text for storing data; a hierarchical file system; treating devices and certain types of inter-process communication (IPC) as files; and the use of a large number of software tools, small programs that can be strung together through a command-line interpreter using pipes, as opposed to using a single monolithic program that includes all of the same functionality. These concepts are collectively known as the "Unix philosophy". Brian Kernighan and Rob Pike summarize this in The Unix Programming Environment as "the idea that the power of a system comes more from the relationships among programs than from the programs themselves".

In an era when a standard computer consisted of a hard disk for storage and a data terminal for input and output (I/O), the Unix file model worked quite well, as I/O was generally linear. In the 1980s, non-blocking I/O and the set of inter-process communication mechanisms were augmented with Unix domain sockets, shared memory, message queues, and semaphores, as well as network sockets to support communication with other hosts. As graphical user interfaces developed, the file model proved inadequate to the task of handling asynchronous events such as those generated by a mouse.

By the early 1980s, users began seeing Unix as a potential universal operating system, suitable for computers of all sizes. The Unix environment and the client–server program model were essential elements in the development of the Internet and the reshaping of computing as centered in networks rather than in individual computers.

Both Unix and the C programming language were developed by AT&T and distributed to government and academic institutions, which led to both being ported to a wider variety of machine families than any other operating system.

Under Unix, the operating system consists of many libraries and utilities along with the master control program, the kernel. The kernel provides services to start and stop programs, handles the file system and other common "low-level" tasks that most programs share, and schedules access to avoid conflicts when programs try to access the same resource or device simultaneously. To mediate such access, the kernel has special rights, reflected in the division between user space and kernel space — although in microkernel implementations, like MINIX or Redox, functions such as network protocols may also run in user space.

Standards

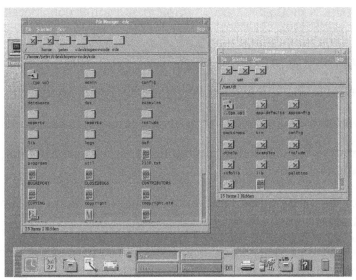

The Common Desktop Environment (CDE), part of the COSE initiative.

In the late 1980s, an open operating system standardization effort now known as POSIX provided a common baseline for all operating systems; IEEE based POSIX around the common structure of the major competing variants of the Unix system, publishing the first POSIX standard in 1988. In the early 1990s, a separate but very similar effort was started by an industry consortium, the Common Open Software Environment (COSE) initiative, which eventually became the Single UNIX Specification (SUS) administered by The Open Group. Starting in 1998, the Open Group and IEEE started the Austin Group, to provide a common definition of POSIX and the Single UNIX Specification, which, by 2008, had become the Open Group Base Specification.

In 1999, in an effort towards compatibility, several Unix system vendors agreed on SVR4's Executable and Linkable Format (ELF) as the standard for binary and object code files. The common format allows substantial binary compatibility among different Unix systems operating on the same CPU architecture.

The Filesystem Hierarchy Standard was created to provide a reference directory layout for Unix-like operating systems, and has mainly been used in Linux.

Components

The Unix system is composed of several components that were originally packaged together. By including the development environment, libraries, documents and the portable, modifiable source code for all of these components, in addition to the kernel of an operating system, Unix was a self-contained software system. This was one of the key reasons it emerged as an important teaching and learning tool and has had such a broad influence.

The inclusion of these components did not make the system large – the original V7 UNIX distribution, consisting of copies of all of the compiled binaries plus all of the source code and documentation occupied less than 10 MB and arrived on a single nine-track magnetic tape. The printed documentation, typeset from the online sources, was contained in two volumes.

The names and filesystem locations of the Unix components have changed substantially across the history of the system. Nonetheless, the V7 implementation is considered by many to have the canonical early structure:

- Kernel – source code in /usr/sys, composed of several sub-components:

    ◦ conf – configuration and machine-dependent parts, including boot code.

    ◦ dev – device drivers for control of hardware (and some pseudo-hardware).

    ◦ sys – operating system "kernel", handling memory management, process scheduling, system calls, etc.

    ◦ h – header files, defining key structures within the system and important system-specific invariables.

- Development environment – early versions of Unix contained a development environment sufficient to recreate the entire system from source code:

    ◦ cc – C language compiler (first appeared in V3 Unix).

    ◦ as – machine-language assembler for the machine.

    ◦ ld – linker, for combining object files.

- lib – object-code libraries (installed in /lib or /usr/lib). libc, the system library with C run-time support, was the primary library, but there have always been additional libraries for things such as mathematical functions (libm) or database access. V7 Unix introduced the first version of the modern "Standard I/O" library stdio as part of the system library. Later implementations increased the number of libraries significantly.

- make – build manager (introduced in PWB/UNIX), for effectively automating the build process.

- include – header files for software development, defining standard interfaces and system invariants.

- Other languages – V7 Unix contained a Fortran-77 compiler, a programmable arbitrary-precision calculator (bc, dc), and the awk scripting language; later versions and implementations contain many other language compilers and toolsets. Early BSD releases included Pascal tools, and many modern Unix systems also include the GNU Compiler Collection as well as or instead of a proprietary compiler system.

- Other tools – including an object-code archive manager (ar), symbol-table lister (nm), compiler-development tools (e.g. lex & yacc), and debugging tools.

- Commands – Unix makes little distinction between commands (user-level programs) for system operation and maintenance (e.g. cron), commands of general utility (e.g. grep), and more general-purpose applications such as the text formatting and typesetting package. Nonetheless, some major categories are:

  - sh – the "shell" programmable command-line interpreter, the primary user interface on Unix before window systems appeared, and even afterward (within a "command window").

  - Utilities – the core toolkit of the Unix command set, including cp, ls, grep, find and many others. Subcategories include:

    - System utilities – administrative tools such as mkfs, fsck, and many others.

    - User utilities – environment management tools such as passwd, kill, and others.

  - Document formatting – Unix systems were used from the outset for document preparation and typesetting systems, and included many related programs such as nroff, troff, tbl, eqn, refer, and pic. Some modern Unix systems also include packages such as TeX and Ghostscript.

  - Graphics – the plot subsystem provided facilities for producing simple vector plots in a device-independent format, with device-specific interpreters to display such files. Modern Unix systems also generally include X11 as a standard windowing system and GUI, and many support OpenGL.

  - Communications – early Unix systems contained no inter-system communication, but did include the inter-user communication programs mail and write. V7 introduced the early inter-system communication system UUCP, and systems beginning with BSD release 4.1c included TCP/IP utilities.

- Documentation – Unix was the first operating system to include all of its documentation online in machine-readable form. The documentation included:

  ◦ man – manual pages for each command, library component, system call, header file, etc.

  ◦ doc – longer documents detailing major subsystems, such as the C language and troff.

Impact

Ken Thompson and Dennis Ritchie,
principal developers of Research Unix.

Photo from USENIX 1984, including
Dennis Ritchie (center).

The Unix system had significant impact on other operating systems. It achieved its reputation by its interactivity, by providing the software at a nominal fee for educational use, by running on inexpensive hardware, and by being easy to adapt and move to different machines. Unix was originally written in assembly language, but was soon rewritten in C, a high-level programming language. Although this followed the lead of Multics and Burroughs, it was Unix that popularized the idea.

Unix had a drastically simplified file model compared to many contemporary operating systems: treating all kinds of files as simple byte arrays. The file system hierarchy contained machine services and devices (such as printers, terminals, or disk drives), providing a uniform interface, but at the expense of occasionally requiring additional mechanisms such as ioctl and mode flags to access features of the hardware that did not fit the simple "stream of bytes" model. The Plan 9 operating system pushed this model even further and eliminated the need for additional mechanisms.

Unix also popularized the hierarchical file system with arbitrarily nested subdirectories, originally introduced by Multics. Other common operating systems of the era had ways to divide a storage device into multiple directories or sections, but they had a fixed number of levels, often only one level. Several major proprietary operating systems eventually added recursive subdirectory capabilities also patterned after Multics. DEC's RSX-11M's "group, user" hierarchy evolved into VMS directories, CP/M's volumes evolved into MS-DOS 2.0+ subdirectories, and HP's MPE group.account hierarchy and IBM's SSP and OS/400 library systems were folded into broader POSIX file systems.

Making the command interpreter an ordinary user-level program, with additional commands provided as separate programs, was another Multics innovation popularized by Unix. The Unix shell used the same language for interactive commands as for scripting (shell scripts – there was no separate job control language like IBM's JCL). Since the shell and OS commands were "just another program", the user could choose (or even write) their own shell. New commands could be added without changing the shell itself. Unix's innovative command-line syntax for creating modular chains of pro-ducer-consumer processes (pipelines) made a powerful programming paradigm (coroutines) widely available. Many later command-line interpreters have been inspired by the Unix shell.

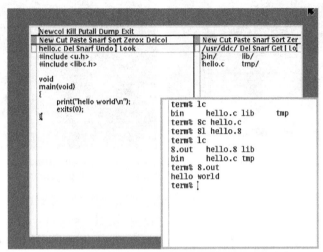

Plan 9 from Bell Labs extends Unix design principles
and was developed as a successor to Unix.

A fundamental simplifying assumption of Unix was its focus on newline-delimited text for nearly all file formats. There were no "binary" editors in the original version of Unix – the entire system was configured using textual shell command scripts. The common denominator in the I/O system was the byte – unlike "record-based" file systems. The focus on text for representing nearly everything made Unix pipes especially useful, and encouraged the development of simple, general tools that could be easily combined to perform more complicated *ad hoc* tasks. The focus on text and bytes made the system far more scalable and portable than other systems. Over time, text-based applications have also proven popular in application areas, such as printing languages (PostScript, ODF), and at the application layer of the Internet protocols, e.g., FTP, SMTP, HTTP, SOAP, and SIP.

Unix popularized a syntax for regular expressions that found widespread use. The Unix programming interface became the basis for a widely implemented operating system interface standard. The C programming language soon spread beyond Unix, and is now ubiquitous in systems and applications programming.

Early Unix developers were important in bringing the concepts of modularity and reusability into software engineering practice, spawning a "software tools" movement. Over time, the leading developers of Unix (and programs that ran on it) established a set of cultural norms for developing software, norms which became as important and influential as the technology of Unix itself; this has been termed the Unix philosophy.

The TCP/IP networking protocols were quickly implemented on the Unix versions widely used on relatively inexpensive computers, which contributed to the Internet explosion of worldwide real-time connectivity, and which formed the basis for implementations on many other platforms.

The Unix policy of extensive on-line documentation and (for many years) ready access to all system source code raised programmer expectations, and contributed to the launch of the free software movement in 1983.

Free Unix and Unix-like Variants

Console screenshots of Debian (left, a popular Linux distribution) and
FreeBSD (right, a popular Unix-like operating system).

In 1983, Richard Stallman announced the GNU (short for "GNU's Not Unix") project, an ambitious effort to create a free software Unix-like system; "free" in the sense that everyone who received a copy would be free to use, study, modify, and redistribute it. The GNU project's own kernel development project, GNU Hurd, had not yet produced a working kernel, but in 1991 Linus Torvalds released the Linux kernel as free software under the GNU General Public License. In addition to their use in the Linux operating system, many GNU packages – such as the GNU Compiler Collection (and the rest of the GNU toolchain), the GNU C library and the GNU core utilities – have gone on to play central roles in other free Unix systems as well.

Linux distributions, consisting of the Linux kernel and large collections of compatible software have become popular both with individual users and in business. Popular distributions include Red Hat Enterprise Linux, Fedora, SUSE Linux Enterprise, openSUSE, Debian GNU/Linux, Ubuntu, Linux Mint, Mandriva Linux, Slackware Linux, Arch Linux and Gentoo.

A free derivative of BSD Unix, 386BSD, was released in 1992 and led to the NetBSD and FreeBSD projects. With the 1994 settlement of a lawsuit brought against the University of California and Berkeley Software Design Inc. (USL v. BSDi) by Unix Systems Laboratories, it was clarified that Berkeley had the right to distribute BSD Unix for free, if it so desired. Since then, BSD Unix has been developed in several different product branches, including OpenBSD and DragonFly BSD.

Linux and BSD are increasingly filling the market needs traditionally served by proprietary Unix operating systems, as well as expanding into new markets such as the consumer desktop and mobile and embedded devices. Because of the modular design of the Unix model, sharing components is relatively common; consequently, most or all Unix and Unix-like systems include at least some BSD code, and some systems also include GNU utilities in their distributions.

In a 1999 interview, Dennis Ritchie voiced his opinion that Linux and BSD operating systems are a continuation of the basis of the Unix design, and are derivatives of Unix:

"I think the Linux phenomenon is quite delightful, because it draws so strongly on the basis that Unix provided. Linux seems to be the among the healthiest of the direct Unix derivatives, though there are also the various BSD systems as well as the more official offerings from the workstation and mainframe manufacturers."

In the same interview, he states that he views both Unix and Linux as "the continuation of ideas that were started by Ken and me and many others, many years ago."

OpenSolaris was the open-source counterpart to Solaris developed by Sun Microsystems, which included a CDDL-licensed kernel and a primarily GNU userland. However, Oracle discontinued the project upon their acquisition of Sun, which prompted a group of former Sun employees and members of the OpenSolaris community to fork OpenSolaris into the illumos kernel. As of 2014, illumos remains the only active open-source System V derivative.

Arpanet

In May 1975, RFC 681 described the development of *Network Unix* by the Center for Advanced Computation at the University of Illinois. The system was said to "present several interesting capabilities as an ARPANET mini-host". At the time Unix required a license from Bell Laboratories that at $20,000(US) was very expensive for non-university users, while an educational license cost just $150. It was noted that Bell was "open to suggestions" for an ARPANET-wide license.

Specific features found beneficial were the local processing facilities, compilers, editors, a document preparation system, efficient file system and access control, mountable and unmountable volumes, unified treatment of peripherals as special files, integration of the network control program (NCP) within the Unix file system, treatment of network connections as special files that can be accessed through standard Unix I/O calls, closing of all files on program exit, and the decision to be "desirable to minimize the amount of code added to the basic Unix kernel".

Branding

Promotional license plate by Digital Equipment Corporation.

In October 1993, Novell, the company that owned the rights to the Unix System V source at the time, transferred the trademarks of Unix to the X/Open Company (now The Open Group), and in 1995 sold the related business operations to Santa Cruz Operation (SCO). Whether Novell also sold the copyrights to the actual software was the subject of a federal lawsuit in 2006, SCO v. Novell, which Novell won. The case was appealed, but on August 30, 2011, the United States Court of Appeals for the Tenth Circuit affirmed the trial decisions, closing the case. Unix vendor SCO Group Inc. accused Novell of slander of title.

The present owner of the trademark UNIX is The Open Group, an industry standards consortium. Only systems fully compliant with and certified to the Single UNIX Specification qualify as "UNIX" (others are called "Unix-like").

By decree of The Open Group, the term "UNIX" refers more to a class of operating systems than to a specific implementation of an operating system; those operating systems which meet The Open

Group's Single UNIX Specification should be able to bear the UNIX 98 or UNIX 03 trademarks today, after the operating system's vendor pays a substantial certification fee and annual trademark royalties to The Open Group. Systems licensed to use the UNIX trademark include AIX, HP-UX, Inspur K-UX, IRIX, Solaris, Tru64 UNIX (formerly "Digital UNIX", or OSF/1), macOS, and a part of z/OS. Notably, Inspur K-UX is a Linux distribution certified as UNIX 03 compliant.

HP9000 workstation running HP-UX, a certified Unix operating system.

Sometimes a representation like Un*x, *NIX, or *N?X is used to indicate all operating systems similar to Unix. This comes from the use of the asterisk (*) and the question mark characters as wildcard indicators in many utilities. This notation is also used to describe other Unix-like systems that have not met the requirements for UNIX branding from the Open Group.

The Open Group requests that UNIX is always used as an adjective followed by a generic term such as system to help avoid the creation of a genericized trademark.

Unix was the original formatting, but the usage of UNIX remains widespread because it was once typeset in small caps (Unix). According to Dennis Ritchie, when presenting the original Unix paper to the third Operating Systems Symposium of the American Association for Computing Machinery (ACM), "we had a new typesetter and troff had just been invented and we were intoxicated by being able to produce small caps." Many of the operating system's predecessors and contemporaries used all-uppercase lettering, so many people wrote the name in upper case due to force of habit. It is not an acronym.

Trademark names can be registered by different entities in different countries and trademark laws in some countries allow the same trademark name to be controlled by two different entities if each entity uses the trademark in easily distinguishable categories. The result is that Unix has been used as a brand name for various products including book shelves, ink pens, bottled glue, diapers, hair driers and food containers.

Several plural forms of Unix are used casually to refer to multiple brands of Unix and Unix-like systems. Most common is the conventional Unixes, but Unices, treating Unix as a Latin noun of the third declension, is also popular. The pseudo-Anglo-Saxon plural form Unixen is not common, although occasionally seen. Sun Microsystems, developer of the Solaris variant, has asserted that the term Unix is itself plural, referencing its many implementations.

LINUX

Linux is a family of open source Unix-like operating systems based on the Linux kernel, an operating system kernel first released on September 17, 1991 by Linus Torvalds. Linux is typically packaged in a Linux distribution.

Distributions include the Linux kernel and supporting system software and libraries, many of which are provided by the GNU Project. Many Linux distributions use the word "Linux" in their name, but the Free Software Foundation uses the name GNU/Linux to emphasize the importance of GNU software, causing some controversy.

Popular Linux distributions include Debian, Fedora, and Ubuntu. Commercial distributions include Red Hat Enterprise Linux and SUSE Linux Enterprise Server. Desktop Linux distributions include a windowing system such as X11 or Wayland, and a desktop environment such as GNOME or KDE Plasma 5. Distributions intended for servers may omit graphics altogether, or include a solution stack such as LAMP. Because Linux is freely redistributable, anyone may create a distribution for any purpose.

Linux was originally developed for personal computers based on the Intel x86 architecture, but has since been ported to more platforms than any other operating system. Linux is the leading operating system on servers and other big iron systems such as mainframe computers, and the only OS used on TOP500 supercomputers (since November 2017, having gradually eliminated all competitors). It is used by around 2.3 percent of desktop computers. The Chromebook, which runs the Linux kernel-based Chrome OS, dominates the US K–12 education market and represents nearly 20 percent of sub-$300 notebook sales in the US.

Linux also runs on embedded systems, i.e. devices whose operating system is typically built into the firmware and is highly tailored to the system. This includes routers, automation controls, televisions, digital video recorders, video game consoles, and smartwatches. Many smartphones and tablet computers run Android and other Linux derivatives. Because of the dominance of Android on smartphones, Linux has the largest installed base of all general-purpose operating systems.

Linux is one of the most prominent examples of free and open-source software collaboration. The source code may be used, modified and distributed—commercially or non-commercially—by anyone under the terms of its respective licenses, such as the GNU General Public License.

Development

The primary difference between Linux and many other popular contemporary operating systems is that the Linux kernel and other components are free and open-source software. Linux is not the only such operating system, although it is by far the most widely used. Some free and open-source software licenses are based on the principle of copyleft, a kind of reciprocity: any work derived from a copyleft piece of software must also be copyleft itself. The most common free software license, the GNU General Public License (GPL), is a form of copyleft, and is used for the Linux kernel and many of the components from the GNU Project.

Linux-based distributions are intended by developers for interoperability with other operating systems and established computing standards. Linux systems adhere to POSIX, SUS, LSB, ISO, and

ANSI standards where possible, although to date only one Linux distribution has been POSIX.1 certified, Linux-FT.

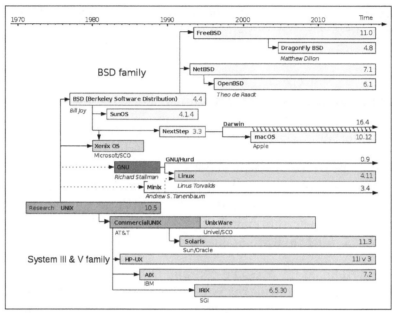

Simplified history of Unix-like operating systems. Linux shares similar architecture and concepts (as part of the POSIX standard) but does not share non-free source code with the original Unix or MINIX.

Free software projects, although developed through collaboration, are often produced independently of each other. The fact that the software licenses explicitly permit redistribution, however, provides a basis for larger scale projects that collect the software produced by stand-alone projects and make it available all at once in the form of a Linux distribution.

Many Linux distributions manage a remote collection of system software and application software packages available for download and installation through a network connection. This allows users to adapt the operating system to their specific needs. Distributions are maintained by individuals, loose-knit teams, volunteer organizations, and commercial entities. A distribution is responsible for the default configuration of the installed Linux kernel, general system security, and more generally integration of the different software packages into a coherent whole. Distributions typically use a package manager such as apt, yum, zypper, pacman or portage to install, remove, and update all of a system's software from one central location.

Community

A distribution is largely driven by its developer and user communities. Some vendors develop and fund their distributions on a volunteer basis, Debian being a well-known example. Others maintain a community version of their commercial distributions, as Red Hat does with Fedora, and SUSE does with openSUSE.

In many cities and regions, local associations known as Linux User Groups (LUGs) seek to promote their preferred distribution and by extension free software. They hold meetings and provide free demonstrations, training, technical support, and operating system installation to new users. Many Internet communities also provide support to Linux users and developers. Most distributions and free software / open-source projects have IRC chatrooms or newsgroups. Online forums are another means for support, with notable examples being LinuxQuestions.org and the various distribution specific support and community forums, such as ones for Ubuntu, Fedora, and Gentoo. Linux distributions host mailing lists; commonly there will be a specific topic such as usage or development for a given list.

There are several technology websites with a Linux focus. Print magazines on Linux often bundle cover disks that carry software or even complete Linux distributions.

Although Linux distributions are generally available without charge, several large corporations sell, support, and contribute to the development of the components of the system and of free software. An analysis of the Linux kernel showed 75 percent of the code from December 2008 to January 2010 was developed by programmers working for corporations, leaving about 18 percent to volunteers and 7% unclassified. Major corporations that provide contributions include Dell, IBM, HP, Oracle, Sun Microsystems (now part of Oracle) and Nokia. A number of corporations, notably Red Hat, Canonical and SUSE, have built a significant business around Linux distributions.

The free software licenses, on which the various software packages of a distribution built on the Linux kernel are based, explicitly accommodate and encourage commercialization; the relationship between a Linux distribution as a whole and individual vendors may be seen as symbiotic. One common business model of commercial suppliers is charging for support, especially for business users. A number of companies also offer a specialized business version of their distribution, which adds proprietary support packages and tools to administer higher numbers of installations or to simplify administrative tasks.

Another business model is to give away the software in order to sell hardware. This used to be the norm in the computer industry, with operating systems such as CP/M, Apple DOS and versions of Mac OS prior to 7.6 freely copyable (but not modifiable). As computer hardware standardized throughout the 1980s, it became more difficult for hardware manufacturers to profit from this tactic, as the OS would run on any manufacturer's computer that shared the same architecture.

Programming on Linux

Linux distributions support dozens of programming languages. The original development tools used for building both Linux applications and operating system programs are found within the GNU toolchain, which includes the GNU Compiler Collection (GCC) and the GNU Build System. Amongst others, GCC provides compilers for Ada, C, C++, Go and Fortran. Many programming languages have a cross-platform reference implementation that supports Linux, for example PHP, Perl, Ruby, Python, Java, Go, Rust and Haskell. First released in 2003, the LLVM project provides an alternative cross-platform open-source compiler for many languages. Proprietary compilers for Linux include the Intel C++ Compiler, Sun Studio, and IBM XL C/C++ Compiler. BASIC in the form of Visual Basic is supported in such forms as Gambas, FreeBASIC, and XBasic, and in terms of terminal programming or QuickBASIC or Turbo BASIC programming in the form of QB64.

A common feature of Unix-like systems, Linux includes traditional specific-purpose programming languages targeted at scripting, text processing and system configuration and management in general. Linux distributions support shell scripts, awk, sed and make. Many programs also have an embedded programming language to support configuring or programming themselves. For example, regular expressions are supported in programs like grep and locate, the traditional Unix MTA Sendmail contains its own Turing complete scripting system, and the advanced text editor GNU Emacs is built around a general purpose Lisp interpreter.

Most distributions also include support for PHP, Perl, Ruby, Python and other dynamic languages. While not as common, Linux also supports C# (via Mono), Vala, and Scheme. Guile Scheme acts as an extension language targeting the GNU system utilities, seeking to make the conventionally small, static, compiled C programs of Unix design rapidly and dynamically extensible via an elegant, functional high-level scripting system; many GNU programs can be compiled with optional Guile bindings to this end. A number of Java Virtual Machines and development kits run on Linux, including the original Sun Microsystems JVM (HotSpot), and IBM's J2SE RE, as well as many open-source projects like Kaffe and JikesRVM.

GNOME and KDE are popular desktop environments and provide a framework for developing applications. These projects are based on the GTK+ and Qt widget toolkits, respectively, which can also be used independently of the larger framework. Both support a wide variety of languages. There are a number of Integrated development environments available including Anjuta, Code::-Blocks, CodeLite, Eclipse, Geany, ActiveState Komodo, KDevelop, Lazarus, MonoDevelop, NetBeans, and Qt Creator, while the long-established editors Vim, nano and Emacs remain popular.

Hardware Support

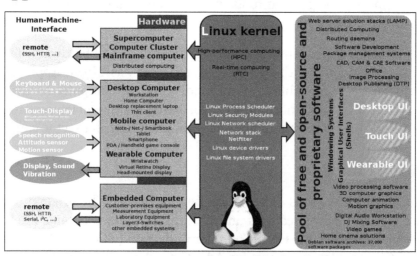

Linux is ubiquitously found on various types of hardware.

The Linux kernel is a widely ported operating system kernel, available for devices ranging from mobile phones to supercomputers; it runs on a highly diverse range of computer architectures, including the hand-held ARM-based iPAQ and the IBM mainframes System z9 or System z10. Specialized distributions and kernel forks exist for less mainstream architectures; for example, the ELKS kernel fork can run on Intel 8086 or Intel 80286 16-bit microprocessors, while the μClinux kernel fork may run on systems without a memory management unit. The kernel also runs on architectures that were only ever intended to use a manufacturer-created operating system, such as Macintosh computers (with both PowerPC and Intel processors), PDAs, video game consoles, portable music players, and mobile phones.

There are several industry associations and hardware conferences devoted to maintaining and improving support for diverse hardware under Linux, such as FreedomHEC. Over time, support for different hardware has improved in Linux, resulting in any off-the-shelf purchase having a "good chance" of being compatible.

Uses

Besides the Linux distributions designed for general-purpose use on desktops and servers, distributions may be specialized for different purposes including: computer architecture support, embedded systems, stability, security, localization to a specific region or language, targeting of specific user groups, support for real-time applications, or commitment to a given desktop environment. Furthermore, some distributions deliberately include only free software. As of 2015, over four hundred Linux distributions are actively developed, with about a dozen distributions being most popular for general-purpose use.

Desktop

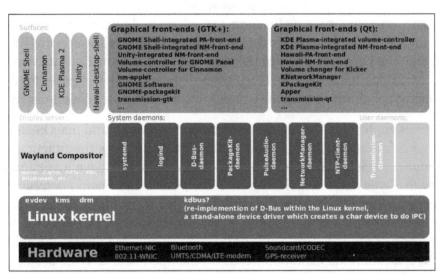

Visible software components of the Linux desktop stack include the display server, widget engines, and some of the more widespread widget toolkits. There are also components not directly visible to end users, including D-Bus and Pulse Audio.

The popularity of Linux on standard desktop computers and laptops has been increasing over the years. Most modern distributions include a graphical user environment, with, as of February 2015, the two most popular environments being the KDE Plasma Desktop and Xfce.

No single official Linux desktop exists: rather desktop environments and Linux distributions select components from a pool of free and open-source software with which they construct a GUI implementing some more or less strict design guide. GNOME, for example, has its human interface guidelines as a design guide, which gives the human–machine interface an important role, not just when doing the graphical design, but also when considering people with disabilities, and even when focusing on security.

The collaborative nature of free software development allows distributed teams to perform language localization of some Linux distributions for use in locales where localizing proprietary systems would not be cost-effective. For example, the Sinhalese language version of the Knoppix distribution became available significantly before Microsoft translated Windows XP into Sinhalese. In this case the Lanka Linux User Group played a major part in developing the localized system by combining the knowledge of university professors, linguists, and local developers.

Performance and Applications

The performance of Linux on the desktop has been a controversial topic; for example in 2007 Con Kolivas accused the Linux community of favoring performance on servers. He quit Linux kernel development out of frustration with this lack of focus on the desktop, and then gave a "tell all" interview on the topic. Since then a significant amount of development has focused on improving the desktop experience. Projects such as Upstart and systemd aim for a faster boot time; the Wayland and Mir projects aim at replacing X11 while enhancing desktop performance, security and appearance.

Many popular applications are available for a wide variety of operating systems. For example, Mozilla Firefox, OpenOffice.org/LibreOffice and Blender have downloadable versions for all major operating systems. Furthermore, some applications initially developed for Linux, such as Pidgin, and GIMP, were ported to other operating systems (including Windows and macOS) due to their popularity. In addition, a growing number of proprietary desktop applications are also supported on Linux, such as Autodesk Maya and The Foundry's Nuke in the high-end field of animation and visual effects. There are also several companies that have ported their own or other companies' games to Linux, with Linux also being a supported platform on both the popular Steam and Desura digital-distribution services.

Many other types of applications available for Microsoft Windows and macOS also run on Linux. Commonly, either a free software application will exist which does the functions of an application found on another operating system, or that application will have a version that works on Linux, such as with Skype and some video games like *Dota 2* and *Team Fortress 2*. Furthermore, the Wine project provides a Windows compatibility layer to run unmodified Windows applications on Linux. It is sponsored by commercial interests including CodeWeavers, which produces a commercial version of the software. Since 2009, Google has also provided funding to the Wine project. CrossOver, a proprietary solution based on the open-source Wine project, supports running Windows versions of Microsoft Office, Intuit applications such as Quicken and QuickBooks, Adobe Photoshop versions through CS2, and many popular games such as *World of Warcraft*. In other cases, where there is no Linux port of some software in areas such as desktop publishing and professional audio, there is equivalent software available on Linux. It is also possible to run applications written for Android on other versions of Linux using Anbox.

Components and Installation

Besides externally visible components, such as X window managers, a non-obvious but quite central role is played by the programs hosted by freedesktop.org, such as D-Bus or PulseAudio; both major desktop environments (GNOME and KDE) include them, each offering graphical front-ends written using the corresponding toolkit (GTK+ or Qt). A display server is another component, which for the longest time has been communicating in the X11 display server protocol with its clients; prominent software talking X11 includes the X.Org Server and Xlib. Frustration over the cumbersome X11 core protocol, and especially over its numerous extensions, has led to the creation of a new display server protocol, Wayland.

Installing, updating and removing software in Linux is typically done through the use of package managers such as the Synaptic Package Manager, PackageKit, and Yum Extender. While most major Linux distributions have extensive repositories, often containing tens of thousands of packages, not all the software that can run on Linux is available from the official repositories. Alternatively, users can install packages from unofficial repositories, download pre-compiled packages directly from websites, or compile the source code by themselves. All these methods come with different degrees of difficulty; compiling the source code is in general considered a challenging process for new Linux users, but it is hardly needed in modern distributions and is not a method specific to Linux.

Samples of graphical desktop interfaces:

  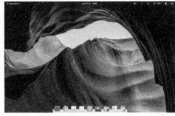

| Budgie | GNOME | Pantheon |

Netbooks

Linux distributions have also become popular in the netbook market, with many devices such as the Asus Eee PC and Acer Aspire One shipping with customized Linux distributions installed.

In 2009, Google announced its Chrome OS as a minimal Linux-based operating system, using the Chrome browser as the main user interface. Chrome OS does not run any non-web applications, except for the bundled file manager and media player (a certain level of support for Android applications was added in later versions). Netbooks that shipped with the operating system, termed Chromebooks, started appearing on the market in June 2011.

Servers, Mainframes and Supercomputers

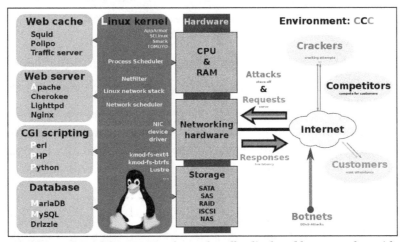

Broad overview of the LAMP software bundle, displayed here together with Squid. A high-performance and high-availability web server solution providing security in a hostile environment.

Linux distributions have long been used as server operating systems, and have risen to prominence in that area; Netcraft reported in September 2006, that eight of the ten (other two with "unknown" OS) most reliable internet hosting companies ran Linux distributions on their web servers, with Linux in the top position. In June 2008, Linux distributions represented five of the top ten, FreeBSD three of ten, and Microsoft two of ten; since February 2010, Linux distributions represented six of the top ten, FreeBSD three of ten, and Microsoft one of ten, with Linux in the top position.

Linux distributions are the cornerstone of the LAMP server-software combination (Linux, Apache, MariaDB/MySQL, Perl/PHP/Python) which has achieved popularity among developers, and which is one of the more common platforms for website hosting.

Linux distributions have become increasingly popular on mainframes, partly due to pricing and the open-source model. In December 2009, computer giant IBM reported that it would predominantly market and sell mainframe-based Enterprise Linux Server. At LinuxCon North America 2015, IBM announced LinuxONE, a series of mainframes specifically designed to run Linux and open-source software.

Linux distributions are also dominant as operating systems for supercomputers. As of November 2017, all supercomputers on the 500 list run some variant of Linux.

Smart Devices

Android smartphones

Several operating systems for smart devices, such as smartphones, tablet computers, smart TVs, and in-vehicle infotainment (IVI) systems, are based on Linux. Major platforms for such systems include Android, Firefox OS, Mer and Tizen.

Android has become the dominant mobile operating system for smartphones, running on 79.3% of units sold worldwide during the second quarter of 2013. Android is also a popular operating system for tablets, and Android smart TVs and in-vehicle infotainment systems have also appeared in the market.

Cellphones and PDAs running Linux on open-source platforms became more common from 2007; examples include the Nokia N810, Openmoko's Neo1973, and the Motorola ROKR E8. Continuing the trend, Palm (later acquired by HP) produced a new Linux-derived operating system, webOS, which is built into its line of Palm Pre smartphones.

Nokia's Maemo, one of the earliest mobile operating systems, was based on Debian. It was later merged with Intel's Moblin, another Linux-based operating system, to form MeeGo. The project was later terminated in favor of Tizen, an operating system targeted at mobile devices as well as IVI. Tizen is a project within The Linux Foundation. Several Samsung products are already running Tizen, Samsung Gear 2 being the most significant example. Samsung Z smartphones will use Tizen instead of Android.

As a result of MeeGo's termination, the Mer project forked the MeeGo codebase to create a basis for mobile-oriented operating systems. In July 2012, Jolla announced Sailfish OS, their own mobile operating system built upon Mer technology.

Mozilla's Firefox OS consists of the Linux kernel, a hardware abstraction layer, a web-standards-based runtime environment and user interface, and an integrated web browser.

Canonical has released Ubuntu Touch, aiming to bring convergence to the user experience on this mobile operating system and its desktop counterpart, Ubuntu. The operating system also provides a full Ubuntu desktop when connected to an external monitor.

Embedded Devices

The Jolla Phone uses the Linux-based Sailfish OS.

In-car entertainment system of the Tesla Model S is based on Ubuntu.

Due to its low cost and ease of customization, Linux is often used in embedded systems. In the non-mobile telecommunications equipment sector, the majority of customer-premises equipment (CPE) hardware runs some Linux-based operating system. OpenWrt is a community driven example upon which many of the OEM firmware releases are based.

Nokia X, a smartphone that runs Linux kernel.

For example, the popular TiVo digital video recorder also uses a customized Linux, as do several network firewalls and routers from such makers as Cisco/Linksys. The Korg OASYS, the Korg KRONOS, the Yamaha Motif XS/Motif XF music workstations, Yamaha S90XS/S70XS, Yamaha MOX6/MOX8 synthesizers, Yamaha Motif-Rack XS tone generator module, and Roland RD-700GX digital piano also run Linux. Linux is also used in stage lighting control systems, such as the WholeHogIII console.

Gaming

In the past, there were few games available for Linux. In recent years, more games have been released with support for Linux (especially Indie games), with the exception of a few AAA title games. Android, a popular mobile platform which uses the Linux kernel, has gained much developer interest and is one of the main platforms for mobile game development along with iOS operating system by Apple for iPhone and iPad devices.

On February 14, 2013, Valve released a Linux version of Steam, a popular game distribution platform on PC. Many Steam games were ported to Linux. On December 13, 2013, Valve released SteamOS, a gaming oriented OS based on Debian, for beta testing, and has plans to ship Steam Machines as a gaming and entertainment platform. Valve has also developed VOGL, an OpenGL debugger intended to aid video game development, as well as porting its Source game engine to desktop Linux. As a result of Valve's effort, several prominent games such as DotA 2, Team Fortress 2, Portal, Portal 2 and Left 4 Dead 2 are now natively available on desktop Linux.

On July 31, 2013, Nvidia released Shield as an attempt to use Android as a specialized gaming platform. Some Linux users play Windows games through Wine or CrossOver Linux.

On 22 August 2018, Valve released their own fork of Wine called Proton, aimed at gaming. It features some improvements over the vanilla Wine such as Vulkan-based DirectX 11 and 12 implementations, Steam integration, better full screen and game controller support and improved performance for multi-threaded games.

Specialized Uses

Due to the flexibility, customizability and free and open-source nature of Linux, it becomes possible to highly tune Linux for a specific purpose. There are two main methods for creating a specialized Linux distribution: building from scratch or from a general-purpose distribution as a base. The distributions often used for this purpose include Debian, Fedora, Ubuntu (which is itself based on Debian), Arch Linux, Gentoo, and Slackware. In contrast, Linux distributions built from scratch do not have general-purpose bases; instead, they focus on the JeOS philosophy by including only necessary components and avoiding resource overhead caused by components considered redundant in the distribution's use cases.

Home Theater PC

A home theater PC (HTPC) is a PC that is mainly used as an entertainment system, especially a home theater system. It is normally connected to a television, and often an additional audio system.

OpenELEC, a Linux distribution that incorporates the media center software Kodi, is an OS tuned specifically for an HTPC. Having been built from the ground up adhering to the JeOS principle, the OS is very lightweight and very suitable for the confined usage range of an HTPC.

There are also special editions of Linux distributions that include the MythTV media center software, such as Mythbuntu, a special edition of Ubuntu.

Digital Security

Kali Linux is a Debian-based Linux distribution designed for digital forensics and penetration testing. It comes preinstalled with several software applications for penetration testing and identifying security exploits. The Ubuntu derivative BackBox provides pre-installed security and network analysis tools for ethical hacking. The Arch-based BlackArch includes over 2100 tools for pentesting and security researching.

There are many Linux distributions created with privacy, secrecy, network anonymity and information security in mind, including Tails, Tin Hat Linux and Tinfoil Hat Linux. Lightweight Portable Security is a distribution based on Arch Linux and developed by the United States Department of Defense. Tor-ramdisk is a minimal distribution created solely to host the network anonymity software Tor.

System Rescue

Linux Live CD sessions have long been used as a tool for recovering data from a broken computer system and for repairing the system. Building upon that idea, several Linux distributions tailored for this purpose have emerged, most of which use GParted as a partition editor, with additional data recovery and system repair software:

- GParted Live – a Debian-based distribution developed by the GParted project.

- Parted Magic – a commercial Linux distribution.

- SystemRescueCD – a Gentoo-based distribution with support for editing Windows registry.

In Space

SpaceX uses multiple redundant flight computers in a fault-tolerant design in its Falcon 9 rocket. Each Merlin engine is controlled by three voting computers, with two physical processors per computer that constantly check each other's operation. Linux is not inherently fault-tolerant (no operating system is, as it is a function of the whole system including the hardware), but the flight computer software makes it so for its purpose. For flexibility, commercial off-the-shelf parts and system-wide "radiation-tolerant" design are used instead of radiation hardened parts. As of July 2019, SpaceX has conducted over 76 launches of the Falcon 9 since 2010, out of which all but one have successfully delivered their primary payloads to the intended orbit, and plans to use it to transport astronauts to the International Space Station.

In addition, Windows was used as an operating system on non-mission critical systems—laptops used on board the space station, for example—but it has been replaced with Linux; the first Linux-powered humanoid robot is also undergoing in-flight testing.

The Jet Propulsion Laboratory has used Linux for a number of years "to help with projects relating to the construction of unmanned space flight and deep space exploration"; NASA uses Linux in robotics in the Mars rover, and Ubuntu Linux to "save data from satellites".

Education

Linux distributions have been created to provide hands-on experience with coding and source code to students, on devices such as the Raspberry Pi. In addition to producing a practical device, the intention is to show students "how things work under the hood".

The Ubuntu derivatives Edubuntu and The Linux Schools Project, as well as the Debian derivative Skolelinux, provide education-oriented software packages. They also include tools for administering and building school computer labs and computer-based classrooms, such as the Linux Terminal Server Project (LTSP).

Others

Instant WebKiosk and Webconverger are browser-based Linux distributions often used in web kiosks and digital signage. Thinstation is a minimalist distribution designed for thin clients. Rocks Cluster Distribution is tailored for high-performance computing clusters.

There are general-purpose Linux distributions that target a specific audience, such as users of a specific language or geographical area. Such examples include Ubuntu Kylin for Chinese language users and BlankOn targeted at Indonesians. Profession-specific distributions include Ubuntu Studio for media creation and DNALinux for bioinformatics. There is also a Muslim-oriented distribution of the name Sabily that consequently also provides some Islamic tools. Certain organizations use slightly specialized Linux distributions internally, including GendBuntu used by the French National Gendarmerie, Goobuntu used internally by Google, and Astra Linux developed specifically for the Russian army.

MAC OS

Mac OS is an operating system (OS) developed by the American computer company Apple Inc. The OS was introduced in 1984 to run the company's Macintosh line of personal computers (PCs). The Macintosh heralded the era of graphical user interface (GUI) systems, and it inspired Microsoft Corporation to develop its own GUI, the Windows OS.

Apple's marketing for the introduction of the Macintosh focused heavily on its operating system's intuitive ease of use. Unlike virtually all other contemporary PCs, the Mac OS (initially designated simply System Software, with a version number appended) was graphically based. Rather than typing commands and directory paths at text prompts, users moved a mouse pointer to visually navigate the Finder—a series of virtual folders and files, represented by icons. Most computer operating systems eventually adopted the GUI model. In the 1980s Apple made an agreement allowing Microsoft to use certain aspects of the Mac interface in early versions of Windows. However, except for a brief period in the 1990s, Mac OS has never been licensed for use with computers made by manufacturers other than Apple.

Later Mac OS releases introduced features such as Internet file sharing, network browsing, and multiple user accounts. In 1996 Apple acquired rival NeXT Computers, which was founded by Steven Jobs after his departure from Apple, and in 2001 the company rolled out Mac OS X, a major redesign based on both the NextStep system and Apple's most recent OS release. OS X ran on a UNIX kernel (core software code) and offered technical advances such as memory protection and preemptive multitasking, along with a more versatile Finder, an elegant-looking interface called Aqua, and a convenient graphical "Dock" bar for launching frequently used applications. Updates to OS X added features such as automated backups and a "Dashboard" manager for small, handy applications called widgets.

From 2007 Apple unveiled a number of mobile devices that could access the Internet, including the iPhone smartphone and the iPad tablet computer. Apple soon emphasized the ability of OS X to connect with these devices. In 2011 Apple introduced iCloud, a cloud computing service that allowed users to share data among all of their Apple devices, for both OS X and the mobile operating system iOS. Apple added more features allowing connectivity between devices to successive updates of OS X, iOS, and later watchOS (the operating system for the Apple Watch smartwatch). These features included the ability to receive phone calls (made to the iPhone) and the means of quickly sharing data among devices.

References

- Aaron Sakovich (2001). "Windows 2000?". The alphant Source. Archived from the original on July 8, 2008. Retrieved January 1, 2007

- Windows, definition: searchwindowsserver.techtarget.com, Retrieved 10 June, 2019

- Cutler, Dave, "Preface", in Russinovich, Mark; Solomon, David A (eds.), Microsoft Windows Internals (fourth ed.), Microsoft Press, ISBN 0-7356-1917-4

- Windows, definition: searchenterprisedesktop.techtarget.com, Retrieved 11 July, 2019

- Vascellaro, Jessica E. (August 3, 2006). "New Ways to Prove You Are Who You Say You Are Online". The Wall Street Journal. Dow Jones & Company. Retrieved March 16, 2016

- Mac-OS, technology: britannica.com, Retrieved 12 August, 2019

- Thadani, Rahul (September 6, 2010). "Windows 7 System Requirements". Buzzle. Archived from the original on July 6, 2017. Retrieved February 27, 2014

4

Process and Threads

The smallest sequence of programmed instructions which can be independently managed by a scheduler is known as a thread. The instance of a computer program which is being executed by a single or multiple threads is termed as a process. The topics elaborated in this chapter will help in gaining a better perspective about processes and threads, as well as the difference between them.

PROCESS

The process is the execution of a program and performs the relevant actions specified in a program, or it is an execution unit where a program runs. The operating system creates, schedules and terminates the processes for the use of the CPU. The other processes created by the main process are known as child process.

A process operations are controlled with the help of PCB (Process control Block) can be considered as the brain of the process, which contains all the crucial information regarding to a process such as a process id, priority, state, PWS and contents CPU register.

PCB is also a kernel-based data structure which uses the three kinds of functions which are scheduling, dispatching and context save:

- Scheduling: It is a method of selecting the sequence of the process in simple words chooses the process which has to be executed first in the CPU.

- Dispatching: It sets up an environment for the process to be executed.

- Context save: This function saves the information regarding to a process when it gets resumed or blocked.

There are certain states included in a process lifecycle such as ready, running, blocked and terminated. Process States are used for keeping the track of the process activity at an instant.

From the programmer's point of view, processes are the medium to achieve the concurrent execution of a program. The chief process of a concurrent program creates a child process. The main process and child process need to interact with each to achieve a common goal.

Interleaving operations of processes enhance the computation speed when i/o operation in one process overlaps with a computational activity in another process.

Properties of a Process

- Creation of each process includes system calls for each process separately.

- A process is an isolated execution entity and does not share data and information.

- Processes use IPC (Inter-process communication) mechanism for communication which significantly increases the number of system calls.

- Process management consumes more system calls.

- Each process has its own stack and heap memory, instruction, data and memory map.

THREAD

In computer science, a thread of execution is the smallest sequence of programmed instructions that can be managed independently by a scheduler, which is typically a part of the operating system. The implementation of threads and processes differs between operating systems, but in most cases a thread is a component of a process. Multiple threads can exist within one process, executing concurrently and sharing resources such as memory, while different processes do not share these resources. In particular, the threads of a process share its executable code and the values of its dynamically allocated variables and non-thread-local global variables at any given time.

Single vs. Multi-processor Systems

Systems with a single processor generally implement multi-threading by time slicing: the central processing unit (CPU) switches between different software threads. This context switching generally happens very often and rapidly enough that users perceive the threads or tasks as running in parallel. On a multi-processor or multi-core system, multiple threads can execute in parallel, with every processor or core executing a separate thread simultaneously; on a processor or core with hardware threads, separate software threads can also be executed concurrently by separate hardware threads.

Threads vs. Processes

Threads differ from traditional multitasking operating system processes in several ways described below:

- Processes are typically independent, while threads exist as subsets of a process.

- Processes carry considerably more state information than threads, whereas multiple threads within a process share process state as well as memory and other resources.

- Processes have separate address spaces, whereas threads share their address space.

- Processes interact only through system-provided inter-process communication mechanisms.

- Context switching between threads in the same process is typically faster than context switching between processes.

Systems such as Windows NT and OS/2 are said to have *cheap* threads and *expensive* processes; in other operating systems there is not so great a difference except the cost of an address space switch which on some architectures (notably x86) results in a translation lookaside buffer (TLB) flush.

Single Threading

In computer programming, single-threading is the processing of one command at a time. The opposite of single-threading is multithreading.

In the formal analysis of the variables' semantics and process state, the term *single threading* can be used differently to mean "backtracking within a single thread", which is common in the functional programming community.

Multithreading

Multithreading is mainly found in multitasking operating systems. Multithreading is a widespread programming and execution model that allows multiple threads to exist within the context of one process. These threads share the process's resources, but are able to execute independently. The threaded programming model provides developers with a useful abstraction of concurrent execution. Multithreading can also be applied to one process to enable parallel execution on a multiprocessing system.

Multithreaded applications have the following advantages:

- Responsiveness: multithreading can allow an application to remain responsive to input. In a one-thread program, if the main execution thread blocks on a long-running task, the entire application can appear to freeze. By moving such long-running tasks to a worker thread that runs concurrently with the main execution thread, it is possible for the application to remain responsive to user input while executing tasks in the background. On the other hand, in most cases multithreading is not the only way to keep a program responsive, with non-blocking I/O and/or Unix signals being available for gaining similar results.

- Faster execution: this advantage of a multithreaded program allows it to operate faster on computer systems that have multiple central processing units (CPUs) or one or more multi-core processors, or across a cluster of machines, because the threads of the program naturally lend themselves to parallel execution, assuming sufficient independence (that they do not need to wait for each other).

- Lower resource consumption: using threads, an application can serve multiple clients concurrently using fewer resources than it would need when using multiple process copies of itself. For example, the Apache HTTP server uses thread pools: a pool of listener threads for listening to incoming requests, and a pool of server threads for processing those requests.

- Better system utilization: as an example, a file system using multiple threads can achieve higher throughput and lower latency since data in a faster medium (such as cache memory) can be retrieved by one thread while another thread retrieves data from a slower medium (such as external storage) with neither thread waiting for the other to finish.

- Simplified sharing and communication: unlike processes, which require a message passing or shared memory mechanism to perform inter-process communication (IPC), threads can communicate through data, code and files they already share.

- Parallelization: applications looking to use multicore or multi-CPU systems can use multi-threading to split data and tasks into parallel subtasks and let the underlying architecture manage how the threads run, either concurrently on one core or in parallel on multiple cores. GPU computing environments like CUDA and OpenCL use the multithreading model where dozens to hundreds of threads run in parallel across data on a large number of cores.

Multithreading has the following drawbacks:

- Synchronization: since threads share the same address space, the programmer must be careful to avoid race conditions and other non-intuitive behaviors. In order for data to be correctly manipulated, threads will often need to rendezvous in time in order to process the data in the correct order. Threads may also require mutually exclusive operations (often implemented using mutexes) to prevent common data from being read or overwritten in one thread while being modified by another. Careless use of such primitives can lead to deadlocks, livelocks or races over resources.

- Thread crashes a process: an illegal operation performed by a thread crashes the entire process; therefore, one misbehaving thread can disrupt the processing of all the other threads in the application.

Scheduling

Operating systems schedule threads either preemptively or cooperatively. On multi-user operating systems, preemptive multithreading is the more widely used approach for its finer grained control over execution time via context switching. However, preemptive scheduling may context switch threads at moments unanticipated by programmers therefore causing lock convoy, priority inversion, or other side-effects. In contrast, cooperative multithreading relies on threads to relinquish control of execution thus ensuring that threads run to completion . This can create problems if a cooperatively multitasked thread blocks by waiting on a resource or if it starves other threads by not yielding control of execution during intensive computation.

Until the early 2000s, most desktop computers had only one single-core CPU, with no support for hardware threads, although threads were still used on such computers because switching between threads was generally still quicker than full-process context switches. In 2002, Intel added support for simultaneous multithreading to the Pentium 4 processor, under the name hyper-threading; in 2005, they introduced the dual-core Pentium D processor and AMD introduced the dual-core Athlon 64 X2 processor.

Processors in embedded systems, which have higher requirements for real-time behaviors, might support multithreading by decreasing the thread-switch time, perhaps by allocating a dedicated register file for each thread instead of saving/restoring a common register file.

Processes, Kernel Threads, User Threads and Fibers

Scheduling can be done at the kernel level or user level, and multitasking can be done preemptively or cooperatively. This yields a variety of related concepts.

At the kernel level, a process contains one or more kernel threads, which share the process's resources, such as memory and file handles – a process is a unit of resources, while a thread is a unit of scheduling and execution. Kernel scheduling is typically uniformly done preemptively or, less commonly, cooperatively. At the user level a process such as a runtime system can itself schedule multiple threads of execution. If these do not share data, as in Erlang, they are usually analogously called processes, while if they share data they are usually called (user) threads, particularly if preemptively scheduled. Cooperatively scheduled user threads are known as fibers; different processes may schedule user threads differently. User threads may be executed by kernel threads in various ways (one-to-one, many-to-one, many-to-many). The term "light-weight process" variously refers to user threads or to kernel mechanisms for scheduling user threads onto kernel threads.

A process is a "heavyweight" unit of kernel scheduling, as creating, destroying, and switching processes is relatively expensive. Processes own resources allocated by the operating system. Resources include memory (for both code and data), file handles, sockets, device handles, windows, and a process control block. Processes are isolated by process isolation, and do not share address spaces or file resources except through explicit methods such as inheriting file handles or shared memory segments, or mapping the same file in a shared way. Creating or destroying a process is relatively expensive, as resources must be acquired or released. Processes are typically preemptively multitasked, and process switching is relatively expensive, beyond basic cost of context switching, due to issues such as cache flushing.

A kernel thread is a "lightweight" unit of kernel scheduling. At least one kernel thread exists within each process. If multiple kernel threads exist within a process, then they share the same memory and file resources. Kernel threads are preemptively multitasked if the operating system's process scheduler is preemptive. Kernel threads do not own resources except for a stack, a copy of the registers including the program counter, and thread-local storage (if any), and are thus relatively cheap to create and destroy. Thread switching is also relatively cheap: it requires a context switch (saving and restoring registers and stack pointer), but does not change virtual memory and is thus cache-friendly (leaving TLB valid). The kernel can assign one thread to each logical core in a system (because each processor splits itself up into multiple logical cores if it supports multithreading, or only supports one logical core per physical core if it does not), and can swap out threads that get blocked. However, kernel threads take much longer than user threads to be swapped.

Threads are sometimes implemented in userspace libraries, thus called user threads. The kernel is unaware of them, so they are managed and scheduled in userspace. Some implementations base their user threads on top of several kernel threads, to benefit from multi-processor machines (M:N model). The term "thread" (without kernel or user qualifier) defaults to referring to kernel threads. User threads as implemented by virtual machines are also called green threads. User threads are generally fast to create and manage, but cannot take advantage of multithreading or multiprocessing, and will get blocked if all of their associated kernel threads get blocked even if there are some user threads that are ready to run.

Fibers are an even lighter unit of scheduling which are cooperatively scheduled: a running fiber must explicitly "yield" to allow another fiber to run, which makes their implementation much easier than kernel or user threads. A fiber can be scheduled to run in any thread in the same process. This permits applications to gain performance improvements by managing scheduling themselves, instead of relying on the kernel scheduler (which may not be tuned for the application). Parallel programming environments such as OpenMP typically implement their tasks through fibers. Closely related to fibers are coroutines, with the distinction being that coroutines are a language-level construct, while fibers are a system-level construct.

Thread and Fiber Issues

Concurrency and Data Structures

Threads in the same process share the same address space. This allows concurrently running code to couple tightly and conveniently exchange data without the overhead or complexity of an IPC. When shared between threads, however, even simple data structures become prone to race conditions if they require more than one CPU instruction to update: two threads may end up attempting to update the data structure at the same time and find it unexpectedly changing underfoot. Bugs caused by race conditions can be very difficult to reproduce and isolate.

To prevent this, threading application programming interfaces (APIs) offer synchronization primitives such as mutexes to lock data structures against concurrent access. On uniprocessor systems, a thread running into a locked mutex must sleep and hence trigger a context switch. On multi-processor systems, the thread may instead poll the mutex in a spinlock. Both of these may sap performance and force processors in symmetric multiprocessing (SMP) systems to contend for the memory bus, especially if the granularity of the locking is fine.

Although threads seem to be a small step from sequential computation, in fact, they represent a huge step. They discard the most essential and appealing properties of sequential computation: understandability, predictability, and determinism. Threads, as a model of computation, are wildly non-deterministic, and the job of the programmer becomes one of pruning that non-determinism.

I/O and Scheduling

User thread or fiber implementations are typically entirely in userspace. As a result, context switching between user threads or fibers within the same process is extremely efficient because it does not require any interaction with the kernel at all: a context switch can be performed by locally saving the CPU registers used by the currently executing user thread or fiber and then loading the registers required by the user thread or fiber to be executed. Since scheduling occurs in userspace, the scheduling policy can be more easily tailored to the requirements of the program's workload.

However, the use of blocking system calls in user threads (as opposed to kernel threads) or fibers can be problematic. If a user thread or a fiber performs a system call that blocks, the other user threads and fibers in the process are unable to run until the system call returns. A typical example of this problem is when performing I/O: most programs are written to perform I/O synchronously. When an I/O operation is initiated, a system call is made, and does not return until the I/O operation has been completed. In the intervening period, the entire process is "blocked" by the kernel and cannot run, which starves other user threads and fibers in the same process from executing.

A common solution to this problem is providing an I/O API that implements a synchronous interface by using non-blocking I/O internally, and scheduling another user thread or fiber while the I/O operation is in progress. Similar solutions can be provided for other blocking system calls. Alternatively, the program can be written to avoid the use of synchronous I/O or other blocking system calls.

SunOS 4.x implemented *light-weight processes* or LWPs. NetBSD 2.x+, and DragonFly BSD implement LWPs as kernel threads (1:1 model). SunOS 5.2 through SunOS 5.8 as well as NetBSD 2 to NetBSD 4 implemented a two level model, multiplexing one or more user level threads on each kernel thread (M:N model). SunOS 5.9 and later, as well as NetBSD 5 eliminated user threads support, returning to a 1:1 model. FreeBSD 5 implemented M:N model. FreeBSD 6 supported both 1:1 and M:N, users could choose which one should be used with a given program using /etc/libmap. conf. Starting with FreeBSD 7, the 1:1 became the default. FreeBSD 8 no longer supports the M:N model.

The use of kernel threads simplifies user code by moving some of the most complex aspects of threading into the kernel. The program does not need to schedule threads or explicitly yield the processor. User code can be written in a familiar procedural style, including calls to blocking APIs, without starving other threads. However, kernel threading may force a context switch between threads at any time, and thus expose race hazards and concurrency bugs that would otherwise lie latent. On SMP systems, this is further exacerbated because kernel threads may literally execute on separate processors in parallel.

Models

1:1 (Kernel-level Threading)

Threads created by the user in a 1:1 correspondence with schedulable entities in the kernel are the simplest possible threading implementation. OS/2 and Win32 used this approach from the start, while on Linux the usual C library implements this approach (via the NPTL or older LinuxThreads). This approach is also used by Solaris, NetBSD, FreeBSD, macOS, and iOS.

N:1 (User-level Threading)

An N:1 model implies that all application-level threads map to one kernel-level scheduled entity; the kernel has no knowledge of the application threads. With this approach, context switching can be done very quickly and, in addition, it can be implemented even on simple kernels which do not support threading. One of the major drawbacks, however, is that it cannot benefit from the hardware acceleration on multithreaded processors or multi-processor computers: there is never more than one thread being scheduled at the same time. For example: If one of the threads needs to execute an I/O request, the whole process is blocked and the threading advantage cannot be used. The GNU Portable Threads uses User-level threading, as does State Threads.

M:N (Hybrid Threading)

M:N maps some M number of application threads onto some N number of kernel entities, or "virtual processors." This is a compromise between kernel-level ("1:1") and user-level ("N:1") threading. In general, "M:N" threading systems are more complex to implement than either kernel or user threads, because changes to both kernel and user-space code are required. In the M:N implementation, the threading library is responsible for scheduling user threads on the available schedulable entities; this makes context switching of threads very fast, as it avoids system calls. However, this increases complexity and the likelihood of priority inversion, as well as suboptimal scheduling without extensive (and expensive) coordination between the userland scheduler and the kernel scheduler.

Hybrid Implementation Examples

- Scheduler activations used by the NetBSD native POSIX threads library implementation (an M:N model as opposed to a 1:1 kernel or userspace implementation model).

- Light-weight processes used by older versions of the Solaris operating system.

- Marcel from the PM2 project.

- The OS for the Tera-Cray MTA-2.

- Microsoft Windows 7 user-mode scheduling.

- The Glasgow Haskell Compiler (GHC) for the language Haskell uses lightweight threads which are scheduled on operating system threads.

Fiber Implementation Examples

Fibers can be implemented without operating system support, although some operating systems or libraries provide explicit support for them.

- Win32 supplies a fiber API (Windows NT 3.51 SP3 and later).

- Ruby as Green threads.

- Netscape Portable Runtime (includes a user-space fibers implementation).

- ribs2.

Programming Language Support

IBM PL/I(F) included support for multithreading (called multitasking) in the late 1960s, and this was continued in the Optimizing Compiler and later versions. The IBM Enterprise PL/I compiler introduced a new model "thread" API. Neither version was part of the PL/I standard.

Many programming languages support threading in some capacity. Many implementations of C and C++ support threading, and provide access to the native threading APIs of the operating system. Some higher level (and usually cross-platform) programming languages, such as Java, Python, and .NET Framework languages, expose threading to developers while abstracting the platform specific differences in threading implementations in the runtime. Several other programming languages and language extensions also try to abstract the concept of concurrency and threading from the developer fully (Cilk, OpenMP, Message Passing Interface (MPI)). Some languages are designed for sequential parallelism instead (especially using GPUs), without requiring concurrency or threads (Ateji PX, CUDA).

A few interpreted programming languages have implementations (e.g., Ruby MRI for Ruby, CPython for Python) which support threading and concurrency but not parallel execution of threads, due to a global interpreter lock (GIL). The GIL is a mutual exclusion lock held by the interpreter that can prevent the interpreter from simultaneously interpreting the applications code on two or more threads at once, which effectively limits the parallelism on multiple core systems. This limits performance mostly for processor-bound threads, which require the processor, and not much for I/O-bound or network-bound ones.

Other implementations of interpreted programming languages, such as Tcl using the Thread extension, avoid the GIL limit by using an Apartment model where data and code must be explicitly "shared" between threads. In Tcl each thread has one or more interpreters.

Event-driven programming hardware description languages such as Verilog have a different threading model that supports extremely large numbers of threads (for modeling hardware).

Practical Multithreading

A standardized interface for thread implementation is POSIX Threads (Pthreads), which is a set of C-function library calls. OS vendors are free to implement the interface as desired, but the application developer should be able to use the same interface across multiple platforms. Most Unix platforms including Linux support Pthreads. Microsoft Windows has its own set of thread functions in the process. h interface for multithreading, like beginthread. Java provides yet another standardized interface over the host operating system using the Java concurrency library java.util. concurrent.

Multithreading libraries provide a function call to create a new thread, which takes a function as a parameter. A concurrent thread is then created which starts running the passed function and ends when the function returns. The thread libraries also offer synchronization functions which make it possible to implement race condition-error free multithreading functions using mutexes, condition variables, critical sections, semaphores, monitors and other synchronization primitives.

Another paradigm of thread usage is that of thread pools where a set number of threads are created at startup that then wait for a task to be assigned. When a new task arrives, it wakes up, completes the task and goes back to waiting. This avoids the relatively expensive thread creation and destruction functions for every task performed and takes thread management out of the application developer's hand and leaves it to a library or the operating system that is better suited to optimize thread management. For example, frameworks like Grand Central Dispatch and Threading Building Blocks.

In programming models such as CUDA designed for data parallel computation, an array of threads run the same code in parallel using only its ID to find its data in memory. In essence, the application must be designed so that each thread performs the same operation on different segments of memory so that they can operate in parallel and use the GPU architecture.

KERNEL AND USER LEVEL THREAD

Kernel-level Threads

To make concurrency cheaper, the execution aspect of process is separated out into threads. As such, the OS now manages threads and processes. All thread operations are implemented in the kernel and the OS schedules all threads in the system. OS managed threads are called kernel-level threads or light weight processes.

- NT: Threads.

- Solaris: Lightweight processes(LWP).

In this method, the kernel knows about and manages the threads. No runtime system is needed in this case. Instead of thread table in each process, the kernel has a thread table that keeps track of all threads in the system. In addition, the kernel also maintains the traditional process table to keep track of processes. Operating Systems kernel provides system call to create and manage threads.

Advantages

- Because kernel has full knowledge of all threads, Scheduler may decide to give more time to a process having large number of threads than process having small number of threads.

- Kernel-level threads are especially good for applications that frequently block.

Disadvantages

- The kernel-level threads are slow and inefficient. For instance, threads operations are hundreds of times slower than that of user-level threads.

- Since kernel must manage and schedule threads as well as processes. It require a full thread control block (TCB) for each thread to maintain information about threads. As a result there is significant overhead and increased in kernel complexity.

User-level Threads

Kernel-Level threads make concurrency much cheaper than process because, much less state to allocate and initialize. However, for fine-grained concurrency, kernel-level threads still suffer from too much overhead. Thread operations still require system calls. Ideally, we require thread operations to be as fast as a procedure call. Kernel-Level threads have to be general to support the needs of all programmers, languages, runtimes, etc. For such fine grained concurrency we need still "cheaper" threads.

To make threads cheap and fast, they need to be implemented at user level. User-Level threads are managed entirely by the run-time system (user-level library). The kernel knows nothing about us-er-level threads and manages them as if they were single-threaded processes. User-Level threads are small and fast, each thread is represented by a PC, register, stack, and small thread control block. Creating a new thread, switiching between threads, and synchronizing threads are done via procedure call. i.e no kernel involvement. User-Level threads are hundred times faster than Kernel-Level threads.

Advantages

*   The most obvious advantage of this technique is that a user-level threads package can be implemented on an Operating System that does not support threads.

*   User-level threads does not require modification to operating systems.

*   Simple Representation: Each thread is represented simply by a PC, registers, stack and a small control block, all stored in the user process address space.

*   Simple Management: This simply means that creating a thread, switching between threads and synchronization between threads can all be done without intervention of the kernel.

*   Fast and Efficient: Thread switching is not much more expensive than a procedure call.

Disadvantages

*   User-Level threads are not a perfect solution as with everything else, they are a trade off. Since, User-Level threads are invisible to the OS they are not well integrated with the OS. As a result, Os can make poor decisions like scheduling a process with idle threads, blocking a process whose thread initiated an I/O even though the process has other threads that can run and unscheduling a process with a thread holding a lock. Solving this requires communication between between kernel and user-level thread manager.

*   There is a lack of coordination between threads and operating system kernel. Therefore, process as whole gets one time slice irrespect of whether process has one thread or 1000 threads within. It is up to each thread to relinquish control to other threads.

*   User-level threads requires non-blocking systems call i.e., a multithreaded kernel. Otherwise, entire process will blocked in the kernel, even if there are runable threads left in the processes. For example, if one thread causes a page fault, the process blocks.

MULTITHREADING MODELS

Multithreading allows the execution of multiple parts of a program at the same time. These parts are known as threads and are lightweight processes available within the process. Therefore, multithreading leads to maximum utilization of the CPU by multitasking.

The main models for multithreading are one to one model, many to one model and many to many model.

One to One Model

The one to one model maps each of the user threads to a kernel thread. This means that many threads can run in parallel on multiprocessors and other threads can run when one thread makes a blocking system call.

A disadvantage of the one to one model is that the creation of a user thread requires a corresponding kernel thread. Since a lot of kernel threads burden the system, there is restriction on the number of threads in the system.

A diagram that demonstrates the one to one model is given as follows:

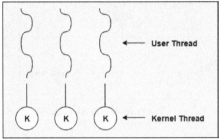

One to One Model.

Many to One Model

The many to one model maps many of the user threads to a single kernel thread. This model is quite efficient as the user space manages the thread management.

A disadvantage of the many to one model is that a thread blocking system call blocks the entire process. Also, multiple threads cannot run in parallel as only one thread can access the kernel at a time.

A diagram that demonstrates the many to one model is given as follows:

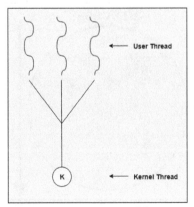

Many to One Model.

Many to Many Model

The many to many model maps many of the user threads to a equal number or lesser kernel threads. The number of kernel threads depends on the application or machine.

The many to many does not have the disadvantages of the one to one model or the many to one model. There can be as many user threads as required and their corresponding kernel threads can run in parallel on a multiprocessor.

A diagram that demonstrates the many to many model is given as follows:

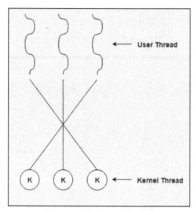

Many to Many Model.

DIFFERENCE BETWEEN PROCESS AND THREAD

In simple words a process is executing a program. But not all, it's only an instance of a computing program. Several processes may be associated with the same program. Process contains program code and its current activity.

Where, as thread is a light weight process. A thread of execution is the smallest sequence of programmed instructions that can be managed independently by scheduler. Threads reside inside the process. Each thread belongs to exactly one process. No thread exists outside the process.

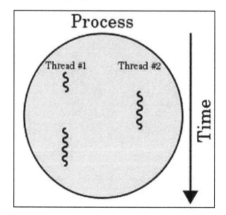

Process	Thread
1. System calls involved in process.	1. No system calls involved.
2. Context switching required.	2. No context switching required.
3. Different process have different copies of code and data.	3. Sharing same copy of code and data can be possible among different threads.

4. Operating system treats different process differently.	4. All user level threads treated as single task for operating system.
5. If a process got blocked, remaining process continue their work.	5. If a user level thread got blocked, all other threads get blocked since they are treated as single task to OS. (Noted: This is can be avoided in kernel level threads).
6. Processes are independent.	6. Threads exist as subsets of a process. They are dependent.
7. Process run in separate memory space.	7. Threads run in shared memory space. And use memory of process which it belong to.
8. Processes have their own program counter (PC), register set, and stack space.	8. Threads share Code section, data section, Address space with other threads.
9. Communication between processes requires some time.	9. Communication between processes requires less time than processes.
10. Processes don't share the memory with any other process.	10. Threads share the memory with other threads of the same process
11. Process have overhead.	11. Threads have no overhead.

Threads are used for small tasks, whereas processes are used for more 'heavyweight' tasks – basically the execution of applications. Another difference between thread and process is that threads within the same process share the same address space, whereas different processes do not.

MULTIPROCESSOR OS

Multiprocessor Operating System refers to the use of two or more central processing units (CPU) within a single computer system. These multiple CPUs are in a close communication sharing the computer bus, memory and other peripheral devices. These systems are referred as tightly coupled systems.

These types of systems are used when very high speed is required to process a large volume of data. These systems are generally used in environment like satellite control, weather forecasting etc. The basic organization of multiprocessing system is shown in figure.

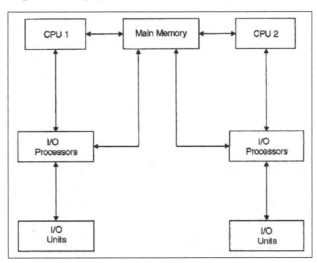

Multiprocessing system is based on the symmetric multiprocessing model, in which each processor runs an identical copy of operating system and these copies communicate with each other. In this system processor is assigned a specific task. A master processor controls the system. This scheme defines a master-slave relationship. These systems can save money in compare to single processor systems because the processors can share peripherals, power supplies and other devices. The main advantage of multiprocessor system is to get more work done in a shorter period of time. Moreover, multiprocessor systems prove more reliable in the situations of failure of one processor. In this situation, the system with multiprocessor will not halt the system; it will only slow it down.

In order to employ multiprocessing operating system effectively, the computer system must have the followings:

1. Motherboard Support: A motherboard capable of handling multiple processors. This means additional sockets or slots for the extra chips and a chipset capable of handling the multiprocessing arrangement.

2. Processor Support: processors those are capable of being used in a multiprocessing system.

The whole task of multiprocessing is managed by the operating system, which allocates different tasks to be performed by the various processors in the system.

Applications designed for the use in multiprocessing are said to be threaded, which means that they are broken into smaller routines that can be run independently. This allows the operating system to let these threads run on more than one processor simultaneously, which is multiprocessing that results in improved performance.

Multiprocessor system supports the processes to run in parallel. Parallel processing is the ability of the CPU to simultaneously process incoming jobs. This becomes most important in computer system, as the CPU divides and conquers the jobs. Generally the parallel processing is used in the fields like artificial intelligence and expert system, image processing, weather forecasting etc.

In a multiprocessor system, the dynamically sharing of resources among the various processors may cause therefore, a potential bottleneck. There are three main sources of contention that can be found in a multiprocessor operating system:

Locking system: In order to provide safe access to the resources shared among multiple processors, they need to be protected by locking scheme. The purpose of a locking is to serialize accesses to the protected resource by multiple processors. Undisciplined use of locking can severely degrade the performance of system. This form of contention can be reduced by using locking scheme, avoiding long critical sections, replacing locks with lock-free algorithms, or, whenever possible, avoiding sharing altogether.

Shared data: The continuous accesses to the shared data items by multiple processors (with one or more of them with data write) are serialized by the cache coherence protocol. Even in a moderate-scale system, serialization delays can have significant impact on the system performance. In addition, bursts of cache coherence traffic saturate the memory bus or the interconnection network, which also slows down the entire system. This form of contention can be eliminated by either avoiding sharing or, when this is not possible, by using replication techniques to reduce the rate of write accesses to the shared data.

False sharing: This form of contention arises when unrelated data items used by different processors are located next to each other in the memory and, therefore, share a single cache line: The effect of false sharing is the same as that of regular sharing bouncing of the cache line among several processors. Fortunately, once it is identified, false sharing can be easily eliminated by setting the memory layout of non-shared data.

Apart from eliminating bottlenecks in the system, a multiprocessor operating system developer should provide support for efficiently running user applications on the multiprocessor. Some of the aspects of such support include mechanisms for task placement and migration across processors, physical memory placement insuring most of the memory pages used by an application is located in the local memory, and scalable multiprocessor synchronization primitives.

References

- Difference-between-process-and-thread: techdifferences.com, Retrieved 13 January, 2019

- Raúl Menéndez; Doug Lowe (2001). Murach's CICS for the COBOL Programmer. Mike Murach & Associates. P. 512. ISBN 978-1-890774-09-7

- Multi-threading-models: tutorialspoint.com, Retrieved 14 February, 2019

- Difference-process-thread: thecrazyprogrammer.com, Retrieved 15 March, 2019

- Multiprocessor-operating-system, disk-operating-system, fundamental: ecomputernotes.com, Retrieved 16 April, 2019

5

Deadlock in Operating Systems

The state in computing where each member within a group is waiting for another member including its own self to send a message is known as a deadlock. There are numerous methods of handling deadlocks, which are broadly categorized as prevention, avoidance, detection and recovery. This chapter discusses in detail the characterization of deadlocks as well as these methods of handling them.

A deadlock happens in operating system when two or more processes need some resource to complete their execution that is held by the other process.

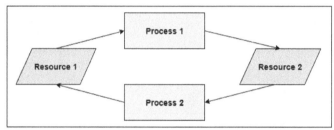

Deadlock in Operating System.

In the above diagram, the process 1 has resource 1 and needs to acquire resource 2. Similarly process 2 has resource 2 and needs to acquire resource 1. Process 1 and process 2 are in deadlock as each of them needs the other's resource to complete their execution but neither of them is willing to relinquish their resources.

DEADLOCK CHARACTERIZATION

A deadlock occurs if the four Coffman conditions hold true. But these conditions are not mutually exclusive. They are given as follows:

Mutual Exclusion

There should be a resource that can only be held by one process at a time. In the diagram below, there is a single instance of Resource 1 and it is held by Process 1 only.

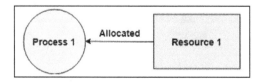

Hold and Wait

A process can hold multiple resources and still request more resources from other processes which are holding them. In the diagram given below, Process 2 holds Resource 2 and Resource 3 and is requesting the Resource 1 which is held by Process 1.

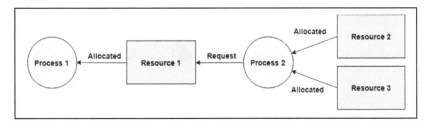

No Preemption

A resource cannot be preempted from a process by force. A process can only release a resource voluntarily. In the diagram below, Process 2 cannot preempt Resource 1 from Process 1. It will only be released when Process 1 relinquishes it voluntarily after its execution is complete.

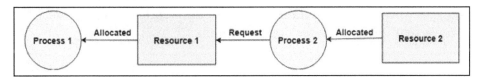

Circular Wait

A process is waiting for the resource held by the second process, which is waiting for the resource held by the third process and so on, till the last process is waiting for a resource held by the first process. This forms a circular chain. For example: Process 1 is allocated Resource2 and it is requesting Resource 1. Similarly, Process 2 is allocated Resource 1 and it is requesting Resource 2. This forms a circular wait loop.

OSTRICH ALGORITHM

In computer science, the ostrich algorithm is a strategy of ignoring potential problems on the basis that they may be exceedingly rare. It is named for the ostrich effect which is defined as "to stick one's head in the sand and pretend there is no problem". It is used when it is more cost-effective to allow the problem to occur than to attempt its prevention.

Use with Deadlocks

This approach may be used in dealing with deadlocks in concurrent programming if they are believed to be very rare and the cost of detection or prevention is high. For example, if each PC deadlocks once per 10 years, the one reboot may be less painful than the restrictions needed to prevent it.

A set of processes is deadlocked if each process in the set is waiting for an event that only another process in the set can cause. Usually the event is release of a currently held resource and none of the processes can run, release resources, and be awakened.

The ostrich algorithm pretends there is no problem and is reasonable to use if deadlocks occur very rarely and the cost of their prevention would be high. The UNIX and Windows operating systems take this approach.

Although using the ostrich algorithm is one of the methods of dealing with deadlocks, other effective methods exist such as dynamic avoidance, banker's algorithm, detection and recovery, and prevention.

Trade-offs

Although efficient, using the Ostrich algorithm trades correctness for convenience. Yet since the algorithm directly deals with extreme cases it is not a large trade-off. In fact, the simplest and most used method to recover from a deadlock is a reboot.

Some algorithms with poor worst-case performance are commonly used because they only exhibit poor performance on artificial cases that do not occur in practice; typical examples are the simplex algorithm and the type-inference algorithm for Standard ML. Issues like integer overflow in programming languages with fixed-width integers are also frequently ignored because they occur only in exceptional cases that do not arise for practical inputs.

METHODS OF HANDLING DEADLOCK

Deadlock Prevention

Deadlock prevention algorithms ensure that at least one of the necessary conditions (Mutual exclusion, hold and wait, no preemption and circular wait) does not hold true. However most prevention algorithms have poor resource utilization, and hence result in reduced throughputs.

Mutual Exclusion

Mutual section from the resource point of view is the fact that a resource can never be used by more than one process simultaneously which is fair enough but that is the main reason behind the deadlock. If a resource could have been used by more than one process at the same time then the process would have never been waiting for any resource.

However, if we can be able to violate resources behaving in the mutually exclusive manner then the deadlock can be prevented.

Spooling

For a device like printer, spooling can work. There is a memory associated with the printer which stores jobs from each of the process into it. Later, Printer collects all the jobs and print each one of them according to FCFS. By using this mechanism, the process doesn't have to wait for the printer and it can continue whatever it was doing. Later, it collects the output when it is produced.

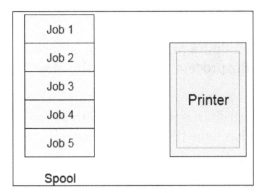

Although, Spooling can be an effective approach to violate mutual exclusion but it suffers from two kinds of problems:

1. This cannot be applied to every resource.

2. After some point of time, there may arise a race condition between the processes to get space in that spool.

We cannot force a resource to be used by more than one process at the same time since it will not be fair enough and some serious problems may arise in the performance. Therefore, we cannot violate mutual exclusion for a process practically.

Hold and Wait

Hold and wait condition lies when a process holds a resource and waiting for some other resource to complete its task. Deadlock occurs because there can be more than one process which are holding one resource and waiting for other in the cyclic order.

However, we have to find out some mechanism by which a process either doesn't hold any resource or doesn't wait. That means, a process must be assigned all the necessary resources before the execution starts. A process must not wait for any resource once the execution has been started.

> (Hold and wait) = hold or wait (negation of hold and wait is, either you don't hold or you don't wait)

This can be implemented practically if a process declares all the resources initially. However, this sounds very practical but can't be done in the computer system because a process can't determine necessary resources initially.

Process is the set of instructions which are executed by the CPU. Each of the instruction may demand multiple resources at the multiple times. The need cannot be fixed by the OS.

The problem with the approach is:

1. Practically not possible.

2. Possibility of getting starved will be increases due to the fact that some process may hold a resource for a very long time.

No Preemption

Deadlock arises due to the fact that a process can't be stopped once it starts. However, if we take the resource away from the process which is causing deadlock then we can prevent deadlock.

This is not a good approach at all since if we take a resource away which is being used by the process then all the work which it has done till now can become inconsistent.

Consider a printer is being used by any process. If we take the printer away from that process and assign it to some other process then all the data which has been printed can become inconsistent and ineffective and also the fact that the process can't start printing again from where it has left which causes performance inefficiency.

Circular Wait

To violate circular wait, we can assign a priority number to each of the resource. A process can't request for a lesser priority resource. This ensures that not a single process can request a resource which is being utilized by some other process and no cycle will be formed.

Condition	Approach	Is Practically Possible?
Mutual Exclusion	Spooling	No
Hold and Wait	Request for all the resources initially	No
No Preemption	Snatch all the resources	No
Circular Wait	Assign priority to each resources and order resources numerically	Yes

Among all the methods, violating Circular wait is the only approach that can be implemented practically.

Deadlock Avoidance

In deadlock avoidance, the request for any resource will be granted if the resulting state of the system doesn't cause deadlock in the system. The state of the system will continuously be checked for safe and unsafe states.

In order to avoid deadlocks, the process must tell OS, the maximum number of resources a process can request to complete its execution.

The simplest and most useful approach states that the process should declare the maximum number of resources of each type it may ever need. The Deadlock avoidance algorithm examines the resource allocations so that there can never be a circular wait condition.

Safe and Unsafe States

The resource allocation state of a system can be defined by the instances of available and allocated resources, and the maximum instance of the resources demanded by the processes.

A state of a system recorded at some random time is shown below:

- Resources Assigned:

Process	Type 1	Type 2	Type 3	Type 4
A	3	0	2	2
B	0	0	1	1
C	1	1	1	0
D	2	1	4	0

- Resources still needed:

Process	Type 1	Type 2	Type 3	Type 4
A	1	1	0	0
B	0	1	1	2
C	1	2	1	0
D	2	1	1	2

$E = (7\ 6\ 8\ 4)$

$P = (6\ 2\ 8\ 3)$

$A = (1\ 4\ 0\ 1)$

Above tables and vector E, P and A describes the resource allocation state of a system. There are 4 processes and 4 types of the resources in a system. Table shows the instances of each resource assigned to each process.

Table shows the instances of the resources, each process still needs. Vector E is the representation of total instances of each resource in the system.

Vector P represents the instances of resources that have been assigned to processes. Vector A represents the number of resources that are not in use.

A state of the system is called safe if the system can allocate all the resources requested by all the processes without entering into deadlock.

If the system cannot fulfill the request of all processes then the state of the system is called unsafe.

The key of Deadlock avoidance approach is when the request is made for resources then the request must only be approved in the case if the resulting state is also a safe state.

Banker's Algorithm

The Banker algorithm, sometimes referred to as the detection algorithm, is a resource allocation and deadlock avoidance algorithm developed by Edsger Dijkstra that tests for safety by simulating the allocation of predetermined maximum possible amounts of all resources, and then makes an "s-state" check to test for possible deadlock conditions for all other pending activities, before deciding whether allocation should be allowed to continue.

The algorithm was developed in the design process for the operating system and originally described in EWD108. When a new process enters a system, it must declare the maximum number of instances of each resource type that it may ever claim; clearly, that number may not exceed the total number of resources in the system. Also, when a process gets all its requested resources it must return them in a finite amount of time.

Resources

For the Banker's algorithm to work, it needs to know three things:

- How much of each resource each process could possibly request[MAX].

- How much of each resource each process is currently holding[ALLOCATED].

- How much of each resource the system currently has available[AVAILABLE].

Resources may be allocated to a process only if the amount of resources requested is less than or equal to the amount available; otherwise, the process waits until resources are available.

Some of the resources that are tracked in real systems are memory, semaphores and interface access.

The Banker's Algorithm derives its name from the fact that this algorithm could be used in a banking system to ensure that the bank does not run out of resources, because the bank would never allocate its money in such a way that it can no longer satisfy the needs of all its customers. By using the Banker's algorithm, the bank ensures that when customers request money the bank never leaves a safe state. If the customer's request does not cause the bank to leave a safe state, the cash will be allocated, otherwise the customer must wait until some other customer deposits enough.

Basic data structures to be maintained to implement the Banker's Algorithm. Let n be the number of processes in the system and m be the number of resource types. Then we need the following data structures:

- Available: A vector of length m indicates the number of available resources of each type. If Available[j] = k, there are k instances of resource type R_j available.

- Max: An $n \times m$ matrix defines the maximum demand of each process. If Max[i,j] = k, then P_i may request at most k instances of resource type R_j.

- Allocation: An $n \times m$ matrix defines the number of resources of each type currently allocated to each process. If Allocation[i,j] = k, then process P_i is currently allocated k instances of resource type R_j.

- Need: An $n \times m$ matrix indicates the remaining resource need of each process. If Need[i,j] = k, then P_i may need k more instances of resource type R_j to complete the task.

    Need[i,j] = Max[i,j] - Allocation[i,j]. n=m-a.

Example:

```
Total system resources are:

15

Processes (currently allocated resources):


P1 2

P2 7

P3 5

Processes (required resources):


P1 3

P2 10

P3 7

Need = maximum resources - currently allocated resources

Processes (possibly needed resources):
 A B C D

P1 2 1 0 1

P2 0 2 0 1

P3 0 1 4 0
```

Safe and Unsafe States

A state (as in the above example) is considered safe if it is possible for all processes to finish executing (terminate). Since the system cannot know when a process will terminate, or how many resources it will have requested by then, the system assumes that all processes will eventually attempt to acquire their stated maximum resources and terminate soon afterward. This is a reasonable assumption in most cases since the system is not particularly concerned with how long each process runs (at least not from a deadlock avoidance perspective). Also, if a process terminates without acquiring its maximum resource it only makes it easier on the system. A safe state is considered to be the decision maker if it's going to process ready queue.

Given that assumption, the algorithm determines if a state is safe by trying to find a hypothetical set of requests by the processes that would allow each to acquire its maximum resources and then terminate (returning its resources to the system). Any state where no such set exists is an unsafe state.

We can show that the state given in the previous example is a safe state by showing that it is possible for each process to acquire its maximum resources and then terminate.

- P1 needs 2 A, 1 B and 1 D more resources, achieving its maximum,

  ○ [available resource: <3 1 1 2> - <2 1 0 1> = <1 0 1 1>];

- ○ The system now still has 1 A, no B, 1 C and 1 D resource available.
- P1 terminates, returning 3 A, 3 B, 2 C and 2 D resources to the system,
  - ○ [available resource: <1 0 1 1> + <3 3 2 2> = <4 3 3 3>];
  - ○ The system now has 4 A, 3 B, 3 C and 3 D resources available.
- P2 acquires 2 B and 1 D extra resources, then terminates, returning all its resources,
  - ○ [available resource: <4 3 3 3> - <0 2 0 1> + <1 2 3 4> = <5 3 6 6>];
  - ○ The system now has 5 A, 3 B, 6 C and 6 D resources.
- P3 acquires 1 B and 4 C resources and terminates,
  - ○ [available resource: <5 3 6 6> - <0 1 4 0> + <1 3 5 0> = <6 5 7 6>];
  - ○ The system now has all resources: 6 A, 5 B, 7 C and 6 D.
- Because all processes were able to terminate, this state is safe.

For an example of an unsafe state, consider what would happen if process 2 was holding 2 units of resource B at the beginning.

Requests

When the system receives a request for resources, it runs the Banker's algorithm to determine if it is safe to grant the request. The algorithm is fairly straightforward once the distinction between safe and unsafe states is understood.

- Can the request be granted?
  - ○ If not, the request is impossible and must either be denied or put on a waiting list.
- Assume that the request is granted.
- Is the new state safe?
  - ○ If so grant the request.
  - ○ If not, either deny the request or put it on a waiting list.

Whether the system denies or postpones an impossible or unsafe request is a decision specific to the operating system.

Example:

Starting in the same state as the previous example started in, assume process 3 requests 2 units of resource C.

- There is not enough of resource C available to grant the request.
- The request is denied.

On the other hand, assume process 3 requests 1 unit of resource C.

- There are enough resources to grant the request.

- Assume the request is granted.

  ○ The new state of the system would be:

```
Available system resources
 A  B  C  D
Free 3  1  0  2
 Processes (currently allocated resources):
 A  B  C  D
P1 1  2  2  1
P2 1  0  3  3
P3 1  2  2  0
 Processes (maximum resources):
 A  B  C  D
P1 3  3  2  2
P2 1  2  3  4
P3 1  3  5  0
```

- Determine if this new state is safe:

  ○ P1 can acquire 2 A, 1 B and 1 D resources and terminate.

  ○ Then, P2 can acquire 2 B and 1 D resources and terminate.

  ○ Finally, P3 can acquire 1 B and 3 C resources and terminate.

  ○ Therefore, this new state is safe.

- Since the new state is safe, grant the request.

Final example: from the state we started at, assume that process 2 requests 1 unit of resource B.

- There are enough resources.

- Assuming the request is granted, the new state would be:

```
Available system resources:
 A  B  C  D
Free 3  0  1  2
 Processes (currently allocated resources):
 A  B  C  D
```

```
P1 1 2 5 1
P2 1 1 3 3
P3 1 2 1 0
 Processes (maximum resources):
 A B C D
P1 3 3 2 2
P2 1 2 3 4
P3 1 3 5 0
```

- Is this state safe? Assuming P1, P2, and P3 request more of resource B and C.

  ○ P1 is unable to acquire enough B resources.

  ○ P2 is unable to acquire enough B resources.

  ○ P3 is unable to acquire enough B resources.

  ○ No process can acquire enough resources to terminate, so this state is not safe.

- Since the state is unsafe, deny the request.

```python
import numpy as np

n_processes = int(input('Number of processes? '))

n_resources = int(input('Number of resources? '))

available_resources = [int(x) for x in input('Claim vector? ').split(' ')]

currently_allocated = np.array([[int(x) for x in input('Currently allocated for
process ' + str(i + 1) + '? ').split(' ')] for i in range(n_processes)])

max_demand = np.array([[int(x) for x in input('Maximum demand from process ' +
str(i + 1) + '? ').split(' ')] for i in range(n_processes)])

total_available = available_resources - np.sum(currently_allocated, axis=0)

running = np.ones(n_processes) # An array with n_processes 1's to indicate if
process is yet to run

while np.count_nonzero(running) > 0:

    at_least_one_allocated = False

    for p in range(n_processes):

        if running[p]:

            if all(i >= 0 for i in total_available - (max_demand[p] - cur-
rently_allocated[p])):

                at_least_one_allocated = True

                print(str(p) + ' is running')

                running[p] = 0
```

```
                    total_available += currently_allocated[p]
        if not at_least_one_allocated:
                print('Unsafe')
                exit()


print('Safe')
```

Limitations

Like the other algorithms, the Banker's algorithm has some limitations when implemented. Specifically, it needs to know how much of each resource a process could possibly request. In most systems, this information is unavailable, making it impossible to implement the Banker's algorithm. Also, it is unrealistic to assume that the number of processes is static since in most systems the number of processes varies dynamically. Moreover, the requirement that a process will eventually release all its resources (when the process terminates) is sufficient for the correctness of the algorithm, however it is not sufficient for a practical system. Waiting for hours (or even days) for resources to be released is usually not acceptable.

Resource Allocation Graph (RAG)

Deadlocks can be described in terms of a directed graph called a system resource-allocation graph.

This graph consists of a set of vertices V and a set of edges E. The set of vertices V is partitioned into two different types of nodes $P = \{PI, P2, ..., Pn\}$, the set consisting of all the active processes in the system, and $R = \{R1, R2, ..., Rm\}$, the set consisting of all resource types in the system.

A directed edge from process Pi to resource type Rj is denoted by PiàRj; it signifies that process Pi requested an instance of resource type Rj and is currently waiting for that resource. A directed edge Pi -> Rj is called a request edge.

A directed edge from resource type Rj to process Pi is denoted by RjàPi; it signifies that an instance of resource type Rj has been allocated to process Pi. A directed edge RjàPi is called an assignment edge.

Pictorially, we represent each process Pi as a circle and each resource type Rj as a square. Since resource type Rj may have more than one instance, we represent each such instance as a dot within the square. A request edge points to only the square Rj, whereas an assignment edge must designate one of the dots in the square.

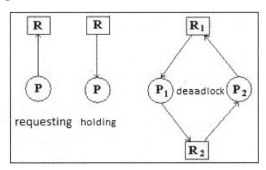

The resource-allocation graph shown below depicts the following situation.

The sets P, R, and E:

P={P1,P2,P3}.

R={R1,R2,R3,R4}.

E={P1®R1, P2®R3, R1®P2, R2®P2, R2®P1, R3®P3}.

Resource instances:

- One instance of resource type R1.

- Two instances of resource type R2.

- One instance of resource type R3.

- Three instances of resource type R4.

Process states:

- Process PI is holding an instance of resource type R2, and is waiting for an instance of resource type R1.

- Process P2 is holding an instance of R1 and R2 and is waiting for an instance of resource type R3.

- Process P3 is holding an instance of R3.

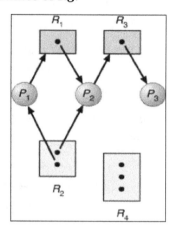

Example of a Resource Allocation Graph

It can be shown that, if the graph contains no cycles, then no process in the system is deadlocked. If the graph does contain a cycle, then a deadlock may exist.

If each resource type has exactly one instance, then a cycle implies that a deadlock has occurred. If the cycle involves only a set of resource types, each of which has only a single instance, then a deadlock has occurred. Each process involved in the cycle is deadlocked. In this case, a cycle in the graph is both a necessary and a sufficient condition for the existence of the deadlock.

If each resource type has several instances, then a cycle does not necessarily imply that a deadlock has occurred. In this case, a cycle in the graph is a necessary but not a sufficient condition for the existence of the deadlock.

To illustrate this concept, let us return to the resource-allocation graph depicted in Figure. Suppose that process P3 requests an instance of resource type R2. Since no resource instance is currently available, a request edge P3® R2 is added to the graph. At this point, two minimal cycles exist in the system:

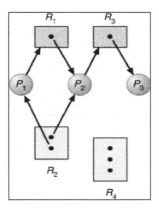

P1®R1® P2® R3® P3® R2® P1.

P2® R3 ® P3® R2® P2.

Processes PI, P2, and P3 are deadlocked. Process P2 is waiting for the resource R3, which is held by process P3. Process P3, on the other hand, is waiting for either process PI or process P2 to release resource R2. In addition, process PI is waiting for process P2 to release resource R1.

Deadlock Detection

In this approach, The OS doesn't apply any mechanism to avoid or prevent the deadlocks. Therefore the system considers that the deadlock will definitely occur. In order to get rid of deadlocks, The OS periodically checks the system for any deadlock. In case, it finds any of the deadlock then the OS will recover the system using some recovery techniques.

The main task of the OS is detecting the deadlocks. The OS can detect the deadlocks with the help of Resource allocation graph.

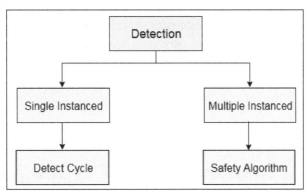

In single instanced resource types, if a cycle is being formed in the system then there will definitely be a deadlock. On the other hand, in multiple instanced resource type graph, detecting a cycle is not just enough. We have to apply the safety algorithm on the system by converting the resource allocation graph into the allocation matrix and request matrix.

Deadlock Recovery

When a detection algorithm determines that a deadlock exists, several alternatives are available. One possibility is to inform the operator that a deadlock has occurred and to let the operator deal with the deadlock manually. Another possibility is to let the system recover from the deadlock automatically. There are two options for breaking a deadlock. One is simply to abort one or more processes to break the circular wait. The other is to preempt some resources from one or more of the deadlocked processes.

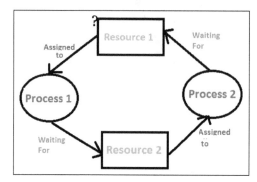

Process Termination

To eliminate deadlocks by aborting a process, we use one of two methods. In both methods, the system reclaims all resources allocated to the terminated processes. Abort all deadlocked processes. This method clearly will break the deadlock cycle, but at great expense; the deadlocked processes may have computed for a long time, and the results of these partial computations must be discarded and probably will have to be recomputed later.

Abort one process at a time until the deadlock cycle is eliminated. This method incurs considerable overhead, since, after each process is aborted, a deadlock-detection algorithm must be invoked to determine whether any processes are still deadlocked. Aborting a process may not be easy. If the process was in the midst of updating a file, terminating it will leave that file in an incorrect state. Similarly, if the process was in the midst of printing data on a printer, the system must reset the printer to a correct state before printing the next job. If the partial termination method is used, then we must determine which deadlocked process (or processes) should be terminated. This determination is a policy decision, similar to CPU-scheduling decisions. The question is basically an economic one; we should abort those processes whose termination will incur the minimum cost. Unfortunately, the term minimum cost is not a precise one. Many factors may affect which process is chosen, including:

1. What the priority of the process is?

2. How long the process has computed and how much longer the process will compute before completing its designated task?

3. How many and what type of resources the process has used (for example, whether the resources are simple to preempt)?

4. How many more resources the process needs in order to complete?

5. How many processes will need to be terminated?

6. Whether the process is interactive or batch?

Resource Preemption

To eliminate deadlocks using resource preemption, we successively preempt some resources from processes and give these resources to other processes until the deadlock cycle is broken. If preemption is required to deal with deadlocks, then three issues need to be addressed:

1. Selecting a victim: Which resources and which processes are to be preempted? As in process termination, we must determine the order of preemption to minimize cost. Cost factors may include such parameters as the number of resources a deadlocked process is holding and the amount of time the process has thus far consumed during its execution.

2. Rollback: If we preempt a resource from a process, what should be done with that process? Clearly, it cannot continue with its normal execution; it is missing some needed resource. We must roll back the process to some safe state and restart it from that state. Since, in general, it is difficult to determine what a safe state is, the simplest solution is a total rollback: Abort the process and then restart it. Although it is more effective to roll back the process only as far as necessary to break the deadlock, this method requires the system to keep more information about the state of all running processes.

3. Starvation: How do we ensure that starvation will not occur? That is, how can we guarantee that resources will not always be preempted from the same process? In a system where victim selection is based primarily on cost factors, it may happen that the same process is always picked as a victim. As a result, this process never completes its designated task, a starvation situation that must be dealt with in any practical system. Clearly, we must ensure that a process can be picked as a victim only a (small) finite number of times. The most common solution is to include the number of rollbacks in the cost factor.

References

- Process-deadlocks-in-operating-system: tutorialspoint.com, Retrieved 17 May, 2019
- Deadlock-characterization: tutorialspoint.com, Retrieved 18 June, 2019
- Deadlock-prevention-avoidance-detection-and-recovery-in-operating-systems: javajee.com, Retrieved 19 July, 2019
- Os-deadlock-prevention: javatpoint.com, Retrieved 20 August, 2019
- Silberschatz, Galvin, & Gagne (2013). Operating System Concepts, 9th Edition. Wiley. p. 330. ISBN 978-1-118-06333-0
- Os-deadlock-avoidance: javatpoint.com, Retrieved 21 January, 2019
- Resource-allocation-graph: basicittopic.com, Retrieved 22 February, 2019
- Os-deadlock-detection-and-recovery: javatpoint.com Retrieved 23 March, 2019

Permissions

We would like to thank the editorial team for lending their expertise to make the book truly unique. They have played a crucial role in the development of this book. Without their invaluable contributions this book wouldn't have been possible. They have made vital efforts to compile up to date information on the varied aspects of this subject to make this book a valuable addition to the collection of many professionals and students.

This book was conceptualized with the vision of imparting up-to-date and integrated information in this field. To ensure the same, a matchless editorial board was set up. Every individual on the board went through rigorous rounds of assessment to prove their worth. After which they invested a large part of their time researching and compiling the most relevant data for our readers.

The editorial board has been involved in producing this book since its inception. They have spent rigorous hours researching and exploring the diverse topics which have resulted in the successful publishing of this book. They have passed on their knowledge of decades through this book. To expedite this challenging task, the publisher supported the team at every step. A small team of assistant editors was also appointed to further simplify the editing procedure and attain best results for the readers.

Apart from the editorial board, the designing team has also invested a significant amount of their time in understanding the subject and creating the most relevant covers. They scrutinized every image to scout for the most suitable representation of the subject and create an appropriate cover for the book.

The publishing team has been an ardent support to the editorial, designing and production team. Their endless efforts to recruit the best for this project, has resulted in the accomplishment of this book. They are a veteran in the field of academics and their pool of knowledge is as vast as their experience in printing. Their expertise and guidance has proved useful at every step. Their uncompromising quality standards have made this book an exceptional effort. Their encouragement from time to time has been an inspiration for everyone.

The publisher and the editorial board hope that this book will prove to be a valuable piece of knowledge for students, practitioners and scholars across the globe.

Index

CPSIA information can be obtained
at www.ICGtesting.com
Printed in the USA
LVHW061157020222
709759LV00167B/274